ALSO BY DAVID GRAEBER

Pirate Enlightenment, or the Real Libertalia

The Dawn of Everything: A New History of Humanity
(with David Wengrow)

Bullshit Jobs: A Theory

On Kings (with Marshall Sahlins)

*The Utopia of Rules: On Technology, Stupidity, and the Secret Joys of
Bureaucracy*

The Democracy Project: A History, a Crisis, a Movement

Debt: The First 5,000 Years

Direct Action: An Ethnography

Lost People: Magic and the Legacy of Slavery in Madagascar

Fragments of an Anarchist Anthropology

*Toward an Anthropological Theory of Value: The False Coin of Our
Own Dreams*

THE ULTIMATE

HIDDEN TRUTH

OF THE WORLD . . .

THE
ULTIMATE
HIDDEN
TRUTH
OF THE
WORLD . . .

ESSAYS

DAVID GRAEBER

Edited and Introduced by
Nika Dubrovsky

Foreword by Rebecca Solnit

Farrar, Straus and Giroux
New York

Farrar, Straus and Giroux
120 Broadway, New York 10271

Printed in the United States of America
First edition, 2024

Owing to limitations of space, all acknowledgments for permission to reprint previously
published and unpublished material can be found on pages 355–356.

Library of Congress Cataloging-in-Publication Data
Names: Graeber, David, author. | Dubrovsky, Nika, 1967– editor. | Solnit, Rebecca,
    author of foreword.
Title: The ultimate hidden truth of the world . . . : essays / David Graeber ; edited and
    introduced by Nika Dubrovsky ; foreword by Rebecca Solnit.
Description: First edition. | New York : Farrar, Straus and Giroux, 2024. | Includes
    bibliographical references and index.
Identifiers: LCCN 2024016455 | ISBN 9780374610227 (hardcover)
Subjects: LCSH: Graeber, David. | Graeber, David—Interviews. | Anthropology—Political
    aspects. | Essays. | LCGFT: Essays.
Classification: LCC GN21.G725 A93 2024 | DDC 301—dc23/eng/20240603
LC record available at https://lccn.loc.gov/2024016455

Designed by Patrice Sheridan

Our books may be purchased in bulk for promotional, educational, or business use. Please
contact your local bookseller or the Macmillan Corporate and Premium Sales Department at
1-800-221-7945, extension 5442, or by email at MacmillanSpecialMarkets@macmillan.com.

www.fsgbooks.com
Follow us on social media at @fsgbooks

10   9   8   7   6   5   4   3   2   1

Contents

Foreword: With Ferocious Joy

Rebecca Solnit

David Graeber's disposition and propensities come through in print the way they did in person. That is, the prose here gallops and invites. He was a joyful, celebratory person—an enthusiast, voluble, on fire with the possibilities in the ideas and ideologies he wrestled with. Every time we met, from New Haven in the early 2000s to London a few years before his death, he was essentially the same: beaming, rumpled, with a restless energy that seemed to echo the constant motion of his mind, words tumbling out as though they were, in their unstoppable abundance, overflowing. But he was also much respected in activist circles for being a good listener, and his radical egalitarianism was lived out in how he related to the people around him.

He was always an anthropologist. After doing fieldwork among traditional peoples in Madagascar, he just never stopped, turning his focus to his own society. He found it both interesting and capable of being analyzed as arising from particular (and often peculiar) beliefs and customs. Essays such as "Dead Zones of the Imagination: On Violence, Bureaucracy, and 'Interpretive Labor'" and his book *Bullshit Jobs* came from using the equipment of an anthropologist on stuff usually regarded as boring, or not regarded at all—the function and impact of bureaucracy. His bestseller on debt reminded us that money and finance are among the social arrangements that could be rearranged for the better.

He insisted, again and again, that industrialized Euro-American civilization was, like other societies past and present, just one way of doing things among the countless options. He returned again and again to moments when societies rejected agriculture or technology or social hierarchy, when social groups chose what has often been dismissed as primitive because it was more free. This work culminated in his 2021 book with David Wengrow, *The Dawn of Everything*, prefigured in the essay here titled "There Never Was a West." And he rejected all the linear narratives that present contemporary human beings as declining from primordial innocence or ascending from primitive barbarism; he offered in place of a single narrative many versions and variations, a vision of societies as ongoing experiments, and human beings as endlessly, restlessly creative. That sheer variety was a source of hope for him, a basis for his recurrent insistence that it doesn't have to be this way.

As Marcus Rediker wrote in his review of David's posthumous book *Pirate Enlightenment*, "Everything Graeber wrote was simultaneously a genealogy of the present and an account of what a just society might look like." He was, as seen throughout these essays and in all his books, concerned about inequality of all kinds, often including gender inequality in this society and others, and the violence that enforces inequality and unfreedom, and how they might be delegitimized and where and when societies might have escaped them. He focused, in short, on freedom and its impediments.

He was often credited with coining the phrase "We are the 99 percent," but he insisted on paring his credit down to having contributed the "99 percent" part to what became an Occupy Wall Street slogan so compelling that "the 1 percent" remains a widely used description of the uppermost elite. "The 99 percent" is itself a hopeful phrase in opposition to the old layer-cake description of the working, middle, and upper classes. It's an assertion that the great majority of us are working and often financially struggling or precarious, that most of us have a lot in common—and a lot of reasons to oppose the super-rich.

The essays gathered here are a reminder that David devoured literature far beyond the field of anthropology, in history, economics, archaeology, and political science. His writing is a synthesis of this material and current events, as digested by his own incendiary imagination. He loved ideas. He took joy in his work and in how that work could and did intersect with actualities on the ground—especially with the radical movements of the late 1990s and the new millennium, including the anti-corporate-globalization movement that peaked with the shutdown of the World Trade Organization Ministerial Conference in Seattle in 1999, the Zapatista uprising in Mexico that began in 1994, and the many forms of radical egalitarianism manifesting as direct-democracy experiments and resistance to unjust institutions and governments, especially 2011's Occupy Wall Street, in which he was deeply involved.

That joy: maybe this is how everyone should feel about ideas and the ways that they open up or close off possibilities, the way that—well, to quote the sentence from which the title of this book comes, "The ultimate hidden truth of the world is that it is something that we make, and could just as easily make differently." If you truly believe that, if you perceive a world that is constructed according to certain assumptions and values, then you see that it can be changed, not least by changing those assumptions and values.

You recognize that ideas matter and that we have some role in choosing which ones generate the realities of our lives, and you recognize that what scholars and thinkers do is tremendously important. While too many anti-intellectuals are dismissive of ideas altogether, even too many of those whose job it is to deal in ideas are dismissive of their power to change the world. Because if they can, we who work with ideas are saddled with responsibility for changing that world or equipping others to do so and helping them dismantle ideas that imprison and degrade. We have to recognize that ideas are tools that we wield, and with them, some power.

David wanted to put those tools in everyone's hands or remind them that they are already there. Which is part of why he worked hard at, and succeeded in, writing in a style that wasn't always simple, but was always as clear and accessible as possible, given the material. Egalitarianism is a prose style, too. Our mutual friend the writer, filmmaker, and debt abolitionist Astra Taylor texted him: "Re-reading Debt. You are such a damn good writer. A rare skill among lefties." He texted back that August, a month before his demise: "Why thanks! Well at least I take care to do so—I call it 'being nice to the reader,' which is an extension of the politics, in a sense."

In order to believe that people can govern themselves in the absence of coercive institutions and hierarchies, anarchists must have great faith in ordinary people, and David did. A sentence Lyndsey Stonebridge wrote about Hannah Arendt could apply equally well to him: "To fixate on her exceptional mind is to miss something that is important about her lessons in thinking: thinking is ordinary, she teaches; that is its secret power."

He had a strained academic career, despite his brilliance and originality—or because of them. In the first book of his that I read, *Fragments of an Anarchist Anthropology*, a literally tiny book bursting with big ideas, he wrote, "In the United States there are thousands of academic Marxists of one sort or another, but hardly a dozen scholars willing openly to call themselves anarchists . . . It does seem that Marxism has an affinity with the academy that anarchism never will. It was, after all, the only great social movement that was invented by a Ph.D., even if afterwards, it became a movement intending to rally the working class." And then he argues that anarchism was not, by comparison, an idea created by a few intellectuals; instead "the basic principles of anarchism—self-organization, voluntary association, mutual aid"— have been around "as long as humanity." David was an anarchist by disposition as well as inclination.

In a 2017 essay, he declared, "There are many mysteries of the academy which would be appropriate objects of ethnographic analysis. One question that never ceases to intrigue me is tenure. How could a system ostensibly designed to give scholars the security to be able to say dangerous things have been transformed into a system so harrowing and psychologically destructive that, by the time scholars find themselves in a secure position, 99 percent of them have forgotten what it would even mean to have a dangerous idea?" That is, he was of the academy and also an outcast and enemy of it, but more than that it was full of animosity toward him, because he did not operate by its rules.

So he also writes, with his usual jaunty bluntness, "I agreed to write this because I have no intention to apply for an academic position in America in the foreseeable future. There is probably not a single paragraph in this essay that I would not have self-censored had that not been the case." I regret he never did a full anthropological analysis of academia, with its strange initiation rites, entrenched hierarchies, dysfunctional systems, absurdist rules, and use of language as a means of exclusion as well as inclusion and communication.

David's recurrent rallying cry as both a scholar and an activist was "It does not have to be this way." Where academia can be cool and guarded, pulling away from direct engagement, he was warm and enthusiastic, wanting to see ideas lead to actions that could change the world. Astra notes, "While he despised the tedium of academic bureaucracy, he loved activist meetings, savoring the ideological debates and reveling in various forms of planning, scheming, and mischief." He was hopeful, not foolishly so, but due to the evidence he had amassed that human societies have taken myriad forms, that the people who are supposed to be powerless can together wield quite a lot of power, and that ideas matter. (One of my favorite scraps of information in *Fragments of an Anarchist Anthropology* is about Madagascar's Sakalava people, who officially revere dead kings—but those kings make their wishes known "through spirit mediums who are usually elderly women of commoner descent." That is, a system officially led by elite men is controlled by non-elite women.)

Hope is a tricky business among intellectuals and activists. Cynicism, though it's often genuinely inaccurate about both human nature and political possibilities, gives the appearance of sophistication; despair is often seen as sophisticated, worldly-wise, and hopefulness is seen as naive, when the opposite is not infrequently true. Hope is risky; you can lose, and you often do, but the records show that if you try, sometimes you win. Which is why David's extended essay "The Shock of Victory," not included in this anthology, begins "The biggest problem facing direct action movements is that we don't know how to handle victory." Another essay not included here, "Despair Fatigue," opens with a similar line: "Is it possible to become bored with hopelessness?"

David's superpower was being an outsider. He did not proceed from widely shared assumptions but sought to dismantle them, urging us to see they're arbitrary, confining, and optional, and inviting everyone into the spaces this opens up (while saluting those already there). So much of his writing says, in essence, "What happens if we don't accept this?"—if we dissect it to see its origins and impacts or if we reject it, if we lift it off like some burden we don't have to carry, some outfit we don't have to wear. What happens is we get free: his is an analysis for the sake of liberation, liberatory in its means and its ends. In that, it's a gift, and a generous one. Thank you, David.

Introduction

Nika Dubrovsky

Since David's death in 2020, much of my life has been entwined with his vast archive of published and unpublished texts, hundreds of notebooks, audio and video recordings, and correspondences. David once said that the real care for a "great man" begins after his death, and is almost always done by women. Now I know what he meant.

When David talked about care, he always added that it has real significance only if it enables freedom. Prisons take care of their inmates, feeding and housing them—but hardly any of us would want to experience that sort of care. Parents take care of their kids so children can play and be free. I ask myself: What kind of care might David need after death, and what posthumous freedom would it enable?

Our Western conception of freedom traces back to the legal authority of Roman patriarchs over their family and slaves. It is based on the idea of private property—understood not as a relation between people, but rather as a relation between a person and a thing, or between two people, one of whom is also a thing (this is how slaves were defined in

Roman law: they were persons who were also *res*, things). Slavery meant social death; a slave was a person deprived of the right to create his or her own social bonds. In turn, the Latin word for "body"—*corpus*—also means a body of writings or a body of laws, and it is linked to the idea of private property and a free man who has autonomy over his body and can own property. In a slight modification it means "corpse," a dead body. A body of work set for eternity, immutable, floating above mere mortals: it would be hard to find a description of writing more alien to David.

David's understanding of freedom was antithetical to Western notions derived from ancient Rome. In his lectures he frequently observed that perhaps we are the only civilization that has been built almost exclusively on the bizarre link between private property and freedom. Virtually all of David's work advanced his theory that true freedom is an underlying principle of the universe, manifested in play and social relationships; freedom, to David, does not derive from laws, and it is not based on individual property rights. (In an essay for the popular magazine *The Baffler*, which concludes this collection, David discusses the crucial themes of freedom and play, which he discussed with the philosophers Roy Bhaskar and Mehdi Belhaj Kacem.)

Writing was an exercise of freedom for David. It was a rebellious project, often created with others to collectively change the social order, literally revising an existing social code. His understanding of change diverged from that of many revolutionaries, especially Vladimir Lenin. David believed that revolution was not about taking over the Louvre or bringing new politicians to power—although sometimes that might help to make the world a better place. Rather, David believed that "revolution happens when there is a transformation of common sense."

David lived with the deep understanding that "the ultimate hidden truth of the world"—the code that drives the invisible social mechanisms of our society that make us kill one another in wars or build free housing, work for years in bullshit jobs or take on caretaking jobs, even if they pay very little—"is that it is something we make and could just as easily make differently."

Borges famously said: "When writers die they become books, which is, after all, not too bad an incarnation." With this sentiment I agree. Though, for it to truly embody David's spirit, his book would have to be open source. In open-source projects, participation remains open to everyone, the methodology and results are transparent, and if the "lead programmers" disappear, the project nevertheless continues to evolve without them.

David was what the French call an "homme de lettres." He lived to share his ideas, expressing them in as many ways as he could. Much like Noam Chomsky, another noted anarchist-scholar, he made himself available to those outside the academy and would speak almost everywhere he was invited.

David understood anarchism not as an identity but as a practice, existing in social relationships with others, and it could be said that David's main intellectual project outside of publishing was the democratization of the writing process itself.

David used to say that when writing in his mind he was talking to his mother, and if he felt that she understood him, he believed that others would, too. His texts were written to be open to discussion and further development by other people. He wanted to change our collective common sense, and this task can only be accomplished collectively.

It seems to me that his social project has been remarkably successful. From book to book, and essay to essay, David was able to challenge assumptions that we hold dear, the way we think—the very essence of our collective social code. David proudly noted that after Occupy Wall Street, the word *inequality* appeared in the speeches of even the most conservative American politicians, and most Americans under the age of thirty-five preferred socialism to capitalism. The Occupy Wall Street movement, to which he later devoted several books, spread around the world. Though often credited to him, the slogan "We are the 99%" was a collective enterprise, born in the struggle, and continues to resonate and have a global impact long after he is gone.

I selected eighteen essays for this collection, in collaboration with David's students and colleagues from both the David Graeber Institute and the Museum of Care, with the aim of mapping his key life projects—or at least those that are already known to us; his archive is vast, and yet to be fully explored. The essays in this collection are a history of his social relationships—an exploration of his friendships, his adversaries, and his conversational partners. They center around the dialogical nature of human consciousness, cooperation as political freedom, and, ultimately, the origins of "common sense."

In the preface to *Pirate Enlightenment*, David describes the book as part of a larger intellectual project, which he first laid out in the 2007 essay "There Never Was a West (Part One)," and continued with *The Dawn of Everything* (coauthored with David Wengrow). He called this project "decolonizing the Enlightenment."

He writes: "There can be no doubt that many of the ideas we now see as products of the eighteenth-century European Lumières were, indeed, used to justify extraordinary cruelty, exploitation and destruction, not just on the working classes at home, but on those who lived on other continents. But the blanket condemnation of Enlightenment thought is in its own way rather odd."

David's lifelong project was to reveal the non-Western origins of the Enlightenment and its strikingly different view of human nature and democracy—thus offering us another Enlightenment we have yet to discover. In *Pirate Enlightenment*, he tells the story of white European settlers in Madagascar who generally avoided committing most of the crimes against humanity that we today call colonialism. It is an example of an alternative colonization, during which the Old World met the New World, mixing with the local population and creating a new culture and even a whole new nation, the Zana-Malata, who still live in Madagascar—all while upholding the ideas of equality, freedom, and democracy we hold dear in the West today.

David articulated many of the central ideas of this project in the 2013 journal article "Dead Zones of the Imagination." But he had begun thinking about this larger project as early as graduate school, when he traveled to Madagascar on the advice of his anthropology professor and intellectual mentor at the University of Chicago, Marshall Sahlins.

David's work builds upon Sahlins's critique of Western economic and cultural models, in large part by incorporating insights gleaned from Russian thinkers—primarily Kropotkin and Bakunin, but also Dostoevsky and Bakhtin. It is noteworthy that he took only two books with him to Madagascar: Dostoevsky's *Brothers Karamazov* and Bakhtin's *Rabelais and His World*. One of the basic ideas to which David would return again and again in his scientific and political projects, as well as his anthropological studies, was that "man is not a final and defined quantity upon which firm calculations can be made; man is free, and can therefore violate any regulating norms which might be thrust upon him . . ." (Mikhail Bakhtin, *Problems of Dostoevsky's Poetics*). Bakhtin and Dostoevsky described human nature as a potentiality that emerges through polyphonic, carnivalesque dialogue with other people.

David used to say, "All human beings are projects of mutual creation. Most of the work we do is on each other." This is how David understood himself and the purpose of his writing.

When choosing texts for the section on economics and care, I remembered how David, at one of his book launches, answered a question from a woman who introduced herself as a nanny in a nursing home. She asked: "Why don't people like me have access to decision-making?" David replied, "Our society is organized in such a way that access to power is conditioned on access to violence. People who are busy taking care of other people have minimal access to make decisions, but army chiefs, CEOs of big corporations, and so on are the ones who decide how we all live our lives." In turn, he asked the woman: "Do we really want to live in a society organized according to the ideals of such people?"

I was in the Berlin auditorium at that moment, and I was personally struck by David's answer, because usually people who have written books of five hundred pages rarely bother to connect their complex constructs, especially economic ones, with the daily reality of ordinary people. It is even more difficult to make your fundamental discoveries—new paradigms of knowledge, history, and power—understandable to people without any specialized education.

But this is exactly what is needed to change public perceptions of common sense.

In the "Against Economics" section, I chose essays I saw as key to David's thinking about power and justice. In the interview "Finance Is Just Another Word for Other People's Debts," David listed some of the people he was in dialogue with, but I would especially like to highlight Michael Hudson, an economist straddling academia and Wall Street, whom David credits for turning him on to creditor-debtor relations, or debt, as a critical turning point in human history. (David also was enchanted by Hudson's incredible biography. As we were heading out to lunch with him one day, David whispered to me, "The most amazing thing is that everything Michael will tell you about himself is really true!" Hudson was the godson of Lev Trotsky, who was murdered with the ice pick belonging to Michael's aunt. Such stories interested David far more than any academic achievement.) Another text included in the "Against Economics" section, "On the Phenomenon of Bullshit Jobs," was born as a follow-up to casual conversations with people who defined their jobs as meaningless or even harmful to society, despite earning good money and enjoying high status. What was remarkable in his approach was his empathy for the very victims of the "spiritualist violence" inflicted upon those holding bullshit jobs. After all, it was these people, occupying the most privileged positions in society, whom the left traditionally scorned for their complicity and blamed for the suffering of the oppressed, and not unfairly so. But David draws attention specifically to their misery, showing how it forms "a scar across our collective soul."

The question of how the power structure of our society works, and, more important, how it might work, was always front and center for David. When he coined the phrase "care and freedom," *care* wasn't a buzzword yet. Today, *care* is invoked in texts frequently and ubiquitously, from academia to the art world to journalism. There is an entire section in this collection, "The Revolt of the Caring Classes," describing David's proposal to integrate Marxist and feminist approaches, creating a new form of the labor theory of value.

In concluding this introduction, I want to refer again to the title of the collection. I hope after reading this book it will become obvious that "the ultimate truth of the world" does not exist somewhere behind the closed doors of museums; it is not kept in archives filled with dusty books by great authors of the past, nor is it to be found in the palaces of kings or in the manifestos and speeches of political party leaders. This truth belongs to all of us, and it is this: we are free to change it as we see fit.

Without magic tricks or a Leninist "bridge and telegraph takeover," David was releasing forces that were already within us—our common human yearning for freedom and care.

With this in mind, I see David's texts—his archive—not as an unchangeable corpus of work, but as a very generous structure that can provide a space for making these horizontal connections, replete with open questions, doubts, and unexpected references to different ways of thinking, with entry points for reader-commentators almost anywhere.

In our essay "Another Art World," we fumbled for a description of what this other world might look like, returning to the Romantics' original idea of culture and to Alexander Bogdanov's Proletkult, an experimental cultural federation in the first years of the Russian Revolution, which created a gigantic network of popular amateur artistic collectives, independent of state and party control.

As I think about the kind of care that might suit David, keeping in mind his ability to make direct emotional and intellectual connections with people—both personally and through his texts—I ponder how to make his legacy a living and ever-evolving project in which all of us, his readers and fellow writers, can participate.

This is the kind of care that David himself not only endorsed but practiced. In this evolving collective space, we can continue to collaborate with David even if he is no longer with us in a corporeal sense.

I hope that these eighteen essays will be the beginning of a series of publications that will include David's unpublished writings, his diaries, his sixty-two lectures, and the complete collection of his archive. But most important, I hope that there will be more and more people who, freely and caringly, in a collective dialogue, will be able to build Another World, exactly as they imagine it to be.

PART I   THERE NEVER
WAS A WEST

There Never Was a West

On the Incoherence of the Notion of the "Western Tradition"

What follows emerges largely from my own experience of the alternative globalization movement, where issues of democracy have been very much at the center of debate. Anarchists in Europe or North America and indigenous organizations in the Global South have found themselves locked in remarkably similar arguments. Is "democracy" an inherently Western concept? Does it refer to a form of governance (a mode of communal self-organization) or a form of government (one particular way of organizing a state apparatus)? Does democracy necessarily imply majority rule? Is representative democracy really democracy at all? Is the word permanently tainted by its origins in Athens, a militaristic, slave-owning society founded on the systematic repression of women? Or does what we now call "democracy" have any real historical

Originally published in *Possibilities: Essays on Hierarchy, Rebellion, and Desire* (Oakland, CA: AK Press, 2007).

connection to Athenian democracy in the first place? Is it possible for those trying to develop decentralized forms of consensus-based direct democracy to reclaim the word? If so, how will we ever convince the majority of people in the world that "democracy" has nothing to do with electing representatives? If not, if we instead accept the standard definition and start calling direct democracy something else, how can we say we're against democracy—a word with such universally positive associations?

These are arguments about words much more than they are arguments about practices. On questions of practice, in fact, there is a surprising degree of convergence; especially within the more radical elements of the movement. Whether one is talking with members of Zapatista communities in Chiapas, unemployed piqueteros in Argentina, Dutch squatters, or anti-eviction activists in South African townships, almost everyone agrees on the importance of horizontal, rather than vertical structures; the need for initiatives to rise up from relatively small, self-organized, autonomous groups rather than being conveyed downward through chains of command; the rejection of permanent, named leadership structures; and the need to maintain some kind of mechanism—whether these be North American–style "facilitation," Zapatista-style women's and youth caucuses, or any of an endless variety of other possibilities—to ensure that the voices of those who would normally find themselves marginalized or excluded from traditional participatory mechanisms are heard. Some of the bitter conflicts of the past, for example, between partisans of majority voting versus partisans of consensus process, have been largely resolved, or perhaps more accurately seem increasingly irrelevant, as more and more social movements use full consensus only within smaller groups and adopt various forms of "modified consensus" for larger coalitions. Something is emerging. The problem is what to call it. Many of the key principles of the movement (self-organization, voluntary association, mutual aid, the refusal of state power) derive from the anarchist tradition. Still, many who embrace these ideas are reluctant, or flat-out refuse, to call themselves "anarchists." Similarly with democracy. My own approach has normally been to openly embrace both terms, to argue, in fact, that anarchism and democracy are—or should be—largely identical. However, as I say, there is no consensus on this issue, nor even a clear majority view.

It seems to me these are tactical, political questions more than anything else. The word *democracy* has meant any number of different things over the course of its history. When first coined, it referred to a system in which the citizens of a community made decisions by equal vote in a collective assembly. For most of its history, it referred to political disorder, rioting, lynching, and factional violence (in fact, the word had much the same associations as *anarchy* does today). Only quite recently has it become identified with a system in which the citizens of a state elect representatives to exercise state power in their name. Clearly there is no true essence to be discovered here. About the only thing these different referents have in common, perhaps, is that they involve some sense that political questions that are normally the concerns of a narrow elite are here thrown open to everyone, and that this is either a very good or a very bad thing. The term has always been so morally loaded that to write a dispassionate, disinterested history of democracy would almost be a contradiction in terms. Most scholars who want to maintain an appearance of disinterest avoid the word. Those who do make generalizations about democracy inevitably have some sort of axe to grind.

I certainly do. That is why I feel it only fair to the reader to make my own axes evident from the start. It seems to me that there's a reason why the word *democracy*, no matter how consistently it is abused by tyrants and demagogues, still maintains its stubborn popular appeal. For most people, democracy is still identified with some notion of ordinary people collectively managing their own affairs. It already had this connotation in the nineteenth century, and it was for this reason that nineteenth-century politicians, who had earlier shunned the term, reluctantly began to adopt the term and refer to themselves as "democrats"—and, gradually, to patch together a history by which they could represent themselves as heirs to a tradition that traced back to ancient Athens. However, I will also assume—for no particular reason, or no particular scholarly reason, since these are not scholarly questions but moral and political ones—that the history of "democracy" should be treated as more than just the history of the word *democracy*. If democracy is simply a matter of communities managing their own affairs through an open and relatively egalitarian process of public discussion, there is no reason why egalitarian forms of decision-making in rural communities in Africa or Brazil should not be at least as worthy of the name as the constitutional systems that govern most nation-states today—and, in many cases, probably a good deal more worthy.

In light of this, I will be making a series of related arguments, and perhaps the best way to proceed would be to just set them all out right away.

1. Almost everyone who writes on the subject assumes "democracy" is a "Western" concept that begins its history in ancient Athens. They also assume that what eighteenth- and nineteenth-century politicians began reviving in Western Europe and North America was essentially the same thing. Democracy is thus seen as something whose natural habitat is Western Europe and its English- or French-speaking settler colonies. Not one of these assumptions is justified. "Western civilization" is a particularly incoherent concept, but, insofar as it refers to anything, it refers to an intellectual tradition. This intellectual tradition is, overall, just as hostile to anything we would recognize as democracy as those of India, China, or Mesoamerica.

2. Democratic practices—processes of egalitarian decision-making—however, occur pretty much anywhere, and are not peculiar to any one given "civilization," culture, or tradition. They tend to crop up wherever human life goes on outside systematic structures of coercion.

3. The "democratic ideal" tends to emerge when, under certain historical circumstances, intellectuals and politicians, usually in some sense navigating their way between states and popular movements and popular practices, interrogate their own traditions—invariably, in dialogue with other ones—citing cases of past or present democratic practice to argue that their

tradition has a fundamental kernel of democracy. I call these moments of "democratic refoundation." From the perspective of the intellectual traditions, they are also moments of recuperation, in which ideals and institutions that are often the product of incredibly complicated forms of interaction among people of very different histories and traditions come to be represented as emerging from the logic of that intellectual tradition itself. Over the course of the nineteenth and twentieth centuries especially, such moments did not just occur in Europe, but almost everywhere.

4. The fact that this ideal is always founded on (at least partly) invented traditions does not mean it is inauthentic or illegitimate or, at least, more inauthentic or illegitimate than any other. The contradiction, however, is that this ideal was always based on the impossible dream of marrying democratic procedures or practices with the coercive mechanisms of the state. The result are not "democracies" in any meaningful sense of the word but republics with a few, usually fairly limited, democratic elements.

5. What we are experiencing today is not a crisis of democracy but rather a crisis of the state. In recent years, there has been a massive revival of interest in democratic practices and procedures within global social movements, but this has proceeded almost entirely outside of statist frameworks. The future of democracy lies precisely in this area.

6. Let me take these in roughly the order I've presented them above. I'll start with the curious idea that democracy is somehow a "Western concept."

A. ON THE INCOHERENCE OF THE NOTION OF THE "WESTERN TRADITION"

I'll begin, then, with a relatively easy target: Samuel P. Huntington's famous essay "The Clash of Civilizations?" Huntington is a professor of international relations at Harvard, a classic Cold War intellectual,

beloved of right-wing think tanks. In 1993, he published an essay arguing that, now that the Cold War was over, global conflicts would come
to center on clashes between ancient cultural traditions. The argument
was notable for promoting a certain notion of cultural humility. Drawing on the work of Arnold Toynbee, he urged Westerners to understand
that theirs is just one civilization among many, that its values should in
no way be assumed to be universal. Democracy in particular, he argued,
is a distinctly Western idea and the West should abandon its efforts to
impose it on the rest of the world:

> At a superficial level, much of Western culture has indeed perme-
> ated the rest of the world. At a more basic level, however, West-
> ern concepts differ fundamentally from those prevalent in other
> civilizations. Western ideas of individualism, liberalism, consti-
> tutionalism, human rights, equality, liberty, the rule of law, de-
> mocracy, free markets, the separation of church and state, often
> have little resonance in Islamic, Confucian, Japanese, Hindu,
> Buddhist, or Orthodox cultures. Western efforts to propagate
> such ideas produce instead a reaction against "human rights im-
> perialism" and a reaffirmation of indigenous values, as can be
> seen in the support for religious fundamentalism by the younger
> generation in non-Western cultures. The very notion that there is
> a "universal civilization" is a Western idea, directly at odds with
> the particularism of most Asian societies and their emphasis on
> what distinguishes one people from another.[1]

The list of Western concepts is fascinating from any number of an-
gles. If taken literally, for instance, it would mean that "the West" only
really took any kind of recognizable form in the nineteenth or even
twentieth centuries, since in any previous one the overwhelming majority of "Westerners" would have rejected just about all these principles
out of hand—if, indeed, they would have been able even to conceive of
them. One can, if one likes, scratch around through the last two or three
thousand years in different parts of Europe and find plausible forerun-

ners to most of them. Many try. Fifth-century Athens usually provides a useful resource in this regard, provided one is willing to ignore, or at least skim over, almost everything that happened between then and perhaps 1215 CE, or maybe 1776. This is roughly the approach taken by most conventional textbooks. Huntington is a bit subtler. He treats Greece and Rome as a separate "Classical civilization," which then splits off into Eastern (Greek) and Western (Latin) Christianity—and later, of course, Islam. When Western civilization begins, it is identical to Latin Christendom. After the upheavals of the Reformation and Counter-Reformation, however, the civilization loses its religious specificity and transforms into something broader and essentially secular. The results, however, are much the same as in conventional textbooks, since Huntington also insists that the Western tradition was all along "far more" the heir of the ideas of Classical civilization than its Orthodox or Islamic rivals.

Now, there are a thousand ways one could attack Huntington's position. His list of "Western concepts" seems particularly arbitrary. Any number of concepts were adrift in Western Europe over the years, and many far more widely accepted. Why choose this list rather than some other? What are the criteria? Clearly, Huntington's immediate aim was to show that many ideas widely accepted in Western Europe and North America are likely to be viewed with suspicion in other quarters. But, even on this basis, could one not equally well assemble a completely different list: say, argue that "Western culture" is premised on science, industrialism, bureaucratic rationality, nationalism, racial theories, and an endless drive for geographic expansion, and then argue that the culmination of Western culture was the Third Reich? (Actually, some radical critics of the West would probably make precisely this argument.) Yet even after criticism, Huntington has been stubborn in sticking to more or less the same arbitrary list.[2] It seems to me the only way to understand why Huntington creates the list he does is to examine his use of the terms *culture* and *civilization*. In fact, if one reads the text carefully, one finds that the phrases "Western culture" and "Western civilization" are used pretty much interchangeably. Each civilization has its own culture. Cultures, in turn, appear to consist primarily of "ideas," "concepts," and "values." In the Western case, these ideas appear to have once been tied to a particular sort of Christianity, but now have developed a basically geographic or national distribution, having set down roots in Western Europe and its English- and French-speaking settler colonies. The other civilizations listed are—with the exception of Japan—not defined in geographic terms. They are still religions: the Islamic, Confucian, Buddhist, Hindu, and Orthodox Christian civilizations. This is already a bit confusing. Why should the West have stopped being primarily defined in religious terms around 1520 (despite the fact that most Westerners continue to call themselves "Christians"), while the others all remain so (despite the fact that most Chinese, for example, would certainly not call themselves "Confucians")? Presumably because, for Huntington to be consistent in this area, he would either have to exclude from the West certain groups he would prefer not to exclude (Catholics or Protestants, Jews, Deists, secular philosophers) or else provide some reason why the West can consist of a complex amalgam of faiths and philosophies while all the other civilizations cannot: despite the fact that if one examines the history of geographical units like India, or China (as opposed to made-up entities like Hinduism or Confucianism), a complex amalgam of faiths and philosophies is precisely what one finds.

It gets worse. In a later clarification called "What Makes the West Western" (1996), Huntington actually does claim that "pluralism" is one of the West's unique qualities:

> Western society historically has been highly pluralistic.[3] What is distinctive about the West, as Karl Deutsch noted, "is the rise and persistence of diverse autonomous groups not based on blood relationship or marriage." Beginning in the sixth and seventh centuries these groups initially included monasteries, monastic orders, and guilds, but afterward expanded in many areas of Europe to include a variety of other associations and societies.[4]

He goes on to explain that this diversity also included class pluralism (strong aristocracies), social pluralism (representative bodies), linguistic diversity, and so on. All this gradually set the stage, he says, for the unique complexity of Western civil society. Now, it would be easy to point out how ridiculous all this is. One could, for instance, remind the reader that China and India in fact had, for most of their histories, a great deal more religious pluralism than Western Europe; that most Asian societies were marked by a dizzying variety of monastic orders, guilds, colleges, secret societies, sodalities, professional and civic groups; that none ever came up with such distinctly Western ways of enforcing uniformity as the war of extermination against heretics, the Inquisition, or the witch hunt. But the amazing thing is that what Huntington is doing here is trying to turn the very incoherence of his category into its defining feature. First, he describes Asian civilizations in such a way that they cannot, by definition, be plural; then, if one were to complain that people he lumps together as "the West" don't seem to have any common features at all—no common language, religion, philosophy, or mode of government—Huntington could simply reply that this pluralism is the West's defining feature. It is the perfect circular argument.

In most ways, Huntington's argument is just typical, old-fashioned Orientalism: European civilization is represented as inherently dynamic, "the East," at least tacitly, as stagnant, timeless, and monolithic. What I really want to draw attention to, however, is just how incoherent Huntington's notions of "civilization" and "culture" really are. The word *civilization*, after all, can be used in two very different ways. It can be used to refer to a society in which people live in cities, in the way an archaeologist might refer to the Indus Valley. Or it can mean refinement, accomplishment, cultural achievement. *Culture* has much the same double meaning. One can use the term in its anthropological sense, as referring to structures of feeling, symbolic codes that members of a given culture absorb in the course of growing up and which inform every aspect of their daily life: the way people talk, eat, marry, gesture, play music, and so on. To use Bourdieu's terminology, one could call this culture *habitus*. Alternately, one can use the word to refer to what is also called "high culture": the best and most profound productions of some artistic, literary, or philosophical elite. Huntington's insistence on defining the West only by its most remarkable, valuable concepts—such as freedom and human rights—suggests that, in either case, it's mainly the latter sense he has in mind. After all, if *culture* were to be defined in the anthropological sense, then clearly the most direct heirs to ancient Greeks would not be modern Englishmen and Frenchmen, but modern Greeks. Whereas, in Huntington's system, modern Greeks parted company with the West more than fifteen hundred years ago, the moment they converted to the wrong form of Christianity.

In short, for the notion of "civilization," in the sense used by Huntington, to really make sense, civilizations have to be conceived basically as traditions of people reading one another's books. It is possible to say Napoleon or Disraeli are more heirs to Plato and Thucydides than a Greek shepherd of their day for one reason only: both men were more likely to have read Plato and Thucydides. Western culture is not just a collection of ideas; it is a collection of ideas that are taught in textbooks and discussed in lecture halls, cafés, or literary salons. If it were not, it would be hard to imagine how one could end up with a civilization that begins in ancient Greece, passes to ancient Rome, maintains a kind of half-life in the Medieval Catholic world, revives in the Italian renaissance, and then passes mainly to dwell in those countries bordering the North Atlantic. It would also be impossible to explain how, for most of their history, "Western concepts" like human rights and democracy existed only in potentia. We could say: this is a literary and philosophical tradition, a set of ideas first imagined in ancient Greece, then conveyed through books, lectures, and seminars over several thousand years, drifting as they did westward, until their liberal and democratic potential was fully realized in a small number of countries bordering the Atlantic a century or two ago. Once they became enshrined in new, democratic institutions, they began to worm their way into ordinary citizens' social and political common sense. Finally, their proponents saw them as having universal status and tried to impose them on the rest of the world. But here they hit their limits, because they cannot ultimately expand to areas where there are equally powerful, rival textual traditions—based in Koranic scholarship, or the teachings of the Buddha—that inculcate other concepts and values.

This position, at least, would be intellectually consistent. One might call it the Great Books theory of civilization. In a way, it's quite compelling. Being Western, one might say, has nothing to do with habitus. It is not about the deeply embodied understandings of the world one absorbs in childhood—that which makes certain people upper-class Englishwomen, others Bavarian farm boys or Italian kids from Brooklyn. The West is, rather, the literary-philosophical tradition into which all of them are initiated, mainly in adolescence—though, certainly, some elements of that tradition do, gradually, become part of everyone's common sense. The problem is that, if Huntington applied this model consistently, it would destroy his argument. If civilizations are not deeply embodied, why, then, should an upper-class Peruvian woman or Bangladeshi farm boy not be able to take the same curriculum and become just as Western as anyone else? But this is precisely what Huntington is trying to deny.

As a result, he is forced to continually slip back and forth between the two meanings of *civilization* and the two meanings of *culture*. Mostly, the West is defined by its loftiest ideals. But sometimes it's defined by its ongoing institutional structure—for example, all those early Medieval guilds and monastic orders, which do not seem to have been inspired by readings of Plato and Aristotle, but cropped up all of their own accord. Sometimes Western individualism is treated as an abstract principle, usually suppressed, an idea preserved in ancient texts, but occasionally poking its head out in documents like the Magna Carta. Sometimes it is treated as a deeply embedded folk understanding, which will never make intuitive sense to those raised in a different cultural tradition.

Now, as I say, I chose Huntington largely because he's such an easy target. The argument in "The Clash of Civilizations?" is unusually sloppy. Critics have duly savaged most of what he's had to say about non-Western civilizations. The reader may, at this point, feel justified to wonder why I'm bothering to spend so much time on him. The reason is that, in part

because they are so clumsy, Huntington's argument brings out the incoherence in assumptions that are shared by almost everyone. None of his
critics, to my knowledge, have challenged the idea that there is an entity
that can be referred to as "the West," that it can be treated simultaneously as a literary tradition originating in ancient Greece, and as the
commonsense culture of people who live in Western Europe and North
America today. The assumption that concepts such as individualism and
democracy are somehow peculiar to it goes similarly unchallenged. All
this is simply taken for granted as the grounds of debate. Some proceed
to celebrate the West as the birthplace of freedom. Others denounce
it as a source of imperial violence. But it's almost impossible to find a
political, philosophical, or social thinker on the left or the right who
doubts one can say meaningful things about "the Western tradition" at
all. Many of the most radical, in fact, seem to feel it is impossible to say
meaningful things about anything else.

Parenthetical Note: On the Slipperiness of the Western Eye

What I am suggesting is that the very notion of the West is founded on
a constant blurring of the line between textual traditions and forms of
everyday practice. To offer a particular vivid example: In the 1920s, a
French philosopher named Lucien Lévy-Bruhl wrote a series of books
proposing that many of the societies studied by anthropologists evinced
a "pre-logical mentality."[5] Where modern Westerners employ logico-
experimental thought, he argued, primitives employ profoundly different principles. The whole argument need not be spelled out. Everything
Lévy-Bruhl said about primitive logic was attacked almost immediately
and his argument is now considered entirely discredited. What his critics did not, generally speaking, point out is that Lévy-Bruhl was comparing apples and oranges. Basically, what he did was assemble the most
puzzling ritual statements or surprising reactions to unusual circumstances he could cull from the observations of European missionaries
and colonial officials in Africa, New Guinea, and similar places, and
try to extrapolate the logic. He then compared this material, not with
similar material collected in France or some other Western country, but

rather, with a completely idealized conception of how Westerners ought to behave, based on philosophical and scientific texts (buttressed, no doubt, by observations about the way philosophers and other academics act while discussing and arguing about such texts). The results are manifestly absurd—we all know that ordinary people do not in fact apply Aristotelian syllogisms and experimental methods to their daily affairs—but it is the special magic of this style of writing that one is never forced to confront this.

Because, in fact, this style of writing is also extremely common. How does this magic work?

Largely, by causing the reader to identify with a human being of unspecified qualities who's trying to solve a puzzle. One sees it in the Western philosophical tradition, especially starting with the works of Aristotle that, especially compared with similar works in other philosophical traditions (which rarely start from such decontextualized thinkers), give us the impression the universe was created yesterday, suggesting no prior knowledge is necessary. Even more, there is the tendency to show a commonsense narrator confronted with some kind of exotic practices—this is what makes it possible, for example, for a contemporary German to read Tacitus's *Germania* and automatically identify with the perspective of the Italian narrator, rather than with his own ancestor, or an Italian atheist to read an Anglican missionary's account of some ritual in Zimbabwe without ever having to think about that observer's dedication to bizarre tea rituals or the doctrine of transubstantiation. Hence, the entire history of the West can be framed as a story of "inventions" and "discoveries." Most of all, there is the fact that it is precisely when one actually begins to write a text to address these issues, as I am doing now, that one effectively becomes part of the canon and the tradition most comes to seem overwhelmingly inescapable.

More than anything else, the "Western individual" in Lévy-Bruhl, or for that matter most contemporary anthropologists, is, more than anything else, precisely that featureless, rational observer, a disembodied eye, carefully scrubbed of any individual or social content, that we are supposed to pretend to be when writing in certain genres of prose.

It has little relation to any human being who has ever existed, grown up, had loves and hatreds and commitments. It's a pure abstraction. Recognizing all of this creates a terrible problem for anthropologists: if the "Western individual" doesn't exist, then what precisely is our point of comparison?

It seems to me, though, it creates an even worse problem for anyone who wishes to see this figure as the bearer of "democracy," as well. If democracy is communal self-governance, the Western individual is an actor already purged of any ties to a community. While it is possible to imagine this relatively featureless, rational observer as the protagonist of certain forms of market economics, to make him (and he is, unless otherwise specified, presumed to be male) a democrat seems possible only if one defines democracy as itself a kind of market that actors enter with little more than a set of economic interests to pursue. This is, of course, the approach promoted by rational choice theory, and, in a way, you could say it is already implicit in the predominant approach to democratic decision-making in the literature since Rousseau, which tends to see "deliberation" merely as the balancing of interests rather than a process through which subjects themselves are constituted, or even shaped.[6] It is very difficult to see such an abstraction, divorced from any concrete community, entering into the kind of conversation and compromise required by anything but the most abstract form of democratic process, such as the periodic participation in elections.

World-Systems Reconfigured

The reader may feel entitled to ask: If "the West" is a meaningless category, how can we talk about such matters? It seems to me we need an entirely new set of categories. While this is hardly the place to develop them, I've suggested elsewhere that there are a whole series of terms—starting with the West, but also including terms such as *modernity*—that effectively substitute for thought.[7] If one looks either at concentrations of urbanism, or literary-philosophical traditions, it becomes hard to avoid the impression that Eurasia was for most of its history divided into three main centers: an Eastern system centered on China, a South Asian one centered on what's now India, and a Western civilization that cen-

tered on what we now call "the Middle East," extending sometimes far-
ther, sometimes less, into the Mediterranean. In world-system terms, for
most of the Middle Ages, Europe and Africa both seem to have almost
precisely the same relation with the core states of Mesopotamia and
the Levant: they were classic economic peripheries, importing manufac-
tures and supplying raw materials like gold and silver, and, significantly,
large numbers of slaves. (After the revolt of African slaves in Basra from
868 to 883 CE, the Abbasid caliphate seem to have begun importing
Europeans instead, as they were considered more docile.) Europe and
Africa were, for most of this period, cultural peripheries as well. Islam
resembles what was later to be called "the Western tradition" in so many
ways—the intellectual efforts to fuse Judeo-Christian scripture with the
categories of Greek philosophy, the literary emphasis on courtly love,
the scientific rationalism, the legalism, puritanical monotheism, missionary impulse, the expansionist mercantile capitalism—even the
periodic waves of fascination with "Eastern mysticism"—that only the
deepest historical prejudice could have blinded European historians to
the conclusion that, in fact, this is the Western tradition; that Islamici-
zation was and continues to be a form of Westernization; that those who
lived in the barbarian kingdoms of the European Middle Ages came
to resemble what we now call "the West" only when they themselves
became more like Islam.

   If so, what we are used to calling "the rise of the West" is probably better thought of, in world-system terms, as the emergence of what
Michel-Rolph Trouillot has called the "North Atlantic system," which
gradually replaced the Mediterranean semi-periphery, and emerged
as a world economy of its own, rivaling, and then gradually, slowly,
painfully incorporating the older world economy that had centered on
the cosmopolitan societies of the Indian Ocean.[8] This North Atlantic
world-system was created through almost unimaginable catastrophe;
the destruction of entire civilizations, mass enslavement, the death of at
least a hundred million human beings. It also produced its own forms
of cosmopolitanism, with endless fusions of African, Native American,
and European traditions. Much of the history of the seaborne, North
Atlantic proletariat is only beginning to be reconstructed, a history of

mutinies, pirates, rebellions, defections, experimental communities, and every sort of Antinomian and populist idea, largely squelched in conventional accounts, much of it permanently lost, but which seems to have played a key role in many of the radical ideas that came to be referred to as "democracy."[9] This is jumping ahead. For now, I just want to emphasize that rather than a history of "civilizations" developing through some Herderian or Hegelian process of internal unfolding, we are dealing with societies that are thoroughly entangled.

B. DEMOCRACY WAS NOT INVENTED

I began this essay by suggesting that one can write the history of democracy in two very different ways. Either one can write a history of the word *democracy*, beginning with ancient Athens, or one can write a history of the sort of egalitarian decision-making procedures that in Athens came to be referred to as "democratic."

Normally, we tend to assume the two are effectively identical because common wisdom has it that democracy—much like, say, science, or philosophy—was invented in ancient Greece. On the face of it this seems an odd assertion. Egalitarian communities have existed throughout human history—many of them far more egalitarian than fifth-century Athens—and they each had some kind of procedure for coming to decisions in matters of collective importance. Often, this involved assembling everyone for discussions in which all members of the community, at least in theory, had equal say. Yet somehow, it is always assumed that these procedures could not have been, properly speaking, "democratic."

The main reason this argument seems to make intuitive sense is because, in these other assemblies, things rarely actually came to a vote. Almost invariably, they used some form of consensus finding. Now, this is interesting in itself. If we accept the idea that a show of hands, or having everyone who supports a proposition stand on one side of the plaza and everyone against stand on the other, are not really such incredibly sophisticated ideas that some ancient genius had to "invent" them, then why are they so rarely employed? Why, instead, did communities invariably prefer the apparently much more difficult task of coming to unanimous decisions?

The explanation I would propose is this: it is much easier, in a face-to-face community, to figure out what most members of that community want to do than to figure out how to change the minds of those who don't want to do it. Consensus decision-making is typical of societies where there would be no way to compel a minority to agree with a majority decision; either because there is no state with a monopoly of coercive force, or because the state has no interest in or does not tend to intervene in local decision-making. If there is no way to compel those who find a majority decision too distasteful to go along with it, then the last thing one would want to do is hold a vote: a public contest that someone will be seen to lose. Voting would be the most likely means to guarantee the sort of humiliations, resentments, and hatreds that ultimately lead to the destruction of communities. As any activist who has gone through a facilitation training for a contemporary direct action group can tell you, consensus process is not the same as parliamentary debate, and finding consensus in no way resembles voting. Rather, we are dealing with a process of compromise and synthesis meant to produce decisions that no one finds so violently objectionable that they are not willing to at least assent. That is to say, two levels we are used to distinguishing—decision-making and enforcement—are effectively collapsed here. It is not that everyone has to agree. Most forms of consensus include a variety of graded forms of disagreement. The point is to ensure that no one walks away feeling that their views have been totally ignored and, therefore, that even those who think the group came to a bad decision are willing to offer their passive acquiescence.

Majority democracy, we might say, can emerge only when two factors coincide:

1. a feeling that people should have equal say in making group decisions, and
2. a coercive apparatus capable of enforcing those decisions.

For most of human history, it has been extremely unusual to have both at the same time. Where egalitarian societies exist, it is also usually considered wrong to impose systematic coercion. Where a machinery of coercion did exist, it did not even occur to those wielding it that they were enforcing any sort of popular will.

It is of obvious relevance that ancient Greece was one of the most competitive societies known to history. It was a society that tended to make everything into a public contest, from athletics to philosophy or tragic drama or just about anything else. So it might not seem entirely surprising that they made political decision-making into a public contest as well. Even more crucial, though, was the fact that decisions were made by a populace in arms. Aristotle, in his *Politics*, remarks that the constitution of a Greek city-state will normally depend on the chief arm of its military: if this is cavalry, it will be an aristocracy, since horses are expensive. If hoplite infantry, it will be oligarchic, as all could not afford the armor and training. If its power was based in the navy or light infantry, one can expect a democracy, as anyone can row, or use a sling. In other words, if a man is armed, then one pretty much has to take his opinions into account. One can see how this worked at its starkest in Xenophon's *Anabasis*, which tells the story of an army of Greek mercenaries who suddenly find themselves leaderless and lost in the middle of Persia. They elect new officers, and then hold a collective vote to decide what to do next. In a case like this, even if the vote was sixty–forty, everyone could see the balance of forces and what would happen if things actually came to blows. Every vote was, in a real sense, a conquest.

In other words, here too decision-making and the means of enforcement were effectively collapsed (or could be), but in a rather different way.

Roman legions could be similarly democratic; this was the main reason they were never allowed to enter the city of Rome. And, when Machiavelli revived the notion of a democratic republic at the dawn of the "modern" era, he immediately reverted to the notion of a populace in arms.

This in turn might help explain the term *democracy* itself, which appears to have been coined as something of a slur by its elitist opponents:

it literally means the "force" or even "violence" of the people. Kratos, not archos. The elitists who coined the term always considered democracy not too far from simple rioting or mob rule; though, of course, their solution was the permanent conquest of the people by someone else. Ironically, when they did manage to suppress democracy for this reason, which was usually, the result was that the only way the general populace's will was known was precisely through rioting, a practice that became quite institutionalized in, say, imperial Rome or eighteenth-century Britain.

One question that bears historical investigation is the degree to which such phenomena were in fact encouraged by the state. Here, I'm not referring to literal rioting, of course, but to what I would call the "ugly mirrors": institutions promoted or supported by elites that reinforced the sense that popular decision-making could only be violent, chaotic, and arbitrary "mob rule." I suspect that these are quite common to authoritarian regimes. Consider, for example, that while the defining public event in democratic Athens was the agora, the defining public event in authoritarian Rome was the circus, assemblies in which the plebs gathered to witness races, gladiatorial contests, and mass executions. Such games were sponsored either directly by the state, or more often, by particular members of the elite.[10] The fascinating thing about gladiatorial contests, in particular, is that they did involve a kind of popular decision-making: lives would be taken, or spared, by popular acclaim. However, where the procedures of the Athenian agora were designed to maximize the dignity of the demos and the thoughtfulness of its deliberations—despite the underlying element of coercion, and its occasional capability of making terrifyingly bloodthirsty decisions— the Roman circus was almost exactly the opposite. It had more the air of regular, state-sponsored lynchings. Almost every quality normally ascribed to "the mob" by later writers hostile to democracy—the capriciousness, overt cruelty, factionalism (supporters of rival chariot teams would regularly do battle in the streets), hero worship, mad passions— all were not only tolerated, but actually encouraged in the Roman amphitheater. It was as if an authoritarian elite was trying to provide the public with constant nightmare images of the chaos that would ensue if they were to take power into their own hands.

My emphasis on the military origins of direct democracy is not meant to imply that popular assemblies in, say, Medieval cities or New England town meetings were not normally orderly and dignified procedures; though one suspects this was in part due to the fact that here, too, in actual practice, there was a certain baseline of consensus-seeking going on. Still, they seem to have done little to disabuse members of political elites of the idea that popular rule would more resemble the circuses and riots of imperial Rome and Byzantium. The authors of the Federalist Papers, like almost all other literate men of their day, took it for granted that what they called "democracy"—by which they meant direct democracy, "pure democracy" as they sometimes put it—was in its nature the most unstable, tumultuous form of government, not to mention one that endangers the rights of minorities (the specific minority they had in mind in this case being the rich). It was only once the term *democracy* could be almost completely transformed to incorporate the principle of representation—a term that itself has a very curious history, since, as Cornelius Castoriadis liked to point out, it referred to representatives of the people before the king, internal ambassadors in fact, rather than those who wielded power in any sense themselves— that it was rehabilitated, in the eyes of well-born political theorists, and took on the meaning it has today. In the next section let me pass, however briefly, to how this came about.[11]

C. ON THE EMERGENCE OF THE "DEMOCRATIC IDEAL"

The remarkable thing is just how long it took. For the first three hundred years of the North Atlantic system, democracy continued to mean "the mob." This was true even in the "Age of Revolutions." In almost every case, the founders of what are now considered the first democratic constitutions in France and the United States rejected any suggestion that they were trying to introduce "democracy." As Francis Dupuis-Déri has observed:

The founders of the modern electoral systems in the United States and France were overtly anti-democratic. This anti-democratism can be explained in part by their vast knowledge of the literary, philosophical and historical texts of Greco-Roman antiquity. Regarding political history, it was common for American and French political figures to see themselves as direct heirs to classical civilization and to believe that, all through history, from Athens and Rome to Boston and Paris, the same political forces have faced off in eternal struggles. The founders sided with the historical republican forces against the aristocratic and democratic ones, and the Roman republic was the political model for both the Americans and the French, whereas Athenian democracy was a despised counter-model.[12]

In the English-speaking world, for example, most educated people in the late eighteenth century were familiar with Athenian democracy largely through a translation of Thucydides by Thomas Hobbes. Their conclusion, that democracy was unstable, tumultuous, prone to factionalism and demagoguery, and marked by a strong tendency to turn into despotism, was hardly surprising.

Most politicians, then, were hostile to anything that smacked of democracy precisely because they saw themselves as heirs to what we now call "the Western tradition." The ideal of the Roman Republic was enshrined, for example, in the American constitution, whose framers were quite consciously trying to imitate Rome's "mixed constitution," balancing monarchical, aristocratic, and democratic elements. John Adams, for example, in his *Defense of the Constitutions* (1797), argued that truly egalitarian societies do not exist; that every known human society has a supreme leader, an aristocracy (whether of wealth or a "natural aristocracy" of virtue) and a public, and that the Roman constitution was the most perfect in balancing the powers of each.[13] The American constitution was meant to reproduce this balance by creating a powerful presidency, a senate to represent the wealthy, and a congress to represent the people—though the powers of the latter were largely limited to ensuring popular control over the distribution of tax money. This republican ideal lies at the basis of all "democratic" constitutions and to this day many conservative thinkers in America like to point out that "America is not a democracy: it's a republic."

On the other hand, as John Markoff notes, "those who called themselves democrats at the tail end of the eighteenth century were likely to be very suspicious of parliaments, downright hostile to competitive political parties, critical of secret ballots, uninterested or even opposed to women's suffrage, and sometimes tolerant of slavery"—again, hardly surprising, for those who wished to revive something along the lines of ancient Athens.[14]

At the time, outright democrats of this sort—men like Tom Paine, for instance—were considered a tiny minority of rabble-rousers even within revolutionary regimes. Things only began to change over the course of the next century. In the United States, as the franchise widened in the first decades of the nineteenth century, and politicians were increasingly forced to seek the votes of small farmers and urban laborers, some began to adopt the term. Andrew Jackson led the way. He started referring to himself as a democrat in the 1820s. Within twenty years, almost all political parties, not just populists but even the most conservative, began to follow suit. In France, socialists began calling for "democracy" in the 1830s, with similar results: within ten or fifteen years, the term was being used by even moderate and conservative republicans forced to compete with them for the popular vote.[15] The same period saw a dramatic reappraisal of Athens, which—again starting in the 1820s—began to be represented as embodying a noble ideal of public participation, rather than a nightmare of violent crowd psychology.[16] This is not, however, because anyone, at this point, was endorsing Athenian-style direct democracy, even on the local level (in fact, one rather imagines it was precisely this fact that made the rehabilitation of Athens possible). For the most part, politicians simply began substituting the word *democracy* for *republic*, without any change in meaning. I suspect the new positive appraisal of Athens had more to do with popular fascination with events in Greece at the time than anything else: specifically, the war of independence against the Ottoman Empire between 1821 and 1829. It was hard not to see it as a modern replay of the clash between the Persian Empire and Greek city-states narrated by Herodotus, a kind of founding text of the opposition between freedom-loving Europe and the despotic East; and, of course, changing one's frame of reference from Thucydides to Herodotus could only do Athens's image good.

When novelists like Victor Hugo and poets like Walt Whitman began touting democracy as a beautiful ideal—as they soon began to do—they were not, however, referring to word games on the part of elites, but to the broader popular sentiment that had caused small farmers and urban laborers to look with favor on the term to begin with, even when the political elite was still largely using it as a term of abuse. The "democratic ideal," in other words, did not emerge from the Western literary-philosophical tradition. It was, rather, imposed on it. In fact, the notion that democracy was a distinctly "Western" ideal only came much later. For most of the nineteenth century, when Europeans defined themselves against "the East" or "the Orient," they did so precisely as "Europeans," not "Westerners." With few exceptions, "the West" referred to the Americas. It was only in the 1890s, when Europeans began to see the United States as part of the same, coequal civilization, that many started using the term in its current sense.[17] Huntington's "Western civilization" comes even later: this notion was first developed in American universities in the years following World War I, at a time when German intellectuals were already locked in debate about whether they were part of the West at all.[18] Over the course of the twentieth century, the concept of "Western civilization" proved perfectly tailored for an age that saw the gradual dissolution of colonial empires, since it managed to lump together the former colonial metropoles with their wealthiest and most powerful settler colonies, at the same time insisting on their shared moral and intellectual superiority, and abandoning any notion that they necessarily had a responsibility to "civilize" anybody else. The peculiar tension evident in phrases like "Western science," "Western freedoms," or "Western consumer goods"—do these reflect universal truths that all human beings should recognize? or are they the products of one tradition among many?—would appear to stem directly from the ambiguities of the historical moment. The resulting formulation is, as I've noted, so riddled with contradictions that it's hard to see how it could have arisen except to fill a very particular historical need.

If you examine these terms more closely, however, it becomes obvious that all these "Western" objects are the products of endless entanglements. "Western science" was patched together out of discoveries made on many continents, and is now largely produced by non-Westerners. "Western consumer goods" were always drawn from materials taken from all over the world, many explicitly imitated Asian products, and nowadays, are all produced in China. Can we say the same of "Western freedoms"?

The reader can probably guess what my answer will be.

D. RECUPERATION

In debates about the origins of capitalism, one of the main bones of contention is whether capitalism—or, alternately, industrial capitalism—emerged primarily within European societies, or whether it can be understood only in the context of a larger world-system connecting Europe and its overseas possessions, markets and sources of labor overseas. It is possible to have the argument, I think, because so many capitalist forms began so early—many could be said to already be present, at least in embryonic form, at the very dawn of European expansion. This can hardly be said for democracy. Even if one is willing to follow by-now accepted convention and identify republican forms of government with that word, democracy emerges only within centers of empire like Britain and France, and colonies like the United States, after the Atlantic system had existed for almost three hundred years.

Giovanni Arrighi, Iftikhar Ahmad, and Min-wen Shih have produced what's to my mind one of the more interesting responses to Huntington: a world-systemic analysis of European expansion, particularly in Asia, over the last several centuries.[19] One of the most fascinating elements in their account is how, at exactly the same time as European powers came to start thinking themselves as "democratic"—in the 1830s, 1840s, and 1850s—those same powers began pursuing an intentional policy of supporting reactionary elites against those pushing for anything remotely resembling democratic reforms overseas. Great Britain was particularly flagrant in this regard: whether in its support for the Ottoman Empire against the rebellion of the Egyptian governor Muhammad Ali after the Balta Limani Treaty of 1838, or in its support for the Qing imperial forces against the Taiping rebellion after the Nanjing Treaty of 1842. In either case, Britain first found some excuse to launch a military attack on one of the great Asian ancien regimes, defeated it militarily, imposed a commercially advantageous treaty, and then, almost immediately upon doing so, swung around to prop that same regime up against political rebels who clearly were closer to their own supposed "Western" values than the regime itself: in the first case a rebellion aiming to turn Egypt into something more like a modern nation-state; in the second, an egalitarian Christian movement calling for universal brotherhood. After the Great Rebellion of 1857 in India, Britain began employing the same strategy in her own colonies, self-consciously propping up "landed magnates and the petty rulers of 'native states' within its own Indian empire."[20] All of this was buttressed on the intellectual level by the development around the same time of Orientalist theories that argued that, in Asia, such authoritarian regimes were inevitable, and democratizing movements were unnatural or did not exist.

In sum, Huntington's claim that Western civilization is the bearer of a heritage of liberalism, constitutionalism, human rights, equality, liberty, the rule of law, democracy, free markets, and other similarly attractive ideals—all of which are said to have permeated other civilizations only superficially—rings false to anyone familiar with the Western record in Asia in the so-called age of nation-states. In this long list of ideals, it is hard to find a single one that was not denied in part or full by the leading Western powers of the epoch in their dealings either with the peoples they subjected to direct colonial rule or with the governments over which they sought to establish suzerainty. And conversely, it is just as hard to find a single one of those ideals that was not upheld by movements of national liberation in their struggle against the Western powers. In upholding these ideals, however, non-Western peoples and governments invariably combined them with ideals derived from their own civilizations in those spheres in which they had little to learn from the West.[21]

Actually, I think one could go much further. Opposition to European expansion in much of the world, even quite early on, appears to have been carried out in the name of "Western values" that the Europeans in question did not yet even have. Engseng Ho, for example, draws our attention to the first known articulation of the notion of jihad against Europeans in the Indian Ocean: a book called *Gift of the Jihad Warriors in Matters Regarding the Portuguese*, written in 1574 by an Arab jurist named Zayn al-Din al-Malibari and addressed to the Muslim sultan of the Deccan state of Bijapur.[22] In it, the author makes a case that it is justified to wage war against the Portuguese specifically because they destroyed a tolerant, pluralistic society in which Muslims, Hindus, Christians, and Jews had always managed to coexist.

In the Muslim trading ecumene of the Indian Ocean, some of Huntington's values—a certain notion of liberty, a certain notion of equality, some very explicit ideas about freedom of trade and the rule of law—had long been considered important; others, such as religious tolerance, might well have become values as a result of Europeans coming onto the scene—if only by point of contrast. My real point is that one simply cannot lay any of these values down to the one particular moral, intellectual, or cultural tradition. They arise, for better or worse, from exactly this sort of interaction.

I also want to make another point, though. We are dealing with the work of a Muslim jurist, writing a book addressed to a South Indian king. The values of tolerance and mutual accommodation he wishes to defend—actually, these are our terms; he himself speaks of "kindness"—

might have emerged from a complex intercultural space, outside the authority of any overarching state power, and they might have crystallized, as values, only in the face of those who wished to destroy that space. Yet, in order to write about them, to justify their defense, he was forced to deal with states and frame his argument in terms of a single literary-philosophical tradition: in this case, the legal tradition of Sunni Islam. There was an act of reincorporation. There inevitably must be, once one reenters the world of state power and textual authority. And, when later authors write about such ideas, they tend to represent matters as if the ideals emerged from that tradition, rather than from the spaces in between.

So do historians. In a way, it's almost inevitable that they should do so, considering the nature of their source material. They are, after all, primarily students of textual traditions, and information about the spaces in between is often very difficult to come by. What's more, they are—at least when dealing with the "Western tradition"—writing, in large part, within the same literary tradition as their sources. This is what makes the real origins of democratic ideals—especially that popular enthusiasm for ideas of liberty and popular sovereignty that obliged politicians to adopt the term to begin with—so difficult to reconstruct. Recall here what I said earlier about the "slipperiness of the Western eye." The tradition has long had a tendency to describe alien societies as puzzles to be deciphered by a rational observer. As a result, descriptions of alien societies were often used, around this time, as a way of making a political point: whether contrasting European societies with the relative freedom of Native Americans, or the relative order of China. But they did not tend to acknowledge the degree to which they were themselves entangled with those societies and to which their own institutions were influenced by them. In fact, as any student of early anthropology knows, even authors who were themselves part Native American or part Chinese, or who had never set foot in Europe, would tend to write this way. As men or women of action, they would negotiate their way between worlds. When it came time to write about their experiences, they would become featureless abstractions. When it came time to write institutional histories, they referred back, almost invariably, to the Classical world.

The "Influence Debate"

In 1977, a historian of the Iroquois Confederacy, Donald A. Grinde (himself a Native American and member of AIM, the American Indian Movement), wrote an essay proposing that certain elements of the U.S. constitution—particularly its federal structure—were inspired in part by the League of Six Nations. He expanded on the argument in the 1980s with another historian, Bruce Johansen, suggesting that, in a larger sense, what we now would consider America's democratic spirit was partly inspired by the example of Native Americans.

Some of the specific evidence they assembled was quite compelling.[23] The idea of forming some sort of federation of colonies was indeed proposed by an Onondaga ambassador named Canassatego, exhausted by having to negotiate with so many separate colonies during negotiations over the Lancaster Treaty in 1744. The image he used to demonstrate the strength of union, a bundle of six arrows, still appears on the Seal of the Union of the United States (the number later increased to thirteen). Ben Franklin, present at the event, took up the idea and promoted it widely through his printing house over the next decade, and, in 1754, his efforts came to fruition with a conference in Albany, New York—with representatives of the Six Nations in attendance—that drew up what came to be known as the Albany Plan of Union. The plan was ultimately rejected both by British authorities and colonial parliaments, but it was clearly an important first step. More important, perhaps, proponents of what has come to be called the "influence theory" argued that the values of egalitarianism and personal freedom that marked so many Eastern Woodlands societies served as a broader inspiration for the equality and liberty promoted by colonial rebels. When Boston patriots triggered their revolution by dressing up as Mohawks and dumping British tea into the harbor, they were making a self-conscious statement of their model for individual liberty.

That Iroquois federal institutions might have had some influence on the U.S. constitution was considered a completely unremarkable notion when it was occasionally proposed in the nineteenth century. When it was proposed again in the 1980s it set off a political maelstrom. Many Native Americans strongly endorsed the idea, Congress passed a bill acknowledging it, and all sorts of right-wing commentators immediately pounced on it as an example of the worst sort of political correctness. At the same time, though, the argument met immediate and quite virulent opposition both from most professional historians considered authorities on the Constitution and from anthropological experts on the Iroquois.

The actual debate ended up turning almost entirely on whether one could prove a direct relation between Iroquois institutions and the thinking of the framers of the Constitution. Payne, for example, noted that some New England colonists were discussing federal schemes before they were even aware of the league's existence; in a larger sense, they argued that proponents of the "influence theory" had essentially cooked the books by picking out every existing passage in the writings of colonial politicians that praised Iroquoian institutions, while ignoring hundreds of texts in which those same politicians denounced the Iroquois, and Indians in general, as ignorant murdering savages.[24] Their opponents, they said, left the reader with the impression that explicit, textual proof of an Iroquoian influence on the Constitution existed, and this was simply not the case. Even the Indians present at constitutional conventions appear to have been there to state grievances, not to offer advice. Invariably, when colonial politicians discussed the origins of their ideas, they looked to classical, biblical, or European examples: the book of Judges, the Achaean League, the Swiss Confederacy, the United Provinces of the Netherlands. Proponents of the influence theory, in turn, replied that this kind of linear thinking was simplistic: no one was claiming the Six Nations were the only or even primary model for American federalism, just one of many elements that went into the mix—and considering that it was the only functioning example of a federal system of which the colonists had any direct experience, to insist it had no influence whatever was simply bizarre. Indeed, some of the objections raised by anthropologists seem so odd—for example, Elisabeth Tooker's objection that, since the league worked by consensus and reserved an important place for women, and the U.S. constitution used a majority system and allowed only men to vote, one could not possibly have served as inspiration for the other, or Dean Snow's remark that such claims "muddle and denigrate the subtle and remarkable features of Iroquois government"—one can only conclude that the Native American activist Vine Deloria probably did have a point in suggesting much of this was simply an effort by scholars to protect what they considered their turf—a matter of intellectual property rights.[25]

The proprietary reaction is much clearer in some quarters. "This myth isn't just silly, it's destructive," wrote one contributor to *The New Republic.* "Obviously 'Western civilization,' beginning in Greece, had provided models of government much closer to the hearts of the Founding Fathers than this one. There was nothing to be gained by looking to the New World for inspiration."[26] If one is speaking of the immediate perceptions of many of the United States' "founding fathers," this may well be true, but if we are trying to understand the Iroquois influence on American democracy, then matters look quite different. As we've seen, the Constitution's framers did indeed identify with the classical tradition, but they were hostile to democracy for that very reason. They identified democracy with untrammeled liberty, equality, and, insofar as they were aware of Indian customs at all, they were likely to see them as objectionable for precisely the same reasons.

If one reexamines some of the mooted passages, this is precisely what one finds. John Adams, remember, had argued in his *Defense of the Constitutions* that egalitarian societies do not exist; political power in every human society is divided among the monarchical, aristocratic, and democratic principles. He saw the Indians as resembling the ancient Germans in that "the democratical branch, in particular, is so determined, that real sovereignty resided in the body of the people," which, he said, worked well enough when one was dealing with populations scattered over a wide territory with no real concentrations of wealth, but, as the Goths found when they conquered the Roman Empire, could only lead to confusion, instability, and strife as soon as such populations became more settled and had significant resources to administer.[27] His observations are typical. Madison, even Jefferson, tended to describe Indians much as did John Locke, as exemplars of an individual liberty untrammeled by any form of state or systematic coercion—a condition made possible by the fact that Indian societies were not marked by significant divisions of property. They considered Native institutions obviously inappropriate for a society such as their own, which did.

Still, Enlightenment theory to the contrary, nations are not really created by the acts of wise lawgivers. Neither is democracy invented in texts; even if we are forced to rely on texts to divine its history. Actually, the men who wrote the Constitution were not only for the most part wealthy landowners, few had a great deal of experience in sitting down with a group of equals—at least, until they became involved in colonial congresses. Democratic practices tend to first get hammered out in places far from the purview of such men, and, if one sets out in search for which of their contemporaries had the most hands-on experience in such matters, the results are sometimes startling. One of the leading contemporary historians of European democracy, John Markoff, in an essay called "Where and When Was Democracy Invented?" remarks, at one point, very much in passing:

> that leadership could derive from the consent of the led, rather than be bestowed by higher authority, and this would have been a likely experience of the crews of pirate vessels in the early modern Atlantic world. Pirate crews not only elected their captains, but were familiar with countervailing power (in the forms of the quartermaster and ship's council) and contractual relations of individual and collective (in the form of written ship's articles specifying shares of booty and rates of compensation for on-the-job injury).[28]

As a matter of fact, the typical organization of eighteenth-century pirate ships, as reconstructed by historians such as Marcus Rediker, appears to have been remarkably democratic.[29] Captains were not only elected, they usually functioned much like Native American war chiefs: granted total power during chase or combat, they were otherwise treated like ordinary crewmen. Those ships whose captains were granted more general powers also insisted on the crew's right to remove them at any time for cowardice, cruelty, or any other reason. In every case, ultimate power rested in a general assembly that often ruled on even the most minor matters, always, apparently, by majority show of hands.

All this might seem less surprising if one considers the pirates' origins. Pirates were generally mutineers, sailors often originally pressed into service against their will in port towns across the Atlantic, who had mutinied against tyrannical captains and "declared war against the whole world." They often became classic social bandits, wreaking vengeance against captains who abused their crews, and releasing or even rewarding those against whom they found no complaints. The makeup of crews was often extraordinarily heterogeneous. "Black Sam Bellamy's crew of 1717 was 'a Mix'd Multitude of all Country's,' including British, French, Dutch, Spanish, Swedish, Native American, African American, and two dozen Africans who had been liberated from a slave ship."[30] In other words, we are dealing with a collection of people in which there was likely to be at least some firsthand knowledge of a very wide range of directly democratic institutions, ranging from Swedish tings to African village assemblies to Native American councils such as those from which the League of Six Nations itself developed, suddenly finding themselves forced to improvise some mode of self-government in the complete absence of any state. It was the perfect intercultural space of experiment. In fact, there was likely to be no more conducive ground for the development of new democratic institutions anywhere in the Atlantic world at the time.

I bring this up for two reasons. One is obvious. We have no evidence that democratic practices developed on Atlantic pirate ships in the early part of the eighteenth century had any influence, direct or indirect, on the evolution of democratic constitutions sixty or seventy years later. Nor could we. While accounts of pirates and their adventures circulated widely, having much the same popular appeal as they do today (and presumably, at the time, were likely to be at least a little more accurate than contemporary Hollywood versions), this would be about the very last influence a French, British, or colonial gentleman would ever have been willing to acknowledge. This is not to say that pirate practices were likely to have influenced democratic constitutions. Only that we would not know if they did. One can hardly imagine things would be too different with those they ordinarily referred to as "the American savages."

The other reason is that frontier societies in the Americas were probably more similar to pirate ships than we would be given to imagine. They might not have been as densely populated as pirate ships, or in as immediate need of constant cooperation, but they were spaces of intercultural improvisation, largely outside the purview of states. Colin Calloway has documented just how entangled the societies of settlers and natives often were, with settlers adopting Indian crops, clothes, medicines, customs, and styles of warfare; trading with them, often living side by side, sometimes intermarrying, and most of all, inspiring endless fears among the leaders of colonial communities and military units that their subordinates were absorbing Indian attitudes of equality and individual liberty.[31] At the same time, as the New England Puritan minister Cotton Mather, for example, was inveighing against pirates as a blaspheming scourge of mankind, he was also complaining that fellow colonists had begun to imitate Indian customs of child-rearing (for example, by abandoning corporal punishment), and increasingly forgetting the principles of proper discipline and "severity" in the governance of families for the "foolish indulgence" typical of Indians, whether in relations between masters and servants, men and women, or young and old.[32] This was true most of all in communities, often made up of escaped slaves and servants who "became Indians," outside the control of colonial governments entirely, or island enclaves of what Linebaugh and Rediker have called the "Atlantic proletariat," the motley collection of freedmen, sailors, ships' whores, renegades, Antinomians, and rebels that developed in the port cities of the North Atlantic world before the emergence of modern racism, and from whom much of the democratic impulse of the American—and other—revolutions seems to have first emerged.[33] But it was true for ordinary settlers as well. The irony is that this was the real argument of Bruce Johansen's book *Forgotten Founders*, which first kicked off the "influence debate"—an argument that largely ended up getting lost in all the sound and fury about the Constitution: that ordinary British and French men settled in the colonies began to think of themselves as "Americans," as a new sort of freedom-loving people, only when they began to see themselves as more like Indians. And that this sense was inspired not primarily by the sort of romanticization at a distance one might encounter in texts by Jefferson or Adam Smith, but rather, by the actual experience of living in frontier societies that were essentially, as Calloway puts it, "amalgams." The colonists who came to America, in fact, found themselves in a unique situation: having largely fled the hierarchy and conformism of Europe, they found themselves confronted with an indigenous population far more dedicated to principles of equality and individualism than they had hitherto been able to imagine; and then proceeded to largely exterminate them, even while adopting many of their customs, habits, and attitudes.

I might add that during this period the Five Nations were something of an amalgam as well. Originally a collection of groups that had made a kind of contractual agreement with one another to create a way of mediating disputes and making peace, they became, during their period of expansion in the seventeenth century, an extraordinary jumble of peoples, with large proportions of the population being war captives adopted into Iroquois families to replace family members who had died. Missionaries in those days often complained that it was difficult to preach to Seneca in their own languages, because a majority were not completely fluent in it.[34] Even during the eighteenth century, for instance, while Canassatego was an Onondaga sachem, the other main negotiator with the colonists, Swatane (called Schickallemy), was actually French—or, at least, born to French parents in what's now Canada. On all sides, then, borders were blurred. We are dealing with a graded succession of spaces of democratic improvisation, from the Puritan

communities of New England with their town councils, to frontier communities, to the Iroquois themselves.

Traditions as Acts of Endless Refoundation

Let me try to pull some of the pieces together now.

Throughout this essay, I've been arguing that democratic practice,
whether defined as procedures of egalitarian decision-making, or government by public discussion, tends to emerge from situations in which
communities of one sort or another manage their own affairs outside
the purview of the state. The absence of state power means the absence
of any systematic mechanism of coercion to enforce decisions; this tends
to result either in some form of consensus process, or, in the case of essentially military formations like Greek hoplites or pirate ships, sometimes a system of majority voting (since, in such cases, the results, if it
did come down to a contest of force, are readily apparent). Democratic
innovation, and the emergence of what might be called democratic values, has a tendency to spring from what I've called zones of cultural improvisation, usually also outside the control of states, in which diverse
sorts of people with different traditions and experiences are obliged to
figure out some way to deal with one another. Frontier communities,
whether in Madagascar or Medieval Iceland, pirate ships, Indian Ocean
trading communities, Native American confederations on the edge of
European expansion, are all examples here.

All of this has very little to do with the great literary-philosophical
traditions that tend to be seen as the pillars of great civilizations: indeed, with few exceptions, those traditions are overall explicitly hostile
to democratic procedures and the sort of people that employ them. Governing elites, in turn, have tended either to ignore these forms or tried
to stomp them out.

At a certain point in time, however, first in the core states of the
Atlantic system—notably Britain and France, the two that had the largest colonies in North America—this began to change. The creation of
that system had been heralded by such unprecedented destruction that
it allowed endless new improvisational spaces for the emerging "Atlantic

proletariat." States, under pressure from social movements, began to institute reforms; eventually, those working in the elite literary tradition started seeking precedents for them. The result was the creation of representative systems modeled on the Roman Republic that then were later redubbed, under popular pressure, "democracies" and traced to Athens.

Actually, I would suggest that this process of democratic recuperation and refoundation was typical of a broader process that probably marks any civilizational tradition, but was at that time entering a phase of critical intensity. As European states expanded and the Atlantic system came to encompass the world, all sorts of global influences appear to have coalesced in European capitals, and to have been reabsorbed within the tradition that eventually came to be known as "Western." The actual genealogy of the elements that came together in the modern state, for example, is probably impossible to reconstruct—if only because the very process of recuperation tends to scrub away the more exotic elements in written accounts, or, if not, integrate them into familiar topoi of invention and discovery. Historians, who tend to rely almost exclusively on texts and pride themselves on exacting standards of evidence, therefore often end up, as they did with the Iroquois influence theory, feeling it is their professional responsibility to act as if new ideas do emerge from within textual traditions. Let me throw out two examples:

African fetishism and the idea of the social contract. The Atlantic system, of course, began to take form in West Africa even before Columbus sailed to America. In a fascinating series of essays, William Pietz has described the life of the resulting coastal enclaves where Venetian, Dutch, Portuguese, and every other variety of European merchant and adventurer cohabited with African merchants and adventurers speaking dozens of different languages, a mix of Muslim, Catholic, Protestant, and a variety of ancestral religions.[35] Trade, within these enclaves, was regulated by objects the Europeans came to refer to as "fetishes," and Pietz does much to elaborate the European merchants' theories of value and materiality to which this notion ultimately gave rise. More interesting, perhaps, is the African perspective. Insofar as it can be reconstructed, it appears strikingly similar to the kind of social contract theories developed by men like Thomas Hobbes in Europe at the same time.[36] Essentially, fetishes were created by a series of contracting parties who wished to enter into ongoing economic relations with one another, and were accompanied by agreements on property rights and the rules of exchange; those violating them were to be destroyed by the objects' power. In other words, just as in Hobbes, social relations are created when a group of men agree to create a sovereign power to threaten them with violence if they fail to respect their property rights and contractual obligations. Later, African texts even praised the fetish as preventing a war of all against all. Unfortunately, it's completely impossible to find evidence that Hobbes was aware of any of this; he lived most of his life in a port town and very likely had met traders familiar with such customs, but his political works contain no references to the African continent whatever.

China and the European nation-state. Over the course of the early modern period, European elites gradually conceived the ideal of governments that ruled over uniform populations, speaking the same language, under a uniform system of law and administration; and eventually that this system also should be administered by a meritocratic elite whose training should consist largely in the study of literary classics in that nation's vernacular language. The odd thing is that nothing approaching a precedent for a state of this sort existed anywhere in previous European history, though it almost exactly corresponded to the system Europeans believed to hold sway (and which to a large extent, did hold sway) in Imperial China. Is there evidence for a Chinese "influence theory"? In this case, there is a little. The prestige of the Chinese government evidently being higher, in the eyes of European philosophers, than African merchants, such influences would not be entirely ignored.

From Leibniz's famous remark that the Chinese should really be sending missionaries to Europe rather than the other way around, to the work of Montesquieu and Voltaire, one sees a succession of political philosophers extolling Chinese institutions—as well as a popular fascination with Chinese art, gardens, fashions, and moral philosophy—at exactly the time that Absolutism took form, only for it to fade away in the nineteenth century once China had become the object of European imperial expansion.[37] Obviously none of this constitutes proof that the modern nation-state is in any way of Chinese inspiration. But considering the nature of the literary traditions we're dealing with, even if it were true, this would be about as much proof as we could ever expect to get.

So, is the modern nation-state really a Chinese model of administration, adopted to channel and control democratic impulses derived largely from the influence of Native American societies and the pressures of the Atlantic proletariat, that ultimately came to be justified by a social contract theory derived from Africa? Probably not. At least, this would no doubt be wildly overstating things. But neither do I think it a coincidence that democratic ideals of statecraft first emerged during a period in which the Atlantic powers were at the center of vast global empires, and an endless confluence of knowledge and influences, or that they eventually developed the theory that those ideals sprang instead exclusively from their own "Western" civilization—despite the fact that, during the period in which Europeans had not been at the center of global empires, they had developed nothing of the kind.

Finally, I think it's important to emphasize that this process of recuperation is by no means limited to Europe. In fact, one of the striking things is how quickly almost everyone else in the world began playing the same game. To some degree, as the example of al-Malibari suggests, it was probably happening in other parts of the world even before it began happening in Europe. Of course, overseas movements only started using the word *democracy* much later—but even in the Atlantic world, that term came into common usage only around the middle of the nineteenth century. It was also around the middle of the nineteenth century—just as European powers began recuperating notions of democracy for their own tradition—when Britain led the way in a very self-conscious policy of suppressing anything that looked like it might even have the potential to become a democratic, popular movement overseas. The ultimate response, in much of the colonial world, was to begin playing the exact same game. Opponents to colonial rule scoured their own literary-philosophical traditions for parallels to ancient Athens, along with examining traditional communal decision-making forms in their hinterlands. As Steve Muhlberger and Phil Paine, for example, have documented, if one simply defines it as decision-making by public discussion, "democracy" is a fairly common phenomenon; examples can be found even under states and empires, if only, usually, in those places or domains of human activity in which the rulers of states and empires took little interest.[38] Greek historians writing about India, for example, witnessed any number of polities they considered worthy of the name. Between 1911 and 1918, a number of Indian historians (K. P. Jayaswal, D. R. Bhandarkar, R. C. Majumdar) began examining some of these sources, not only Greek accounts of Alexander's campaigns but also early Buddhist documents in Pali, and early Hindu vocabularies and works of political theory. They discovered dozens of local equivalents to fifth-century Athens on South Asian soil: cities and political confederations in which all men formally classified as warriors—which in some cases meant a very large proportion of adult males—were expected to make important decisions collectively, through public deliberation in communal assemblies. The literary sources of the time were mostly just as hostile to popular rule as Greek ones, but, at least until around 400 CE, such polities definitely existed, and the deliberative mechanisms they employed continue to be employed, in everything from the governance of Buddhist monasteries to craft guilds, until the present day. It was possible, then, to say that the Indian, or even Hindu, tradition was always inherently democratic; and this became a strong argument for those seeking independence.

These early historians clearly overstated their case. After independence came the inevitable backlash. Historians began to point out that these "clan republics" were very limited democracies at best, that the overwhelming majority of the population—women, slaves, those defined as outsiders—were completely disenfranchised. Of course, all this was true of Athens as well, and historians have pointed that out at length. But it seems to me questions of authenticity are of at best secondary importance. Such traditions are always largely fabrications. To some degree, that's what traditions are: the continual process of their own fabrication. The point is that, in every case, what we have are political elites—or would-be political elites—identifying with a tradition of democracy in order to validate essentially republican forms of government. Also, not only was democracy not the special invention of "the West," neither was this process of recuperation and refoundation. True, elites in India started playing the game some sixty years later than those in Britain and France, but, historically, this is not a particularly long period of time. Rather than seeing Indian, or Malagasy, or Tswana, or Maya claims to being part of an inherently democratic tradition as an attempt to ape the West, it seems to me we are looking at different aspects of the same planetary process: a crystallization of long-standing democratic practices in the formation of a global system, in which ideas were flying back and forth in all directions, and the gradual, usually grudging adoption of some by ruling elites.

The temptation to trace democracy to some particular cultural "origins," though, seems almost irresistible. Even serious scholars continue to indulge it. Let me return to Harvard to provide one final, to my mind particularly ironic, example: a collection of essays called *The Breakout: The Origins of Civilization*, put together by leading American symbolic archaeologists.[39] The line of argument sets out from a suggestion by K. C. Chang that early Chinese civilization was based on a fundamentally different sort of ideology than Egypt or Mesopotamia. It was essentially a continuation of the cosmos of earlier hunting societies, in which the monarch replaced the shaman as having an exclusive and personal connection with divine powers. The result was absolute authority. Chang was fascinated by the similarities between early China and the Classic Maya, as reconstructed through recently translated inscriptions: the "stratified universe with bird-perched cosmic tree and religious personnel interlinking the Upper, Middle, and Under Worlds," animal messengers, use of writing mainly for politics and ritual, veneration of ancestors, and so on.[40] The states that emerged in the third millennium in the Middle East, in contrast, represented a kind of breakthrough to an alternate, more pluralistic model that began when gods and their priesthoods came to be seen as independent from the state.

Most of the resulting volume consists of speculations as to what this breakthrough really involved. C. C. Lamberg-Karlovsky argued that the key was the first appearance of notions of freedom and equality in ancient Mesopotamia, in royal doctrines that saw a social contract between the rulers of individual city-states and their subjects—which he calls a "breakout," and which most contributors agreed should be seen as "pointing the way towards Western Democracy."[41] In fact, the main topic of debate soon became who, or what, deserved the credit. Mason Hammond argued in "The Indo-European Origins of the Concept of a Democratic Society" that notions of democracy "did not reach Greece from contact with the Near East or Mesopotamia—where equity and justice were the gift of the ruler—but stemmed from an Indo-European concept of a social organization in which sovereignty might be said to rest, not with the chief, but with the council of elders and the assembly of arms-bearing males."[42] Gordon Willey, on the other hand, sees democratic urges as arising from the free market, which he thinks was more developed in Mesopotamia than China, and largely absent under Maya kingdoms, where rulers ruled by divine right "and there is no evidence of any counterbalancing power within the chiefdom or state that could have held him in check."[43] Linda Schele, the foremost authority on the Classic Maya, concurs, adding that this shamanic cosmos "is still alive and functioning today" in "modern Maya communities."[44] Other scholars try to put in a good word for their own parts of the ancient world: Egypt, Israel, the Harappan civilization.

At times, these arguments seem almost comical parodies of the kind of logic I've been criticizing in historians: most obviously, the line of reasoning that assumes that, if there is no direct evidence for something, it can be treated as if it does not exist. This seems especially inappropriate when dealing with early antiquity, an enormous landscape on which archaeology and linguistics can at best throw open a few tiny windows. For example: the fact that "primitive Celts and Germans" met in communal assemblies does not in itself prove that communal assemblies have an Indo-European origin—unless, that is, one can demonstrate that stateless societies speaking non-Indo-European languages at the time did not. In fact, the argument seems almost circular, since by "primitive," the author seems to mean "stateless" or "relatively egalitarian," and such societies almost by definition cannot be ruled autocratically, no matter what language people speak. Similarly, when characterizing the Classic Maya as lacking any form of "countervailing institutions" (Willey describes even the bloodthirsty Aztecs as less authoritarian, owing to their more developed markets), it doesn't seem to occur to any of the authors to wonder what ancient Rome or Medieval England might look like if they had to be reconstructed exclusively through ruined buildings and official statements carved in stone.

In fact, if my argument is right, what these authors are doing is searching for the origins of democracy precisely where they are least likely to find it: in the proclamations of the states that largely suppressed local forms of self-governance and collective deliberation, and the literary-philosophical traditions that justified their doing so. (This, at least, would help explain why, in Italy, Greece, and India alike, sovereign assemblies appear at the beginnings of written history and disappear quickly thereafter.) The fate of the Maya is instructive here. Sometime in the late first millennium, Classic Maya civilization collapsed. Archaeologists argue about the reasons—presumably they always will—but most theories assume popular rebellions played at least some role. By the time the Spaniards arrived six hundred years later, Mayan societies were thoroughly decentralized, with an endless variety of tiny city-states, some apparently with elected leaders. Conquest took much longer than it did in Peru and Mexico, and Maya communities have proved so consistently rebellious that, over the last five hundred years, there has been virtually no point during which at least some have not been in a state of armed insurrection. Most ironic of all, the current wave of the global justice movement was largely kicked off by the EZLN, or Zapatista Army of National Liberation, a group of largely Maya-speaking rebels in Chiapas, mostly drawn from campesinos who had resettled in new communities in the Lacandon rain forest. Their insurrection in 1994 was carried out explicitly in the name of democracy, by which they meant something much more like Athenian-style direct democracy than the republican forms of government that have since appropriated the name. The Zapatistas developed an elaborate system in which communal assemblies, operating on consensus, supplemented by women and youth caucuses to counterbalance the traditional dominance of adult males, are knitted together by councils with recallable delegates. They claim it to be rooted in, but a radicalization of, the way that Maya-speaking communities have governed themselves for thousands of years. We do know that most highland Maya communities have been governed by some kind of consensus system since we have records: that is, for at least five hundred years. While it's possible that nothing of the sort existed in rural communities during the Classic Maya heyday, a little over a thousand years ago, it seems rather unlikely.

Certainly, modern rebels make their own views on the Classic Maya clear enough. As a Ch'ol-speaking Zapatista remarked to a friend of mine recently, pointing to the ruins of Palenque, "We managed to get rid of those guys. I don't suppose the Mexican government could be all that much of a challenge in comparison."

E. THE CRISIS OF THE STATE

We're finally back, then, where we began, with the rise of global movements calling for new forms of democracy. In a way, the main point of this piece has been to demonstrate that the Zapatistas are nothing unusual. They are speakers of a variety of Maya languages—Tzeltal, Tojalobal, Ch'ol, Tzotzil, Mam—originally from communities traditionally allowed a certain degree of self-governance (largely so they could function as indigenous labor reserves for ranches and plantations located elsewhere), who had formed new largely multiethnic communities in newly opened lands in the Lacandon.[45] In other words, they inhabit a classic example of what I've been calling spaces of democratic improvisation, in which a jumbled amalgam of people, most with at least some initial experience of methods of communal self-governance, find themselves in new communities outside the immediate supervision of the state. Neither is there anything particularly new about the fact that they are at the fulcrum of a global play of influences: absorbing ideas from everywhere, and their own example having an enormous impact on social movements across the planet. The first Zapatista encuentro in 1996, for example, eventually led to the formation of an international network (People's Global Action, or PGA), based on principles of autonomy, horizontality, and direct democracy, that included such disparate groups as the Movimento dos Trabalhadores Rurais Sem Terra (MST) in Brazil; the Karnataka State Farmers' Association (KRSS), a Gandhian socialist direct action group in India; the Canadian Postal Workers' Union; and a whole host of anarchist collectives in Europe and the Americas, along with indigenous organizations on every continent. It was PGA, for instance, that put out the original call to action against the WTO meetings in Seattle in November 1999. Even more, the principles of Zapatismo, the rejection of vanguardism, the emphasis on creating viable alternatives in one's own community as a way of subverting the logic of global capital, has had an enormous influence on participants in social movements that, in some cases, are at best vaguely aware of the Zapatistas themselves and have certainly never heard of PGA. No doubt the growth of the internet and global communications have allowed the process to proceed much faster than ever before, and allowed for more formal, explicit alliances; but this does not mean we are dealing with an entirely unprecedented phenomenon.

One might gauge the importance of the point by considering what happens when it's not borne constantly in mind. Let me turn here to an author whose position is actually quite close to my own. In a book called *Cosmopolitanism*, the literary theorist Walter Mignolo provides a beautiful summary of just how much Kant's cosmopolitanism, or the UN discourse on human rights, was developed within a context of conquest and imperialism; then he invokes Zapatista calls for democracy to counter an argument by Slavoj Žižek that leftists need to temper their critiques of Eurocentrism in order to embrace democracy as "the true European legacy from ancient Greece onward."[46] Mignolo writes:

> The Zapatistas have used the word democracy, although it has a different meaning for them than it has for the Mexican government. Democracy for the Zapatistas is not conceptualized

in terms of European political philosophy but in terms of Maya social organization based on reciprocity, communal (instead of individual) values, the value of wisdom rather than epistemology, and so forth . . . The Zapatistas have no choice but to use the word that political hegemony imposed, though using that word does not mean bending to its mono-logic interpretation. Once democracy is singled out by the Zapatistas, it becomes a connector through which liberal concepts of democracy and indigenous concepts of reciprocity and community social organization for the common good must come to terms.[47]

This is a nice idea. Mignolo calls it "border thinking." He proposes it as a model for how to come up with a healthy, "critical cosmopolitanism," as opposed to the Eurocentric variety represented by Kant or Žižek. The problem though, it seems to me, is that in doing so, Mignolo himself ends up falling into a more modest version of the very essentializing discourse he's trying to escape.

First of all, to say "the Zapatistas have no choice but to use the word" *democracy* is simply untrue. Of course they have a choice. Other indigenous-based groups have made very different ones. The Aymara movement in Bolivia, to select one fairly random example, chose to reject the word *democracy* entirely, on the grounds that, in their people's historical experience, the name has only been used for systems imposed on them through violence. They therefore see their own traditions of egalitarian decision-making as having nothing to do with democracy. The Zapatista decision to embrace the term, it seems to me, was more than anything else a decision to reject anything that smacked of a politics of identity, and to appeal for allies, in Mexico and elsewhere, among those interested in a broader conversation about forms of self-organization—in much the same way as they also sought to begin a conversation with those interested in reexamining the meaning of words like *revolution*. Second, Mignolo, not entirely unlike Lévy-Bruhl, ends up producing yet another confrontation between apples and oranges. He ends up contrasting Western theory and indigenous practice. In fact, Zapatismo is not simply an emanation of traditional Maya practices: its origins have to be sought in a prolonged confrontation between those practices and, among other things, the ideas of local Maya intellectuals (many, presumably, not entirely unfamiliar with the work of Kant), liberation theologists (who drew inspiration from prophetic texts written in ancient Palestine), and mestizo revolutionaries (who drew inspiration from the works of Chairman Mao, who lived in China). Democracy, in turn, did not emerge from anybody's discourse. It is as if simply taking the Western literary tradition as one's starting point—even for purposes of critique—means authors like Mignolo always somehow end up trapped within it.

In reality, the "word that political hegemony imposed" is in this case itself a fractured compromise. If it weren't, we would not have a Greek word originally coined to describe a form of communal self-governance applied to representative republics to begin with. It's exactly this contradiction the Zapatistas were seizing on. In fact, it seems impossible to get rid of. Liberal theorists do occasionally evince a desire to simply brush aside Athenian democracy entirely, to declare it irrelevant and be done with it, but for ideological purposes, such a move would be simply inadmissible.[48] After all, without Athens, there would be no way to claim that "the Western tradition" had anything inherently democratic about it. We would be left tracing back our political ideals to the totalitarian musings of Plato, or if not, perhaps, to admit there's really no such thing as "the West." In effect, liberal theorists have boxed themselves into a corner. Obviously, the Zapatistas are hardly the first revolutionaries to have seized on this contradiction; but their doing so has found an unusually powerful resonance this time—in part because this is a moment of a profound crisis of the state.

The Impossible Marriage

In its essence, I think, the contradiction is not simply one of language. It reflects something deeper. For the last two hundred years, democrats have been trying to graft ideals of popular self-governance onto the coercive apparatus of the state. In the end, the project is simply unworkable. States cannot, by their nature, ever truly be democratized. They are, after all, basically ways of organizing violence. The American Federalists were being quite realistic when they argued that democracy is inconsistent with a society based on inequalities of wealth; since, in order to protect wealth, one needs an apparatus of coercion to keep down the very "mob" that democracy would empower. Athens was a unique case in this respect because it was, in effect, transitional: there were certainly inequalities of wealth, even, arguably, a ruling class, but there was virtually no formal apparatus of coercion. Hence there's no consensus among scholars whether it can really be considered a state at all.

It's precisely when one considers the problem of the modern state's monopoly of coercive force that the whole pretense of democracy dissolves into a welter of contradictions. For example: while modern elites have largely put aside the earlier discourse of the "mob" as a murderous "great beast," the same imagery still pops back, in almost exactly the form it had in the sixteenth century, the moment anyone proposes democratizing some aspect of the apparatus of coercion. In the United States, for example, advocates of the "fully informed jury movement," who point out that the Constitution actually allows juries to decide on questions of law, not just of evidence, are regularly denounced in the media as wishing to go back to the days of lynchings and "mob rule." It's no coincidence that the United States, a country that still prides itself on its democratic spirit, has also led the world in mythologizing, even deifying, its police.

Francis Dupuis-Déri has coined the term "political agoraphobia" to refer to the suspicion of public deliberation and decision-making that runs through the Western tradition, just as much in the works of Constant, Sieyés, or Madison as in Plato or Aristotle.[49] I would add that even the most impressive accomplishments of the liberal state, its most genuinely democratic elements—for instance, its guarantees on freedom of speech and freedom of assembly—are premised on such agoraphobia. It is only once it becomes absolutely clear that public speech and assembly is no longer itself the medium of political decision-making, but at best an attempt to criticize, influence, or make suggestions to political decision-makers, that they can be treated as sacrosanct. Critically, this agoraphobia is not just shared by politicians and professional journalists, but in large measure by the public itself. The reasons, I think, are not far to seek. While liberal democracies lack anything resembling the Athenian agora, they certainly do not lack equivalents to Roman circuses. The ugly mirror phenomenon, by which ruling elites encourage forms of popular participation that continually remind the public just how much it is unfit to rule, seems, in many modern states, to have been brought to a condition of unprecedented perfection. Consider here, for example, the view of human nature one might derive generalizing from the experience of driving to work on the highway, as opposed to the view one might derive from the experience of public transportation. Yet the American—or German—love affair with the car was the result of conscious policy decisions by political and corporate elites beginning in the 1930s. One could write a similar history of the television, or consumerism, or, as Polanyi long ago noted, "the market."

Jurists, meanwhile, have long been aware that the coercive nature of the state ensures that democratic constitutions are founded on a fundamental contradiction. Walter Benjamin summed it up nicely by pointing out that any legal order that claims a monopoly of the use of violence has to be founded by some power other than itself, which inevitably means by acts that were illegal according to whatever system of law came before.[50] The legitimacy of a system of law thus necessarily rests on acts of criminal violence. American and French revolutionaries were, after all, by the law under which they grew up, guilty of high treason. Of course, sacred kings from Africa to Nepal have managed to solve this logical conundrum by placing themselves, like God, outside the system. But as political theorists from Agamben to Negri remind us, there is no obvious way for "the people" to exercise sovereignty in the same way. Both the right-wing solution (constitutional orders are founded by, and can be set aside by, inspired leaders—whether Founding Fathers, or a Führer—who embody the popular will) and the left-wing solution (constitutional orders usually gain their legitimacy through violent popular revolutions) lead to endless practical contradictions. In fact, as the sociologist Michael Mann has hinted, much of the slaughter of the twentieth century derives from some version of this contradiction.[51] The demand to simultaneously create a uniform apparatus of coercion within every piece of land on the surface of the planet, and to maintain the pretense that the legitimacy of that apparatus derives from "the people," has led to an endless need to determine who, precisely, "the people" are supposed to be.

In all the varied German law courts of the last eighty years—from Weimar to Nazi to Communist DDR to the Bundesrepublik— the judges have used the same opening formula: *In Namen des Volkes*, "In the Name of the People." American courts prefer the formula "The Case of the People versus X."[52]

In other words, "the people" must be evoked as the authority behind the allocation of violence, despite the fact that any suggestion that the proceedings be in any way democratized is likely to be greeted with horror by all concerned. Mann suggests that pragmatic efforts to work out this contradiction, to use the apparatus of violence to identify and constitute a "people" which those maintaining that apparatus feel are worthy of being the source of their authority, has been responsible for at least sixty million murders in the twentieth century alone.

It is in this context that I might suggest that the anarchist solution— that there really is no resolution to this paradox—is really not all that unreasonable. The democratic state was always a contradiction. Globalization has simply exposed the rotten underpinnings, by creating the need for decision-making structures on a planetary scale where any attempt to maintain the pretense of popular sovereignty, let alone participation, would be obviously absurd. The neoliberal solution, of course, is to declare the market the only form of public deliberation one really needs, and to restrict the state almost exclusively to its coercive function. In this context, the Zapatista response—to abandon the notion that revolution is a matter of seizing control over the coercive apparatus of the state, and instead proposing to refound democracy in the self-organization of autonomous communities—makes perfect sense. This is the reason an otherwise obscure insurrection in southern Mexico caused such a sensation in radical circles to begin with. Democracy, then, is for the moment returning to the spaces in which it originated: the spaces in between. Whether it can then proceed to engulf the world depends perhaps less on what kind of theories we make about it, but on whether we honestly believe that ordinary human beings, sitting down together in deliberative bodies, would be capable of managing their own affairs as well as elites, whose decisions are backed up by the power of weapons, are of managing it for them—or even whether, even if they wouldn't, they have the right to be allowed to try. For most of human history, faced with such questions, professional intellectuals have almost universally taken the side of the elites. It is rather my impression that, if it really comes down to it, the overwhelming majority are still seduced by the various ugly mirrors and have no real faith in the possibilities of popular democracy. But perhaps this, too, could change.

PART II AGAINST ECONOMICS

Finance Is Just Another Word for Other People's Debts

Odd things happened in fall 2011 as Occupy Wall Street began to inhabit downtown Manhattan. People rode the subway carrying signs that touted the merits of the Glass-Steagall Act; they started sidewalk conversations about corporate personhood and about the social purpose of derivatives. Legislation, legal precedent, and financial products that had once been obscure emerged in public in new ways.

In the months after city officials forcibly evicted occupiers from Liberty Square (née Zuccotti Park), this public conversation—like the occupiers themselves—dispersed. The talk did not stop so much as it spread out, changed forms, and took root through and beyond New York. Those signs on the subway and the initial conversations about financial regulation (and its discontents) yielded to new referents and signifiers, not least among which were debt—whether student, medical, foreclosure, municipal, or sovereign—and a substantial red-jacketed

An interview with Hannah Chadeayne Appel; originally published in *Radical History Review*, no. 118, Fall 2014, pp. 159–73.

book by the same name. *Debt: The First 5,000 Years* established an intellectual reference point almost immediately, but it also became the visual sign of membership in a new kind of political dialogue about who owes what to whom.

I sat down with David Graeber in late fall 2012, more than a year after he had been among Occupy's first organizers and after *Debt* had been widely reviewed as one of the year's most influential books—not only within anthropology, or even academia, but in *The New York Times Book Review, Financial Times, The Guardian*, and elsewhere. Perhaps most important to David himself, the book has become a must-read in activist networks that stretch from New York to Oakland, Greece to Germany. He and I ducked into a hole-in-the-wall café in downtown San Francisco to record this interview. David ordered a coffee at the counter, while I—famished and (unbeknownst to David) four months pregnant—ordered the most substantial breakfast on offer: eggs, sausage, toast, orange juice, and fruit. When I moved to pay for what was essentially my breakfast, David insisted on picking up the tab, declaring behind an incredulous smile that writing a book on debt had at last provided him with a little disposable income, which he insisted on distributing. I owe David a thank-you for that breakfast and for this interview. May all of our future debts be comparably repayable.

HANNAH CHADEAYNE APPEL: There is much radical lore about your childhood. Tell us about your family background and your own political coming-of-age.

DAVID GRAEBER: I guess my childhood was full of radical politics, but I wasn't entirely aware of it. My father was from Lawrence, Kansas. He was one of two people from the university at Lawrence who volunteered to fight in Spain, where he served as an ambulance driver. I think he always had an anarchistic streak himself. When he first got involved politically, the only thing really happening on campus was the local Communist Party league, and they were the ones who recruited him. He was never a party member, and he broke with the youth league too, pretty early on. And was always in the anti-CP [Communist Party] faction of the Spanish veterans' group. But he did tell me a story of all the volunteers coming over the Pyrenees and a very inspiring moment when, as soon as they crossed into Spain, they all started singing "The International" at the same time, except in twelve different languages at once.

And then they went to basic training. And basic training is like basic training anywhere—the obstacle course, you jump over things and crawl under things, and they shoot machine guns over your head. As my father was waiting in line, he was watching this and went to the officer directing things and said, "These guys shooting machine guns, are they just recruits too? Or are they experienced troops?" The officer replied, "I don't know. I think they're guys who went through basic training yesterday who we drafted to do this." "What!?" my father responded. "They don't know what they're doing? We could get killed." The officer's response, essentially, was, "You're in the army, dude. Do what you're told." My dad thought that was ridiculous. "I'm not going to get killed in basic training. I'm not going to do this." So the officer got mad and went off to get the commanding officer, who heard the story and said, "All right, Graeber, you got a driver's license? You're in the ambulance car." Clearly, my dad did not have what it took to be a foot soldier, to just blindly follow stupid orders, so he became an ambulance driver in the ambulance corps. He was posted in Barcelona, but they were wherever the action was, so in a way it was the most dangerous job. You were positioned wherever people were getting killed. But he had incredible luck. He was never wounded or hurt in any way. The other guy who joined from Lawrence got killed almost immediately, which caused a small scandal back in Kansas when his parents found out.

After the war my dad went back to the United States and finished his degree. He ended up in World War II as part of the merchant marines. Again, he didn't figure foot soldier was really the job for him. He met my mother, who had come to America when she was ten, from Ostrov, Poland. Ironically, the places where my parents' families come from are not that far apart. The Graeber family is originally from Bartenstein, East Prussia. Johann Graeber actually fought in the battles of Leipzig and Waterloo. He was my great-great-grandfather, a shoemaker and soldier. They were all shoemakers. I now discover there is a fairly strong history of radical shoemakers from Bartenstein. Johann's son, Carl August Graeber (or Charlie, as he came to be known), came to the United States shortly after 1848—a suspicious date already. He settled in Lawrence, Kansas, which at the time was the very center of American abolitionism and radicalism right in the middle of the Civil War. Apparently, the family was hiding in the haystack when Quantrel's Raiders came through—or he was. The women and children came out to meet them and said that the men were in town. That story is in the family.

Charlie's son, Gustavus Adolphus Graeber, or Dolly, as everyone called him, was actually a musician for a long time on the western frontier. This is our big family claim to fame: he was apparently the man who introduced the mandolin to American music. He got the first mandolin, this is really true, from a band of gypsies who were coming through town. He bought it. It had no strings. He didn't know what to do with it. He went to the university, and they figured out that you string it like a violin. He sent away for sheet music all the way to Europe, and eventually he formed the first mandolin band, in which he actually played guitar. Later he was the guy who ran the boathouse in Lawrence where kids from the college would rent boats. He was famous for being able to hunt catfish by tying a hook to his wrist and guiding it over the dam. He was a river guy. My father grew up there, in Lawrence, and Dolly had him later in life. That's why my grandfather, my father's father, was born before the Civil War, because he was in his fifties when my father was born. My father was in his late forties when I was born. That was my father's background.

So he met my mom, who was born in Poland to a Jewish family and came to America. She was a very precocious kid. She got into college at age sixteen and dropped out again a year later because it was the Depression and they needed help supporting the family, so she got a job at a brassiere factory. She was in the ILGWU (International Ladies' Garment Workers' Union). At the time, they went to a seven-hour day. The union manager got that through, so they had all these union activities in their free time, and one of them they decided [was] to put on a musical comedy. At the time, labor drama had this reputation for being didactic and boring, so they wanted to do something funny. She was involved in that. They had a show called *Pins and Needles*, which became a surprise hit on Broadway. It was very successful. And so my mom had this curious rags-to-riches-to-rags story where she was suddenly famous as a female lead on Broadway, with a profile in *Life* magazine—Ruth Rubenstein was her name at the time. She toured the country for a couple of years; they played the White House. And then she went back to working in the factory after three or four years. When she married my dad, she met him at some lefty summer camp or something. They were Zionists and all that, but they were the radical socialists, you know, Martin Buber type, Hashomel Hatzair, who considered the measure of the success of the Zionist project to be how successfully they integrated with the local Palestinian population. Extremely antireligious. My cousin Chesky grew up on a kibbutz in Israel where they raised pigs, just to annoy the religious people. It was that kind of tradition. My mother's family disowned her when she married my dad. Not only was he not Jewish, he was German by background, despite the fact that he was what they called then a "premature antifascist" who fought in Spain. I mean, you can't get much less Nazi than that. It didn't matter to them. So I never actually met my grandmother, for example, even though she continued to live in Brooklyn and only died when I was about sixteen. There was a profound rift there.

The funny thing about anybody growing up is that it's hard to

conceive of your parents being cool. In fact, your parents are the definition of what is not cool. So it was only kind of gradually that I figured it out . . . I remember there was one time I was talking to my dad, before he moved to the co-op, and they were living on St. Mark's Place in the Village over, I think, what's now Yaffa's. It was an Armenian place at the time. I talked about going to a hockey game and Dad said something like, "I haven't been to a hockey game in about thirty years. I think the last time I went was with that Beat poet. What was his name?" And I remember thinking to myself, "Wait a minute, you're actually cool." I didn't know that my family was extraordinary. I gradually realized that while they were still alive, so they were still there when I figured out how cool they were, but it took a long time.

I think my father was very sympathetic with anarchism because he'd seen it work. He was in Barcelona when it was basically organized on anarchist principles. It worked fine. There were problems, but the problems got resolved. So the way I always put it is that most people don't think of anarchism as a bad idea; they think of it as insane, right? "That would never work! C'mon!" My dad knew that was not the case. It was never treated as insane in my family. So it's hardly surprising that I came into it at an early age. I had all sorts of weird interests and obsessions when I was a kid which weren't explicitly political. I was really into Robert Graves and his ideas on poetry. I had a fascination with Mayan hieroglyphics. That's how I ended up getting into Andover. I went from PS 11 and IS 70—public schools in New York—to an elite private school on a scholarship, and then back to SUNY [State University of New York] Purchase. From private to state school again and then finally to Chicago. I bounced back and forth.

APPEL: When did you begin to identify as an anarchist?

GRAEBER: Some of it has to do with a cousin of mine who I never knew all that well, but I think he considered himself an anarchist and suggested that I look into the thing. As a late teenager, I hadn't really thought of myself as having a specific political identity. I was sort of default radicalism. The cousin said I should read up on Spain. I asked my dad, and he was trying to be fair, so he gave me George Orwell, *Homage to Catalonia*. Dad cautioned me, "Bear in mind that the guy has a total bias, and a lot of what he says is bullshit. But it's a good place to start." And my father was brought in by the very antianarchist people, and he propagandized against them all the time. But he knew many anarchists personally when he was there and they got along. The position he ended up taking on Spain was that it was necessary to build a modern army to fight the Fascists, but suppressing the actual revolution was insane and suicidal. The anarchist military structure wasn't going to work, but the anarchist social structure and political economic structure [were]. When they shot that down, that was the beginning of the end. So I read Orwell and I read up on Spain and politics, and, you know, I came around to the realization that anarchism is a reasonable position.

APPEL: Can you give us a brief history of your own political engagement since coming to anarchism? Perhaps situating Occupy in a longer durée of political involvement?

GRAEBER: The globalization movement itself was, as I've written, the result of a confluence of movements, that you can trace it back as long as you like, but the seventies were when the pieces really came together in the antinuclear movement. And it was a convergence between anarchist traditions, feminism—which played the most important role in bringing about the whole emphasis on consensus—and certain spiritual traditions including [those of] the Quakers, who until that time had resisted actually teaching anybody how to do consensus meetings because they felt it was a form of proselytizing, and they didn't want to do that. They understood it as a spiritual exercise. So the pieces—affinity groups, spokes-councils—all that really came together in the antinuclear movement and kind of faded in and out in terms of large-scale organizing. It was always there in small-scale organizing. Food Not Bombs is a great example that comes out of the antinuclear movement and endures and then pops back up again as organizing the food for all the big mobilizations of the globalization movement. This is a very American-centric view, obviously. The globalization movement itself doesn't come out of the North at all but [comes] from the Zapatistas, MST (Landless Workers Movement) in Brazil, KRRS (Karnataka State Farmers' Association) in India. It was one of the first global social movements where the organizational initiatives all were coming from the South instead of the North. But in the American context that took on a particular form of direct democracy that people think of as anarchist process. It's just as much feminist process in terms of where it comes from.

So I got involved in 2000 after I heard about Seattle. I had kind of been in my own academic cloud. I had tried to get involved in anarchist stuff periodically, in the eighties, for example, and I wasn't that impressed by what I saw. I like to call the eighties the Bob Black period in American anarchism, where everybody was in these little screaming sectarian parties made up of one person. So I would try. I mean there were very good things going on; I just didn't happen to stumble across them. But I remember very well stepping out of a lecture I had given at Yale in a course called "Power, Violence, and Cosmology." I had given the last lecture of the course. I walked out and I see this little newspaper box that says "Martial Law Declared in Seattle." And I was like "what?!" That's what happens when there's a press blackout on organizing, and then, suddenly, they do something really big. "Where the hell did that come from?!" Which is what a lot of people in New York were saying at the time. So my reaction was, "This is the movement that I always wished existed, and they put it together. It came about when I wasn't paying attention. Where do I go?" So I got involved. A16—the April 16, 2000, actions against the IMF [International Monetary Fund] and World

Bank in Washington, D.C.—was my first action. Gradually, I became deeply involved in Direct Action Network in New York.

Then, after 9/11, there were increasing levels of repression, and the rules of engagement really tilted in their favor. A lot of people burned out during this time. They gave up; they went to live on an organic farm, went to grad school, [and] otherwise despaired. I was one of the stalwarts. We would say, "Maybe this year. It's gonna be back." We kept trying and trying and knocking our head against the wall. It was not like it ever really disappeared. I was in Japan for the G8 [Group of Eight summit]. I was in Gleneagles. That was the time a bomb went off in London just at the height of the actions, for reasons having nothing to do with us, but afterward, everything collapsed. Each time it never quite clicked into the thing it used to be. But we kept banging our heads against the wall.

One of the things I would say about the emergence of Occupy is, at some point, you find yourself organizing your life around something that, on some level, you don't think is going to happen. We'd always had this idea that direct democracy is contagious. It will be. You can't explain it to people, but if people actually experience it, it changes their life; they can't go back. But the question is how to get them in the room. So we thought, "This is going to happen eventually." It's going to happen, but at some level we didn't believe it was going to happen, because at some level you have to create this armor to cover up the continual disappointment. And then it happened, and we were like, "Oh, my God! It worked! Finally! How do you like that?" I actually talked to someone in Egypt who told me exactly the same thing. All of these years you organize a rally, a demonstration, only twenty-five people show up, you're depressed. Three hundred people show up and you're happy! And then one day three hundred thousand people show up and you're like, "What?! What did we do differently?" So it was like that. I think one of my most important roles in the origins of Occupy was actually just being that generational bridge. Calling up all these people to say, "No, really, it's actually happening this time. I know you've heard me say this before . . ."

APPEL: From that longer genealogy out of which Occupy emerges, what differentiates what's happening now from what happened in the past?

GRAEBER: Occupy is constantly reinventing itself. Strike Debt is a good example. But let's talk about the holding-space tactic—the importance of the camp or the community. As in the globalization movement, this did not start in the North. That technique of holding space starts in Tahrir Square and Tunisia, and it goes on through Syntagma and Plaça de Catalunya. In contrast, the core thematic center of the globalization movement was the carnival or the festival—festival of resistance, carnival against capitalism, hence the whole clown-and-puppets theme. And it made sense when you're dealing with what's basically a solidarity movement trying to make a mockery of, or attack, the whole structure of global governance. Whereas this round, you don't see so many puppets and clowns at the center. You see some, but it wasn't so central to what we were doing. Rather, again, it was the camp, the community. But, still, there's some continuity here: We're going to create forms of organization which not only show that organizations we're contesting are bad, which everybody knows, but that they're unnecessary. We're going to put an alternative directly in their face as the most potent way of destroying their legitimacy and authority. The carnival made sense for the first round, but the most potent thing we could possibly create as a symbol against Wall Street specifically was a community of people who care about one another. And there's nothing more radical than performing exemplary love in front of this symbol of the impossibility of a society based on that.

APPEL: What about various projects coming out of Occupy after the camps—Strike Debt, debtors' unions, and new tactics?

GRAEBER: One of the most effective tools that began to undercut the Washington Consensus and neoliberal hegemony in France was unemployed unions. Unions of the unemployed which formed all over France and were critical in 1996, when they basically blunted the austerity drive there. France became the only country, really, not to go through those policies. So there's a long history of unions based in things other than labor. Part of the problem is that labor unions have been so completely politically defanged they might as well be useless in larger terms. Yet debtors are notoriously difficult to organize. It's a real challenge. And there's a strange paradox about this: the first effect of debt is to create isolation, shame, humiliation, a fear of even talking about it. On the other hand, if you look at history, the vast majority of revolts and insurrections are about debt. So in a sense it's incredibly effective, ideologically, at isolating people. But once people overcome that isolation, the results are always explosive. Debt is something people are most likely to revolt about. So the stakes are high; it's really difficult. But if we can do it, it's going to be very, very effective.

APPEL: Can you help us understand the relationship between debt and finance?

GRAEBER: The way we talk about finance, it's almost completely removed from actual social relations, let alone class, which is of course what Occupy has always been about—reminding us that class power specifically does exist. That was the whole point of "the 99 percent." But the way finance is always represented is, "Wow, these guys have figured out a way to scam everybody by just making up money out of nothing!" You have this idea that these guys are sitting around, playing with computer blips and pieces of paper, saying, "Ooh, look, money!" Or that they're going in the casino and gambling, and somehow by buying chips they produce more of them. Of course, they very much encouraged that misunderstanding. There's all this rhetoric . . . I remember, right before the crash in 2007, I would go to these conferences and there would be these culture theory guys, very slick, trendy, whose work didn't differentiate at all between forms of knowledge, forms of power, and physical reality. So therefore they were like, "This is amazing! They're using forms of securitization to change the very material nature of reality, of time! We have to learn from these guys who can create value out of nothing." I remember sitting in the back thinking, "I think in the business world those are called scams." They couldn't put it together. They fell for it. And the scamsters were totally encouraging this by tossing up specters of expertise: "Oh, yeah, we have these programs that only an astrophysicist can run. There are only five people in the world who can understand." I saw an interview with one of those astrophysicists, and he was like, "Ya know, we were just making this up as we went along." So everybody was scamming everybody. But what was really going on, what financialization actually means is they collude with the government through various elaborate forms of bribery to change the law so as to put everyone deeper and deeper in debt, directly turning their income over to the FIRE [finance, insurance, and real estate] sector.

I don't know the exact numbers. It's telling that you can't get these numbers. But something around 15 to 25 percent, at least, of average American household income is directly removed in the form of interest, penalties, fees, insurance, et cetera. And it's obviously much more than that, because 25 percent are either too rich or too poor to be indebted. They are taking money out of your pockets. If you look at the profits of Wall Street, smaller and smaller percentages have anything to do with commerce or industry. I think it's 9 to 11 percent that is industrial, and that's way overstated because for companies like General Motors (GM) (at least in 2007–2008) none of their profits came from the cars. It all came from lending people money for the cars, and that's counted as industrial. In fact, it's almost all from financial profits, basically indebting people.

I like to describe it like this: look at the fifties—when there was the expression "What's good for GM is good for America," which was coined by the head of GM. That made sense at the time when you consider that GM was taxed at 60 to 70 percent and the executives were taxed at 90 percent. They were producing enormous profits, and most of their profits went to the government, which in turn used that money to build roads and highways and infrastructure for the cars, so it became this virtuous circle. And then all sorts of bribes and kickback money circulated in the contracting process, and everybody got rich. Well, not quite everybody, but the money got spread around. Fast-forward fifty years, and companies like that are paying no taxes. They're getting all their money from the financial sector, not from the cars, which are not profitable anymore. Instead, they charge people interest, and use that money to bribe politicians to change the laws that regulate them to be able to extract even more. And that's basically how the American system works, and that's why Wall Street and the government become almost indistinguishable. Government coercive force becomes a means through which profit is extracted, and that's why suddenly you have this change of how people perceive one another in relation to this system.

First of all, fewer and fewer people see themselves as middle class. Being middle class means you see the basic bureaucratic apparatus around you as existing in your favor, which is hard to see when you have some illegal robo-signed mortgage guys taking away your home. Second of all, it means that suddenly we have this alliance between the working poor and indebted college students. You never would have seen that in the past. They would've been archenemies. All of this is directly attributable to the changing nature of capital extraction. I always think of the proliferation of storefront banks as this beautiful symbol of that change. There are hundreds and hundreds of these Bank of America branches or Citibank branches opening up. In New York, they're everywhere. Every block has one. And what do they sell? Nothing. They sell money. So they have these stores with no merchandise, but they have lots of guards with guns wandering around. It's a perfect expression—these beautiful, shiny, nothing stores with armed security everywhere. That's what it is.

Both nationally and internationally we're ruled by a ruling class whose profits are based primarily on complex forms of rent extraction, backed by coercive force.

APPEL: Which thinkers and which theoretical or political approaches have been helpful to you in making sense of finance, debt, and contemporary capitalism?

GRAEBER: I like the Midnight Notes Collective. Often Marxists take me to task for ignoring the basic tenets of Marxism. I don't think I ignore them, but I actually take them rather for granted. I'm just emphasizing other parts of the equation. I find that the autonomist tradition—not the Negri/Deleuzian branch of the autonomist tradition, but more the kind of thing that comes from people like Harry Cleaver, Massimo De Angelis; Silvia Federici is a big hero of mine, George Caffentzis too—this tradition really has the best, or what I've found to be the most illuminating, approach to contemporary changes in capitalism, the two cycles of postwar capitalism. I've found their works useful. I've found the work of Michael Hudson, coming from a very different tradition, equally useful. And then modern money theory people . . . While I don't agree with everything they say, I find them useful. People like L. Randall Wray, from Kansas City. This is a whole post-Keynesian tradition which is totally excluded from mainstream political discourse, but they are extremely interesting and doing important work. So I'm pulling on a lot of different strands.

In terms of the *Debt* book, probably my biggest influence was Keith Hart, one of the first people to talk about heterodox economics in anthropology. He talked about the distinction between bullion theories of money and credit theories of money and how money is this paradoxical thing which is both. I took that and said, "Yes. But over history the weight varies back and forth between the two forms." Hart has said to me that he hadn't realized that. So I'm in that theoretical tradition as well. So I'm synthesizing particularly the autonomous postworkerist school of Marxism with post-Keynesian and anthropological traditions.

APPEL: Let's talk about the *Debt* book. It has obviously enjoyed tremendous success far beyond the disciplinary confines of anthropology. Where did it come from?

GRAEBER: I was approached by the publisher, who said, "We think you could be someone who could write for the public. What are you working on?" When I said debt, they got very excited. This was back in 2007, before the crash, though not long before. People did have a sense that something was off, not in mainstream media, but anyone with any common sense.

I used to say, "I don't want to be famous, I just want to be famous among those people I actually respect, whose opinions I respect." In a way I had almost achieved that already, in the sense that activists and anthropologists knew who I was, as did other scholars who were working on things I thought were important. But with this project I thought, all right, it would be interesting to write for a broader audience and see what kind of impact you can have on arguments going on. In particular, I was really shocked by the degree to which, after 2008, for example, there was this moment that lasted maybe a month or so, where suddenly you could talk about anything. Everything was in doubt. Even *The Economist* ran headlines effectively asking: "Capitalism: Was It a Good Idea?" Obviously, they concluded yes; they're *The Economist*. But, nonetheless, it seemed like everything was up for grabs. You could think big thoughts again and wonder why it was all here. Why do we have an economy? And that lasted about four weeks, until everyone said, "Shut up and stop thinking about this. It will come back if we just close our eyes and ears and keep carrying on as if nothing is happening."

It seemed obvious that denial would not last forever. You can't put that conversation off. I mean they did everything they could to put it off. I fervently believe that the attack on the British educational systems was a reaction . . . All of the lines they've been telling us to legitimate themselves have been completely destroyed. Now we know that markets don't run themselves and that these guys running them aren't incredible geniuses we couldn't possibly understand. The idea that the market and the state are somehow separate entities is absurd. So once all moral justifications for the system have been blown away, all they have left is to destroy any locus from which alternatives might emerge. The only line they have left is, "Okay, the system isn't so great, but it's the only one that can possibly exist." That's basically their only remaining argument, hence the attack on the educational system, where they tried to rewrite the British school systems along a financial/business model. From the perspective of common sense, on the one side, you have the financiers who do their job so badly they trash the world economy, and, on the other, you have the educational people who do their job perfectly well. You'd think a logical reaction to the crisis would be to make the financial system more like the educational system, but instead they do it the other way around, taking the failed model. Clearly, they felt they had to organize education—a place where legitimate alternatives might come from—in such a way that it couldn't actually produce anything outside of our model. There's this kind of desperation. At that moment it seemed like anyone who had a position from which they could open up the conversation that others were so desperately trying to stop had a certain responsibility to try and intervene. You know, I didn't think it would work. But it kind of did!

APPEL: And where has the book gone?

GRAEBER: The most incredible story is Germany. [The] German [edition] was the first translation to come out. I did a tour there, and I knew something weird was going on. It was crazy. Every day I gave one talk and sixteen interviews—radio, TV, major TV shows. I was on the Maybrit Illner show, a big TV news thing with politicians, on a panel. It was one of those hot talk-politics shows. It was fascinating to watch how the conversation unfolded. They were all in their usual mode where 2 percent of what people are actually thinking seems allowable to say on TV. It was an incredibly stale, boring debate with a Greek economist and a bunch of German politicians. And as soon as I walked in, it was almost as if they felt liberated: "Here's a crazy anarchist guy! Let's say my crazy thought." So I heard central bankers saying, "A jubilee might actually work!" The interviewer's first question to me was, "So, is capitalism on the way out?" I thought it was a joke, and then I later found out that she was a former East German TV personality. She had already seen one system go . . .

The book was actually a bestseller for eleven weeks in Germany. We've sold over one hundred thousand copies by now in German. I was trying to figure out why, and the conclusion I finally came to was that a lot of the German intellectual class feel they've boxed themselves into a hole. They have this moral discourse about debt that's so effective that there's almost no way out of it, but at the same time they realize that it's about to destroy the EU [European Union], which is the last thing they want. The reason I think an anthropologist's book was perfect was because, while there is a tradition of anthropology in Germany, there's no tradition of popular anthropology, and they've preempted other approaches. If you're an economist, they'll say, "Oh, you're a Marxist" or "Oh, you're a post-Keynesian." You're a this, you're a that. But anthropology is so far out of the box . . .

APPEL: How do you situate *Debt* in your own intellectual trajectory, in relation to *Toward an Anthropological Theory of Value*, for example?

GRAEBER: In a larger sense I have constantly been working in this juncture between Marxian and Maussian traditions, though I find Maussian approaches much more radical than people realize. Marcel

Mauss himself was a cooperativist and a political organizer. One way to think of it is [that] the Marxian critique tradition is all about seeing how everything integrates in the way of reproducing some totality, which is ultimately one of exploitation in some way. Now, this is very true, and if you forget it, you become very naive. But if that's all you do, you become so cynical that there doesn't seem to be much point in resisting at all. "Everything [is] encompassed in giant totalities" is pretty much what everybody says who doesn't want to be political but doesn't like capitalism. On the other hand, the Maussian tradition is the cooperativist tradition, where rather than seeing everything at its essence coming from its role in reproducing a totality, you see everything, all social possibilities, as simultaneously present. In fact, everything is always there. Mauss stressed that democracy, dictatorship, oligarchy, and everything in between is present in all societies at some level or another, that individualism and communism, rather than being in any way contradictory, are mutually reinforcing of each other and always there. So I think I took a lot from that. So I've been trying to reconcile those two traditions throughout my intellectual life.

APPEL: Mindful that this interview is intended for a history journal, how does an anthropologist deal with five thousand years differently from a historian?

GRAEBER: The only people who would write a book like that would be anthropologists, or maybe historical sociologists or economists. I find that historians obviously do the most detailed, empirically informed work, but they have this rigorous refusal to talk about anything for which they do not have specific, concrete evidence, to the extent that you have to treat things that you can't prove as if they didn't happen, which is insane. So people write things about the origin of democratic institutions based on where they find the first written evidence for people sitting around making decisions together. And we have to pretend that before that they didn't do that.

It's absurd. On the other hand, economists go all the way the other way. It's all models. They don't really care what's there. They listen until they can have enough evidence to plug in to a model where they can show some signs that people are doing what they think they really ought to have been doing, and then they create a model saying they did that. I think anthropology is a happy medium. We can fill in the blank spaces, but we can do so based on empirical observation of what people in analogous situations actually have tended to do. That's what I think we can add.

APPEL: Where are we now? Help us to think through this moment.

GRAEBER: The impression I get right now is that the vast majority of the ruling class have trained themselves to have no more than a two- to three-year horizon. They don't really care what happens. There's still about 10 percent with a certain statesmanlike instinct to think about the long-term interest and preservation of the system. Those guys are scared as fuck. I know that because some of them are talking to me, and if they're talking to me, you know they're in trouble. I've had the IMF's chief research economist sending me papers which are saying things like, "Maybe we should get rid of fractional reserve banking entirely. What would that be like?" Really. I'll show you the paper. While they're telling everyone, "Nothing to see here, carry on, carry on," in fact those guys are panicking like crazy. You can see all these clear struggles going on where we don't really know what is at stake. Dominique Strauss-Kahn—first he comes out saying stop austerity; spend, spend. Then he says maybe we should move away from the dollar as the world currency. And oops, sex scandal! He's gone. I'm not saying he didn't do it. Obviously, he did. But somebody didn't make the usual phone call.

So there are titanic struggles going on between people saying, "This is an emergency, we have to address this situation," and people who have a different long-term view or others who are just blindly saying, "Absolutely not." They're just going to hold on to this thing until cataclysms embrace us. I've talked to people at the Federal Reserve. Not very important people, but nonetheless people who say they're really worried. They released a white paper calling for mortgage cancellation. They did. Look it up. They know that there's going to be a huge collapse if they don't. They'd never call for it otherwise. That's the Federal Reserve! So on top there are people who are really worried. Radical things might happen. We have a juncture where they're listening.

What does the ruling class always do? They take the best ideas coming out of social movements and turn them into something horrible. And that's going to happen. And for years, I must say this, those of us involved in the globalization movement were writing up our position papers. The Midnight Notes guys were involved in this. We weren't making demands but making an analysis. I remember for the G8 in Sapporo, Japanese people asked us to write something up, so we wrote up an analysis in which we said, look, there's only one way to save the system. They'll have to announce an emergency and declare that green capitalism is the only thing to save the planet. Then they'll divert all that money accumulating to sovereign wealth funds in the Global South and places that are not supposed to have it back into the system. It was the only logical thing they could do from their point of view. Except they kept not doing it. They kept sitting around arguing with one another instead. And there we were saying, "Can't they come up with their evil plan? We can't fight their evil plan unless they have their evil plan. We can think of a better evil plan than that! Hire us. Give us a million dollars to come up with an evil plan for you, and then give us a million dollars to fight you." It sounds like that's what's happening right now. They're asking me for a plan, and they'll make it evil. So we're at that kind of moment. But which one they adopt, who knows?

It could be [that] we could move in a direction of democratization of finance. It could happen. I don't know what that would look like or what it would mean. I do think one of the most important things we could be doing right now is to think about that. There are people like Charles Eisenstein who are coming up with all sorts of crazy ideas about what to do with money—ideas that might well work. The reaction, the hypothetical IMF plan to get rid of the private banking system and substitute a public banking system, of course gives even more power to states. Obviously, as an anarchist it's not really the approach I would take. But as I was talking to the guy at the Fed, I was thinking, what would a democratic money-creation system look like? We haven't spent a lot of time thinking about it. And I think it's a priority. If we're going to look back happy from 2020, rather than from a devastated planet half underwater, it's got to be something like that.

This is a provocation, but it is this line of thinking that has often led me to say, if Occupy is going to have a demand (and I'm not saying we should), it would be something like this: start with jubilee. But the question is, what happens after the jubilee? And I say, four-hour days, because the debt machine is a work machine (see *Tidal*, issue 3). It's the same thing. We have an economy which is based on the assumption of at least 5 percent growth. No one can pull that off anymore except maybe China, and who knows how long they'll be able to do that. Therefore, we just keep promising ourselves to increase production at the same rate as we used to, even though we don't do it, so the debt piles up, which is this constant promise of greater future exploitation and productivity. This is exactly what we don't need right now if we want to preserve a habitable planet. So it seems to me that canceling the debt also offers a unique possibility to cancel these idiotic promises we've made to one another, primarily that we're going to have to satisfy ever-increasing rent demands of the rich by producing even more for even less reward in the future. Decelerating the work machine would be probably the only way, at this point, to save the planet.

We could go to a basic income system. There are a million ways to do it. If you go to a four-hour day, for example, it's not like people don't do anything during the rest of the hours. They do whatever they want. They'll be producing things, but hopefully things that don't require so much coal.

Looking back on this moment, we know the debt will be canceled. Among those taking a long-term perspective, everyone agrees on that. The question is, How will that be done, and what's going to happen after that? Are they going to admit they're canceling the debt? Will there be some acknowledgment that we're living in a different monetary age? Money is something we promise one another. We need to think democratically about what kinds of promises we want to make to one another and how we can create a just social order on that basis. It could happen. Anything could happen. As an optimistic perspective, I would look back to today as a moment of break, where we finally realize that we've shifted into a different sort of regime than we'd been in before. That's one reason I point out in the book [Debt]—periods of bullion money, which is what we've been moving out of for the past thirty years, tend to be periods of large empires based on standing armies and some or another form of slavery, of which wage slavery is just one form. When you move back to virtual credit money you need to set up institutions that protect debtors.

I personally don't see how capitalism could really, ultimately, be preserved in any meaningful sense of the term within that virtual money environment. In fact, the very meaning of money itself will shift into something radically different. The potential for that happening is there. And something like that will happen eventually if history rings true. But, of course, we're talking about five-hundred-year cycles, so thirty years at the beginning of a new cycle is nothing. The first thirty years of the Middle Ages were pretty rough too. The cycles are getting shorter, but they're not that much shorter. The Fed and the IMF have all the information. They know that what they're doing right now is not going to work over the long term. And there are people on the top who realize they have to start listening to other perspectives. Again, they boxed themselves into a hole much like the German situation, where they've been so effective with the ideology, in convincing everybody that nothing else is conceivable, that the moment the thing starts to collapse everyone is sitting there with their mouths gaping open, saying, "But wait, this was supposed to be there forever. Now what do we do?" Some of them are smart enough to start looking around. And you know radical change is coming when they call an anthropologist.

On the Phenomenon of Bullshit Jobs

A Work Rant

In the year 1930, John Maynard Keynes predicted that, by century's end, technology would have advanced sufficiently that countries like the United Kingdom or the United States would have achieved a fifteen-hour work week. There's every reason to believe he was right. In technological terms, we are quite capable of this. And yet it didn't happen. Instead, technology has been marshaled, if anything, to figure out ways to make us all work more. In order to achieve this, jobs have had to be created that are, effectively, pointless. Huge swaths of people, in Europe and North America in particular, spend their entire working lives performing tasks they secretly believe do not really need to be performed. The moral and spiritual damage that comes from this situation is profound. It is a scar across our collective soul. Yet virtually no one talks about it.

Why did Keynes's promised utopia—still being eagerly awaited in

Originally published in *STRIKE! Magazine*, no. 3, Summer 2013, strikemag.org/bullshit-jobs.

the '60s—never materialize? The standard line today is that he didn't figure in the massive increase in consumerism. Given the choice between fewer hours and more toys and pleasures, we've collectively chosen the latter. This presents a nice morality tale, but even a moment's reflection shows it can't really be true. Yes, we have witnessed the creation of an endless variety of new jobs and industries since the '20s, but very few have anything to do with the production and distribution of sushi, iPhones, or fancy sneakers.

So what are these new jobs, precisely? A recent report comparing employment in the United States between 1910 and 2000 gives us a clear picture (and I note, one pretty much exactly echoed in the United Kingdom). Over the course of the last century, the number of workers employed as domestic servants, in industry, and in the farm sector has collapsed dramatically. At the same time, "professional, managerial, clerical, sales, and service workers" tripled, growing "from one-quarter to three-quarters of total employment." In other words, productive jobs have, just as predicted, been largely automated away. (Even if you count industrial workers globally, including the toiling masses in India and China, such workers are still not nearly so large a percentage of the world population as they used to be.)

But rather than allowing a massive reduction of working hours to free the world's population to pursue their own projects, pleasures, visions, and ideas, we have seen the ballooning not even so much of the "service" sector as of the administrative sector, up to and including the creation of whole new industries such as financial services or telemarketing, or the unprecedented expansion of sectors like corporate law, academic and health administration, human resources, and public relations. And these numbers do not even reflect on all those people whose job is to provide administrative, technical, or security support for these industries, or for that matter the whole host of ancillary industries (dog washers, all-night pizza delivery) that exist only because everyone else is spending so much of their time working in all the other ones.

These are what I propose to call "bullshit jobs."

It's as if someone were out there making up pointless jobs just for the sake of keeping us all working. And here, precisely, lies the mystery. In capitalism, this is precisely what is not supposed to happen. Sure, in the old inefficient socialist states like the Soviet Union, where employment was considered both a right and a sacred duty, the system made up as many jobs as it had to (this is why in Soviet department stores it took three clerks to sell a piece of meat). But, of course, this is the very sort of problem market competition is supposed to fix. According to economic theory, at least, the last thing a profit-seeking firm is going to do is shell out money to workers it doesn't really need to employ. Still, somehow, it happens.

While corporations may engage in ruthless downsizing, the layoffs and speed-ups invariably fall on that class of people who are actually making, moving, fixing, and maintaining things; through some strange alchemy no one can quite explain, the number of salaried paper pushers ultimately seems to expand, and more and more employees find themselves, not unlike Soviet workers actually, working forty- or even fifty-hour weeks on paper, but effectively working fifteen hours just as Keynes predicted, since the rest of their time is spent organizing or attending motivational seminars, updating their Facebook profiles, or downloading TV box sets.

The answer clearly isn't economic: it's moral and political. The ruling class has figured out that a happy and productive population with free time on their hands is a mortal danger (think of what started to happen when this even began to be approximated in the '60s). And, on the other hand, the feeling that work is a moral value in itself, and that anyone not willing to submit themselves to some kind of intense work discipline for most of their waking hours deserves nothing, is extraordinarily convenient for them.

Once, when contemplating the apparently endless growth of administrative responsibilities in British academic departments, I came up with one possible vision of hell. Hell is a collection of individuals who are spending the bulk of their time working on a task they don't like and are not especially good at. Say they were hired because they were excellent cabinetmakers, and then discover they are expected to spend a great deal of their time frying fish. Neither does the task really need to be done—at least, there's only a very limited number of fish that need to be fried. Yet somehow, they all become so obsessed with resentment at the thought that some of their coworkers might be spending more time making cabinets, and not doing their fair share of the fish-frying responsibilities, that before long there are endless piles of useless badly cooked fish piling up all over the workshop and it's all that anyone really does. I think this is actually a pretty accurate description of the moral dynamics of our own economy.

Now, I realize any such argument is going to run into immediate objections: "Who are you to say what jobs are really 'necessary'? What's necessary anyway? You're an anthropology professor, what's the 'need' for that?" (And indeed a lot of tabloid readers would take the existence of my job as the very definition of wasteful social expenditure.) And on one level, this is obviously true. There can be no objective measure of social value.

I would not presume to tell someone who is convinced they are making a meaningful contribution to the world that, really, they are not. But what about those people who are themselves convinced their jobs are meaningless? Not long ago I got back in touch with a school friend who I hadn't seen since I was twelve. I was amazed to discover that in the interim, he had become first a poet, then the front man in an indie rock band. I'd heard some of his songs on the radio having no idea the singer was someone I actually knew. He was obviously brilliant, innovative, and his work had unquestionably brightened and improved the lives of people all over the world. Yet, after a couple of unsuccessful albums, he'd lost his contract, and plagued with debts and a newborn daughter, ended up, as he put it, "taking the default choice of so many directionless folk: law school." Now he's a corporate lawyer working in a prominent New York firm. He was the first to admit that his job was utterly meaningless, contributed nothing to the world, and, in his own estimation, should not really exist.

There's a lot of questions one could ask here, starting with, what does it say about our society that it seems to generate an extremely limited demand for talented poet-musicians, but an apparently infinite demand for specialists in corporate law? (Answer: if 1 percent of the population controls most of the disposable wealth, what we call 'the market' reflects what they think is useful or important, not anybody else.) But even more, it shows that most people in these jobs are ultimately aware of it. In fact, I'm not sure I've ever met a corporate lawyer who didn't think their job was bullshit. The same goes for almost all the new industries outlined above. There is a whole class of salaried professionals that, should you meet them at parties and admit that you do something that might be considered interesting (an anthropologist, for example), will want to avoid even discussing their line of work entirely (one or t'other?). Give them a few drinks, and they will launch into tirades about how pointless and stupid their job really is.

This is a profound psychological violence here. How can one even begin to speak of dignity in labor when one secretly feels one's job should not exist? How can it not create a sense of deep rage and resentment? Yet it is the peculiar genius of our society that its rulers have figured out a way, as in the case of the fish-fryers, to ensure that rage is directed precisely against those who actually do get to do meaningful work. For instance: in our society, there seems a general rule that, the more obviously one's work benefits other people, the less one is likely to be paid for it. Again, an objective measure is hard to find, but one easy way to get a sense is to ask: What would happen were this entire class of people to simply disappear? Say what you like about nurses, garbage collectors, or mechanics, it's obvious that were they to vanish in a puff of smoke, the results would be immediate and catastrophic. A world without teachers or dockworkers would soon be in trouble, and even one without science fiction writers or ska musicians would clearly be a lesser place. It's not entirely clear how humanity would suffer were all private equity CEOs, lobbyists, PR researchers, actuaries, telemarketers, bailiffs, or legal consultants to similarly vanish. (Many suspect it might markedly improve.) Yet apart from a handful of well-touted exceptions (doctors), the rule holds surprisingly well.

Even more perverse, there seems to be a broad sense that this is the way things should be. This is one of the secret strengths of right-wing populism. You can see it when tabloids whip up resentment against Tube workers for paralyzing London during contract disputes: the very fact that Tube workers can paralyze London shows that their work is actually necessary, but this seems to be precisely what annoys people. It's even clearer in the U.S., where Republicans have had remarkable success mobilizing resentment against schoolteachers, or autoworkers (and not, significantly, against the school administrators or auto-industry managers who actually cause the problems), for their supposedly bloated wages and benefits. It's as if they are being told "but you get to teach children! Or make cars! You get to have real jobs! And on top of that you have the nerve to also expect middle-class pensions and health care?"

If someone had designed a work regime perfectly suited to maintaining the power of finance capital, it's hard to see how they could have done a better job. Real, productive workers are relentlessly squeezed and exploited. The remainder are divided between a terrorized stratum of the universally reviled unemployed and a larger stratum who are basically paid to do nothing, in positions designed to make them identify with the perspectives and sensibilities of the ruling class (managers, administrators, etc.)—and particularly its financial avatars—but, at the same time, foster a simmering resentment against anyone whose work has clear and undeniable social value. Clearly, the system was never consciously designed. It emerged from almost a century of trial and error. But it is the only explanation for why, despite our technological capacities, we are not all working three- to four-hour days.

Against Economics

There is a growing feeling, among those who have the responsibility of managing large economies, that the discipline of economics is no longer fit for purpose. It is beginning to look like a science designed to solve problems that no longer exist.

A good example is the obsession with inflation. Economists still teach their students that the primary economic role of government—many would insist, its only really proper economic role—is to guarantee price stability. We must be constantly vigilant over the dangers of inflation. For governments to simply print money is therefore inherently sinful. If, however, inflation is kept at bay through the coordinated action of government and central bankers, the market should find its "natural rate of unemployment," and investors, taking advantage of clear price signals, should be able to ensure healthy growth. These assumptions came with the monetarism of the 1980s, the idea that government should restrict itself to managing the money supply, and by the 1990s had come to be accepted as such elementary common sense that pretty

Originally published in *The New York Review of Books*, December 5, 2019, nybooks.com.

much all political debate had to set out from a ritual acknowledgment of the perils of government spending. This continues to be the case, despite the fact that, since the 2008 recession, central banks have been printing money frantically in an attempt to create inflation and compel the rich to do something useful with their money, and have been largely unsuccessful in both endeavors.

We now live in a different economic universe than we did before the crash. Falling unemployment no longer drives up wages. Printing money does not cause inflation. Yet the language of public debate, and the wisdom conveyed in economic textbooks, remain almost entirely unchanged.

One expects a certain institutional lag. Mainstream economists nowadays might not be particularly good at predicting financial crashes, facilitating general prosperity, or coming up with models for preventing climate change, but when it comes to establishing themselves in positions of intellectual authority, unaffected by such failings, their success is unparalleled. One would have to look at the history of religions to find anything like it. To this day, economics continues to be taught not as a story of arguments—not, like any other social science, as a welter of often warring theoretical perspectives—but rather as something more like physics, the gradual realization of universal, unimpeachable mathematical truths. "Heterodox" theories of economics do, of course, exist (institutionalist, Marxist, feminist, "Austrian," post-Keynesian . . .), but their exponents have been almost completely locked out of what are considered "serious" departments, and even outright rebellions by economics students (from the post-autistic economics movement in France to post-crash economics in Britain) have largely failed to force them into the core curriculum.

As a result, heterodox economists continue to be treated as just a step or two away from crackpots, despite the fact that they often have a much better record of predicting real-world economic events. What's more, the basic psychological assumptions on which mainstream (neoclassical) economics is based—though they have long since been disproved by actual psychologists—have colonized the rest of the academy, and have had a profound impact on popular understandings of the world.

Nowhere is this divide between public debate and economic reality more dramatic than in Britain, which is perhaps why it appears to be the first country where something is beginning to crack. It was the center-left New Labour that presided over the pre-crash bubble, and voters' throw-the-bastards-out reaction brought a series of Conservative governments that soon discovered that a rhetoric of austerity—the Churchillian evocation of common sacrifice for the public good—played well with the British public, allowing them to win broad popular acceptance for policies designed to pare down what little remained of the British welfare state and redistribute resources upward, toward the rich. "There is no magic money tree," as Theresa May put it during the snap election of 2017—virtually the only memorable line from one of the most lackluster campaigns in British history. The phrase has been repeated endlessly in the media, whenever someone asks why England is the only country in Western Europe that charges university tuition, or whether it is really necessary to have quite so many people sleeping on the streets.

The truly extraordinary thing about May's phrase is that it isn't true. There are plenty of magic money trees in Britain, as there are in any developed economy. They are called "banks." Since modern money is simply credit, banks can and do create money literally out of nothing, simply by making loans. Almost all of the money circulating in Britain at the moment is bank-created in this way. Not only is the public largely unaware of this, but a recent survey by the British research group Positive Money discovered that an astounding 85 percent of members of Parliament had no idea where money really came from (most appeared to be under the impression that it was produced by the Royal Mint).

Economists, for obvious reasons, can't be completely oblivious to the role of banks, but they have spent much of the twentieth century arguing about what actually happens when someone applies for a loan. One school insists that banks transfer existing funds from their reserves, another that they produce new money, but only on the basis of a multiplier effect (so that your car loan can still be seen as ultimately rooted in some retired grandmother's pension fund). Only a minority—mostly heterodox economists, post-Keynesians, and modern money theorists—uphold what is called the "credit creation theory of banking": that bankers simply wave a magic wand and make the money appear, secure in the confidence that even if they hand a client a credit for $1 million, ultimately the recipient will put it back in the bank again, so that, across the system as a whole, credits and debts will cancel out. Rather than loans being based in deposits, in this view, deposits themselves were the result of loans.

The one thing it never seemed to occur to anyone to do was to get a job at a bank, and find out what actually happens when someone asks to borrow money. In 2014 a German economist named Richard Werner did exactly that, and discovered that, in fact, loan officers do not check their existing funds, reserves, or anything else. They simply create money out of thin air, or, as he preferred to put it, "fairy dust."

That year also appears to have been when elements in Britain's notoriously independent civil service decided that enough was enough. The question of money creation became a critical bone of contention. The overwhelming majority of even mainstream economists in the UK had long since rejected austerity as counterproductive (which, predictably, had almost no impact on public debate). But at a certain point, demanding that the technocrats charged with running the system base all policy decisions on false assumptions about something as elementary as the nature of money becomes a little like demanding that architects proceed on the understanding that the square root of 47 is actually π. Architects are aware that buildings would start falling down. People would die.

Before long, the Bank of England (the British equivalent of the Federal Reserve, whose economists are most free to speak their minds since they are not formally part of the government) rolled out an elaborate official report called "Money Creation in the Modern Economy," replete with videos and animations, making the same point: existing economics textbooks, and particularly the reigning monetarist orthodoxy, are wrong. The heterodox economists are right. Private banks create money. Central banks like the Bank of England create money as

well, but monetarists are entirely wrong to insist that their proper function is to control the money supply. In fact, central banks do not in any
sense control the money supply; their main function is to set the interest
rate—to determine how much private banks can charge for the money
they create. Almost all public debate on these subjects is therefore based
on false premises. For example, if what the Bank of England was saying
were true, government borrowing didn't divert funds from the private
sector; it created entirely new money that had not existed before.

One might have imagined that such an admission would create
something of a splash, and in certain restricted circles, it did. Central
banks in Norway, Switzerland, and Germany quickly put out similar papers. Back in the UK, the immediate media response was simply silence.
The Bank of England report has never, to my knowledge, been so much
as mentioned on the BBC or any other TV news outlet. Newspaper columnists continued to write as if monetarism was self-evidently correct.
Politicians continued to be grilled about where they would find the cash
for social programs. It was as if a kind of entente cordiale had been
established, in which the technocrats would be allowed to live in one
theoretical universe, while politicians and news commentators would
continue to exist in an entirely different one.

Still, there are signs that this arrangement is temporary. Britain—
and the Bank of England in particular—prides itself on being a
bellwether for global economic trends. Monetarism itself got its launch
into intellectual respectability in the 1970s after having been embraced
by Bank of England economists. From there it was ultimately adopted
by the insurgent Thatcher regime, and only after that by Ronald Reagan
in the United States, and it was subsequently exported almost everywhere else.

It is possible that a similar pattern is reproducing itself today. In
2015, a year after the appearance of the Bank of England report, the
Labour Party for the first time allowed open elections for its leadership, and the left wing of the party, under Jeremy Corbyn and shadow
chancellor of the exchequer John McDonnell, took hold of the reins of
power. At the time, the Labour left were considered even more marginal

extremists than was Thatcher's wing of the Conservative Party in 1975; it is also (despite the media's constant efforts to paint them as unreconstructed 1970s socialists) the only major political group in the UK that has been open to new economic ideas. While pretty much the entire political establishment has been spending most of its time these last few years screaming at one another about Brexit, McDonnell's office— and Labour youth support groups—have been holding workshops and floating policy initiatives on everything from a four-day workweek and universal basic income to a Green Industrial Revolution and "Fully Automated Luxury Communism," and inviting heterodox economists to take part in popular education initiatives aimed at transforming conceptions of how the economy really works. Corbynism has faced near-histrionic opposition from virtually all sectors of the political establishment, but it would be unwise to ignore the possibility that something historic is afoot.

One sign that something historically new has indeed appeared is if scholars begin reading the past in a new light. Accordingly, one of the most significant books to come out of the UK in recent years would have to be Robert Skidelsky's *Money and Government: The Past and Future of Economics*. Ostensibly an attempt to answer the question of why mainstream economics rendered itself so useless in the years immediately before and after the crisis of 2008, it is really an attempt to retell the history of the economic discipline through a consideration of the two things—money and government—that most economists least like to talk about.

Skidelsky is well positioned to tell this story. He embodies a uniquely English type: the gentle maverick, so firmly ensconced in the establishment that it never occurs to him that he might not be able to say exactly what he thinks, and whose views are tolerated by the rest of the establishment precisely for that reason. Born in Manchuria, trained at Oxford, professor of political economy at Warwick, Skidelsky is best known as the author of the definitive, three-volume biography of John Maynard Keynes, and has for the last three decades sat in the House of Lords as Baron Skidelsky of Tilton, affiliated at different times with a variety of political parties, and sometimes none at all. During the early Blair years, he was a Conservative, and even served as opposition spokesman on economic matters in the upper chamber; currently he's a cross-bench independent, broadly aligned with left Labour. In other words, he follows his own flag. Usually, it's an interesting flag. Over the last several years, Skidelsky has been taking advantage of his position in the world's most elite legislative body to hold a series of high-level seminars on the reformation of the economic discipline.

What it reveals is an endless war between two broad theoretical perspectives in which the same side always seems to win—for reasons that rarely have anything to do with either theoretical sophistication or greater predictive power. The crux of the argument always seems to turn on the nature of money. Is money best conceived of as a physical commodity, a precious substance used to facilitate exchange, or is it better to see money primarily as a credit, a bookkeeping method or circulating IOU—in any case, a social arrangement? This is an argument that has been going on in some form for thousands of years. What we call "money" is always a mixture of both, and, as I myself noted in *Debt* (2011), the center of gravity between the two tends to shift back and forth over time. In the Middle Ages everyday transactions across Eurasia were typically conducted by means of credit, and money was assumed to be an abstraction. It was the rise of global European empires in the sixteenth and seventeenth centuries, and the corresponding flood of gold and silver looted from the Americas, that really shifted perceptions. Historically, the feeling that bullion actually is money tends to mark periods of generalized violence, mass slavery, and predatory standing armies—which for most of the world was precisely how the Spanish, Portuguese, Dutch, French, and British empires were experienced. One important theoretical innovation that these new bullion-based theories of money allowed was, as Skidelsky notes, what has come to be called the quantity theory of money (usually referred to in textbooks—since economists take endless delight in abbreviations—as QTM).

The QTM argument was first put forward by a French lawyer named Jean Bodin, during a debate over the cause of the sharp, destabilizing price inflation that immediately followed the Iberian conquest of the

Americas. Bodin argued that the inflation was a simple matter of supply and demand: the enormous influx of gold and silver from the Spanish colonies was cheapening the value of money in Europe. The basic principle would no doubt have seemed a matter of common sense to anyone with experience of commerce at the time, but it turns out to have been based on a series of false assumptions. For one thing, most of the gold and silver extracted from Mexico and Peru did not end up in Europe at all, and certainly wasn't coined into money. Most of it was transported directly to China and India (to buy spices, silks, calicoes, and other "oriental luxuries"), and insofar as it had inflationary effects back home, it was on the basis of speculative bonds of one sort or another. This almost always turns out to be true when QTM is applied: it seems self-evident, but only if you leave most of the critical factors out.

In the case of the sixteenth-century price inflation, for instance, once one takes account of credit, hoarding, and speculation—not to mention increased rates of economic activity, investment in new technology, and wage levels (which, in turn, have a lot to do with the relative power of workers and employers, creditors and debtors)—it becomes impossible to say for certain which is the deciding factor: whether the money supply drives prices, or prices drive the money supply. Technically, this comes down to a choice between what are called exogenous and endogenous theories of money. Should money be treated as an outside factor, like all those Spanish doubloons supposedly sweeping into Antwerp, Dublin, and Genoa in the days of Philip II, or should it be imagined primarily as a product of economic activity itself, mined, minted, and put into circulation, or more often, created as credit instruments such as loans, in order to meet a demand—which would, of course, mean that the roots of inflation lie elsewhere?

To put it bluntly: QTM is obviously wrong. Doubling the amount of gold in a country will have no effect on the price of cheese if you give all the gold to rich people and they just bury it in their yards, or use it to make gold-plated submarines (this is, incidentally, why quantitative easing, the strategy of buying long-term government bonds to put money into circulation, did not work either). What actually matters is spending.

Nonetheless, from Bodin's time to the present, almost every time there was a major policy debate, the QTM advocates won. In England, the pattern was set in 1696, just after the creation of the Bank of England, with an argument over wartime inflation between Secretary of the Treasury William Lowndes, Sir Isaac Newton (then warden of the mint), and the philosopher John Locke. Newton had agreed with the treasury that silver coins had to be officially devalued to prevent a deflationary collapse; Locke took an extreme monetarist position, arguing that the government should be limited to guaranteeing the value of property (including coins) and that tinkering would confuse investors and defraud creditors. Locke won. The result was deflationary collapse. A sharp tightening of the money supply created an abrupt economic contraction that threw hundreds of thousands out of work and created mass penury, riots, and hunger. The government quickly moved to moderate the policy (first by allowing banks to monetize government war debts in the form of bank notes, and eventually by moving off the silver standard entirely), but in its official rhetoric, Locke's small-government, pro-creditor, hard-money ideology became the grounds of all further political debate.

According to Skidelsky, the pattern was to repeat itself again and again, in 1797, the 1840s, the 1890s, and, ultimately, the late 1970s and early 1980s, with Thatcher's and Reagan's (in each case brief) adoption of monetarism. Always we see the same sequence of events:

1. The government adopts hard-money policies as a matter of principle.
2. Disaster ensues.
3. The government quietly abandons hard-money policies.
4. The economy recovers.
5. Hard-money philosophy nonetheless becomes, or is reinforced as, simple universal common sense.

How was it possible to justify such a remarkable string of failures? Here a lot of the blame, according to Skidelsky, can be laid at the feet of the Scottish philosopher David Hume. An early advocate of QTM, Hume was also the first to introduce the notion that short-term shocks—such as Locke produced—would create long-term benefits if they had the effect of unleashing the self-regulating powers of the market:

> Ever since Hume, economists have distinguished between the short-run and long-run effects of economic change, including the effects of policy interventions. The distinction has served to protect the theory of equilibrium, by enabling it to be stated in a form that took some account of reality. In economics, the short run now typically stands for the period during which a market (or an economy of markets) temporarily deviates from its long-term equilibrium position under the impact of some "shock," like a pendulum temporarily dislodged from a position of rest. This way of thinking suggests that governments should leave it to markets to discover their natural equilibrium positions. Government interventions to "correct" deviations will only add extra layers of delusion to the original one.

There is a logical flaw to any such theory: there's no possible way to disprove it. The premise that markets will always right themselves in the end can be tested only if one has a commonly agreed definition of when the "end" is; but for economists, that definition turns out to be "however long it takes to reach a point where I can say the economy has returned to equilibrium." (In the same way, statements like "the barbarians always win in the end" or "truth always prevails" cannot be proved wrong, since in practice they just mean "whenever barbarians win, or truth prevails, I shall declare the story over.")

At this point, all the pieces were in place: tight-money policies (which benefited creditors and the wealthy) could be justified as "harsh medicine" to clear up price signals so the market could return to a healthy state of long-run balance. In describing how all this came about, Skidelsky is providing us with a worthy extension of a history Karl Polanyi first began to map out in the 1940s: the story of how supposedly self-regulating national markets were the product of careful social engineering. Part of that involved creating government policies

self-consciously designed to inspire resentment of "big government."
Skidelsky writes:

> A crucial innovation was income tax, first levied in 1814, and re-
> newed by [Prime Minister Robert] Peel in 1842. By 1911–14, this
> had become the principal source of government revenue. Income
> tax had the double benefit of giving the British state a secure
> revenue base, and aligning voters' interests with cheap govern-
> ment, since only direct taxpayers had the vote . . . "Fiscal probity,"
> under Gladstone, "became the new morality."

In fact, there's absolutely no reason a modern state should fund itself
primarily by appropriating a proportion of each citizen's earnings. There
are plenty of other ways to go about it. Many—such as land, wealth, commercial, or consumer taxes (any of which can be made more or less
progressive)—are considerably more efficient, since creating a bureaucratic apparatus capable of monitoring citizens' personal affairs to the
degree required by an income tax system is itself enormously expensive.
But this misses the real point: income tax is supposed to be intrusive and
exasperating. It is meant to feel at least a little bit unfair. Like so much
of classical liberalism (and contemporary neoliberalism), it is an ingenious political sleight of hand—an expansion of the bureaucratic state
that also allows its leaders to pretend to advocate for small government.

The one major exception to this pattern was the mid-twentieth century, what has come to be remembered as the Keynesian age. It was a
period in which those running capitalist democracies, spooked by the
Russian Revolution and the prospect of the mass rebellion of their own
working classes, allowed unprecedented levels of redistribution—which,
in turn, led to the most generalized material prosperity in human history. The story of the Keynesian revolution of the 1930s, and the neoclassical counterrevolution of the 1970s, has been told innumerable times,
but Skidelsky gives the reader a fresh sense of the underlying conflict.

Keynes himself was staunchly anti-Communist, but largely because
he felt that capitalism was more likely to drive rapid technological ad-

vance that would largely eliminate the need for material labor. He wished for full employment not because he thought work was good, but because he ultimately wished to do away with work, envisioning a society in which technology would render human labor obsolete. In other words, he assumed that the ground was always shifting under the analysts' feet; the object of any social science was inherently unstable. Max Weber, for similar reasons, argued that it would never be possible for social scientists to come up with anything remotely like the laws of physics, because by the time they had come anywhere near to gathering enough information, society itself, and what analysts felt was important to know about it, would have changed so much that the information would be irrelevant. Keynes's opponents, on the other hand, were determined to root their arguments in just such universal principles.

It's difficult for outsiders to see what was really at stake here, because the argument has come to be recounted as a technical dispute between the roles of micro- and macroeconomics. Keynesians insisted that the former is appropriate to studying the behavior of individual households or firms, trying to optimize their advantage in the marketplace, but that as soon as one begins to look at national economies, one is moving to an entirely different level of complexity, where different sorts of laws apply. Just as it is impossible to understand the mating habits of an aardvark by analyzing all the chemical reactions in its cells, so patterns of trade, investment, or the fluctuations of interest or employment rates were not simply the aggregate of all the microtransactions that seemed to make them up. The patterns had, as philosophers of science would put it, "emergent properties." Obviously, it was necessary to understand the micro level (just as it was necessary to understand the chemicals that made up the aardvark) to have any chance of understanding the macro, but that was not, in itself, enough.

The counterrevolutionaries, starting with Keynes's old rival Friedrich Hayek at the London School of Economics and the various luminaries who joined him in the Mont Pelerin Society, took aim directly at this notion that national economies are anything more than the sum of their parts. Politically, Skidelsky notes, this was due to a hostility to the very idea of statecraft (and, in a broader sense, of any collective good). National economies could indeed be reduced to the aggregate effect of millions of individual decisions, and, therefore, every element of macroeconomics had to be systematically "micro-founded."

One reason this was such a radical position was that it was taken at exactly the same moment that microeconomics itself was completing a profound transformation—one that had begun with the marginal revolution of the late nineteenth century—from a technique for understanding how those operating on the market make decisions, to a general philosophy of human life. It was able to do so, remarkably enough, by proposing a series of assumptions that even economists themselves were happy to admit were not really true: let us posit, they said, purely rational actors motivated exclusively by self-interest, who know exactly what they want and never change their minds, and have complete access to all relevant pricing information. This allowed them to make precise, predictive equations of exactly how individuals should be expected to act.

Surely there's nothing wrong with creating simplified models. Arguably, this is how any science of human affairs has to proceed. But an empirical science then goes on to test those models against what people actually do, and adjust them accordingly. This is precisely what economists did not do. Instead, they discovered that, if one encased those models in mathematical formulae completely impenetrable to the noninitiate, it would be possible to create a universe in which those premises could never be refuted. ("All actors are engaged in the maximization of utility. What is utility? Whatever it is that an actor appears to be maximizing.") The mathematical equations allowed economists to plausibly claim theirs was the only branch of social theory that had advanced to anything like a predictive science (even if most of their successful predictions were of the behavior of people who had themselves been trained in economic theory).

This allowed *Homo economicus* to invade the rest of the academy, so that by the 1950s and 1960s almost every scholarly discipline in the business of preparing young people for positions of power (political science, international relations, etc.) had adopted some variant of "rational choice theory" culled, ultimately, from microeconomics. By the 1980s and 1990s, it had reached a point where even the heads of art founda-tions or charitable organizations would not be considered fully qualified if they were not at least broadly familiar with a "science" of human af-fairs that started from the assumption that humans were fundamentally selfish and greedy.

These, then, were the "microfoundations" to which the neoclassi-cal reformers demanded macroeconomics be returned. Here they were able to take advantage of certain undeniable weaknesses in Keynes-ian formulations, above all its inability to explain 1970s stagflation, to brush away the remaining Keynesian superstructure and return to the same hard-money, small-government policies that had been dominant in the nineteenth century. The familiar pattern ensued. Monetarism didn't work; in the UK and then the USA, such policies were quickly abandoned. But ideologically, the intervention was so effective that even when "new Keynesians" such as Joseph Stiglitz or Paul Krugman re-turned to dominate the argument about macroeconomics, they still felt obliged to maintain the new microfoundations.

The problem, as Skidelsky emphasizes, is that if your initial assump-tions are absurd, multiplying them a thousandfold will hardly make them less so. Or, as he puts it, rather less gently, "lunatic premises lead to mad conclusions":

> The efficient market hypothesis (EMH), made popular by Eugene Fama . . . is the application of rational expectations to financial markets. The rational expectations hypothesis (REH) says that agents optimally utilize all available information about the econ-omy and policy instantly to adjust their expectations . . .
>
> Thus, in the words of Fama, . . . "In an efficient market, com-petition among the many intelligent participants leads to a sit-uation where . . . the actual price of a security will be a good estimate of its *intrinsic value*." [Skidelsky's italics]

In other words, we were obliged to pretend that markets could not, by definition, be wrong—if in the 1980s the land on which the Imperial compound in Tokyo was built, for example, was valued higher than that of all the land in New York City, then that would have to be because that was what it was actually worth. If there are deviations, they are purely random, "stochastic" and therefore unpredictable, temporary, and, ultimately, insignificant. In any case, rational actors will quickly step in to sweep up any undervalued stocks. Skidelsky drily remarks:

> There is a paradox here. On the one hand, the theory says that there is no point in trying to profit from speculation, because shares are always correctly priced and their movements cannot be predicted. But on the other hand, if investors did not try to profit, the market would not be efficient because there would be no self-correcting mechanism . . .
>
> Secondly, if shares are always correctly priced, bubbles and crises cannot be generated by the market . . .
>
> This attitude leached into policy: "government officials, starting with [Federal Reserve Chairman] Alan Greenspan, were unwilling to burst the bubble precisely because they were unwilling to even judge that it was a bubble." The EMH made the identification of bubbles impossible because it ruled them out a priori.

If there is an answer to the queen's famous question of why no one saw the crash coming, this would be it.

At this point, we have come full circle. After such a catastrophic embarrassment, orthodox economists fell back on their strong suit—academic politics and institutional power. In the UK, one of the first moves of the new Conservative–Liberal Democratic coalition in 2010 was to reform the higher education system by tripling tuition and instituting an American-style regime of student loans. Common sense might have suggested that if the education system was performing successfully (for all its foibles, the university system in Britain was considered among the best in the world), while the financial system was operating so badly that it had nearly destroyed the global economy, the sensible thing might be to reform the financial system to be a bit more like the educational system, rather than the other way around. An aggressive effort to do the opposite could only be an ideological move. It was a full-on assault on the very idea that knowledge could be anything other than an economic good.

Similar moves were made to solidify control over the institutional structure. The BBC, a once proudly independent body, under the Tories has increasingly come to resemble a state broadcasting network, their political commentators often reciting almost verbatim the latest talking points of the ruling party—which, at least economically, were premised on the very theories that had just been discredited. Political debate simply assumed that the usual "harsh medicine" and Gladstonian "fiscal probity" were the only solution; at the same time, the Bank of England began printing money like mad and, effectively, handing it out to the 1 percent in an unsuccessful attempt to kick-start inflation. The practical results were, to put it mildly, uninspiring. Even at the height of the eventual recovery, in the fifth-richest country in the world, something like one British citizen in twelve experienced hunger, up to and including going entire days without food. If an "economy" is to be defined as the means by which a human population provides itself with its material needs, the British economy is increasingly dysfunctional. Frenetic efforts on the part of the British political class to change the subject (Brexit) can hardly go on forever. Eventually, real issues will have to be addressed.

Economic theory as it exists increasingly resembles a shed full of broken tools. This is not to say there are no useful insights here, but fundamentally the existing discipline is designed to solve another century's problems. The problem of how to determine the optimal distribution of work and resources to create high levels of economic growth is simply not the same problem we are now facing: i.e., how to deal with increasing technological productivity, decreasing real demand for labor, and the effective management of care work, without also destroying the Earth. This demands a different science. The "microfoundations" of current economics are precisely what stands in the way of this. Any new, viable science will either have to draw on the accumulated knowledge of feminism, behavioral economics, psychology, and even anthropology to come up with theories based on how people actually behave, or once again embrace the notion of emergent levels of complexity—or, most likely, both.

Intellectually, this won't be easy. Politically, it will be even more difficult. Breaking through neoclassical economics' lock on major institutions, and its near-theological hold over the media—not to mention all the subtle ways it has come to define our conceptions of human motivations and the horizons of human possibility—is a daunting prospect. Presumably, some kind of shock would be required. What might it take? Another 2008-style collapse? Some radical political shift in a major world government? A global youth rebellion? However it will come about, texts like this—and quite possibly this text—will play a crucial part.

Soak the Rich

An Exchange on Capital, Debt, and the Future

This exchange is from a conversation in Paris between David Graeber and Thomas Piketty, discoursing on the deep shit we're all in and what we might do about climbing out. It was held at the École Normale Supérieure; moderated by Joseph Confavreux and Jade Lindgaard; edited by Edwy Plenel; first published by the French magazine *Mediapart*; and translated from the French for *The Baffler* by Donald Nicholson-Smith.

MODERATORS: You both appear to think that the prevailing economic and financial system has run its course, and cannot endure much longer in its present form. I would like to ask each of you to explain why.

An exchange with Thomas Piketty; originally published in *The Baffler*, no. 25, July 2014, thebaffler.com.

THOMAS PIKETTY: I am not sure that we are on the eve of a collapse of the system, at least not from a purely economic viewpoint. A lot depends on political reactions and on the ability of the elites to persuade the rest of the population that the present situation is acceptable. If an effective apparatus of persuasion is in place, there is no reason why the system should not continue to exist as it is. I do not believe that strictly economic factors can precipitate its fall.

Karl Marx thought that the falling rate of profit would inevitably bring about the fall of the capitalist system. In a sense, I am more pessimistic than Marx, because even given a stable rate of return on capital, say around 5 percent on average, and steady growth, wealth would continue to concentrate, and the rate of accumulation of inherited wealth would go on increasing.

But, in itself, this does not mean an economic collapse will occur. My thesis is thus different from Marx's, and also from David Graeber's. An explosion of debt, especially American debt, is certainly happening, as we have all observed, but at the same time there is a vast increase in capital—an increase far greater than that of total debt.

The creation of net wealth is thus positive, because capital growth surpasses even the increase in debt. I am not saying that this is necessarily a good thing. I am saying that there is no purely economic justification for claiming that this phenomenon entails the collapse of the system.

MODERATORS: But you still say the level of inequality has become intolerable?

PIKETTY: Yes. But there again, the apparatus of persuasion—or of repression, or a combination of the two, depending on what country you are considering—may allow the present situation to persist. A century ago, despite universal suffrage, the elites of the industrialized countries succeeded in preventing any progressive taxes. It took World War I to bring about a progressive income tax.

DAVID GRAEBER: But the indebtedness of one person has to imply the enrichment of another, don't you think?

PIKETTY: That is an interesting question. I loved your book, by the way. The only criticism I would have is that capital cannot be reduced to debt. It is true that more debt for some, public or private, is bound to increase the resources of others. But you do not directly address possible differences between debt and capital. You argue as if the history of capital were indistinguishable from that of debt. I think you are right to say that debt plays a much more significant historical part than has been assumed—especially when you dismiss the fairy tales retailed by economists concerning capital accumulation, barter, the invention of money, or monetary exchange. The way you redirect our attention by stressing the relationships of power and domination that underlie relationships of indebtedness is admirable. The fact remains that capital is useful in itself. The inequalities associated with it are problematic, but not capital per se. And there is much more capital today than formerly.

GRAEBER: I do not mean to say that capital is reducible to debt. But the absolute opposite is what everybody is told, and it is our task to fill in the blanks left by that account with respect to the history of wage labor, industrial capitalism, and early forms of capital. Why do you say that resources increase even as debt increases?

PIKETTY: Net wealth has increased—"wealth" meaning resources inasmuch as we can calculate them. And this is true even when debt is taken into account.

GRAEBER: You mean to say that there is now more wealth per capita than before?

PIKETTY: Clearly, yes. Take housing. Not only is there more housing now than fifty or a hundred years ago, but, by year of production, housing, net of debt, is increasing. On the basis of annual GNP, if you calculate national capital (defined as all revenue engendered by economic activity) and then the total indebtedness of all public and private actors in the country, the former will be seen to have increased relative to the latter in all the rich countries. This increase is somewhat less spectacular in the United States than in Europe and Japan, but it exists nevertheless. Resources are increasing much faster than debt.

GRAEBER: Getting back to the original question, the possible collapse of the system, I think that historical forecasts of this kind are a trap. What is certain is that all systems must end, but it is very hard to predict when the end might come. Signs of a slowing down of the capitalist system are visible. So far as technology is concerned, we no longer have the sense, as we did in the 1960s and 1970s, that we are about to see great innovations. In terms of political visions, we seem to be very far from the grand projects of the postwar period, such as the United Nations or the initiation of a space program. U.S. elites can't act on climate change, even though it puts our ecosystem and human life itself in jeopardy. Our feelings of helplessness stem from the fact that for thirty years the tools of persuasion and coercion have been mobilized to wage an ideological war for capitalism, rather than to create conditions for capitalism to remain viable. Neoliberalism places political and ideological considerations above economic ones. The result has been a campaign of fantasy manipulation, a campaign so effective that people with dead-end jobs now believe that there is no alternative.

It is quite clear that this ideological hegemony has now reached its limit. Does this mean that the system is on the point of collapse? It's hard to say. But capitalism is not old. It hasn't been around forever, and it seems just as reasonable to imagine it can be transformed into something completely different as to imagine it will necessarily continue existing until the sun blows up, or until it annihilates us through some ecological catastrophe.

MODERATORS: Is capitalism itself the cause of the problem, or can it be reformed?

PIKETTY: One of the points that I most appreciate in David Graeber's book is the link he shows between slavery and public debt. The most extreme form of debt, he says, is slavery: slaves belong forever to somebody else, and so, potentially, do their children. In principle, one of the great advances of civilization has been the abolition of slavery. As Graeber explains, the intergenerational transmission of debt that slavery embodied has found a modern form in the growing public debt, which allows for the transfer of one generation's indebtedness to the next. It is possible to picture an extreme instance of this, with an infinite quantity of public debt amounting to not just one, but ten or twenty years of GNP, and in effect creating what is, for all intents and purposes, a slave society, in which all production and all wealth creation is dedicated to the repayment of debt. In that way, the great majority would be slaves to a minority, implying a reversion to the beginnings of our history.

In actuality, we are not yet at that point. There is still plenty of capital to counteract debt. But this way of looking at things helps us understand our strange situation, in which debtors are held culpable and we are continually assailed by the claim that each of us "owns" between thirty and forty thousand euros of the nation's public debt.

This is particularly crazy because, as I say, our resources surpass our debt. A large portion of the population owns very little capital individually, since capital is so highly concentrated. Until the nineteenth century, 90 percent of accumulated capital belonged to 10 percent of the population. Today things are a little different. In the United States, 73 percent of capital belongs to the richest 10 percent. This degree of concentration still means that half the population owns nothing but debt. For this half, the per capita public debt thus exceeds what they possess. But the other half of the population owns more capital than debt, so it is an absurdity to lay the blame on populations in order to justify austerity measures.

But for all that, is the elimination of debt the solution, as Graeber writes? I have nothing against this, but I am more favorable to a progressive tax on inherited wealth along with high tax rates for the upper brackets. Why? The question is: What about the day after? What do we do once debt has been eliminated? What is the plan? Eliminating debt implies treating the last creditor, the ultimate holder of debt, as the responsible party. But the system of financial transactions as it actually operates allows the most important players to dispose of letters of credit well before debt is forgiven. The ultimate creditor, thanks to the system of intermediaries, may not be especially rich. Thus canceling debt does not necessarily mean that the richest will lose money in the process.

GRAEBER: No one is saying that debt abolition is the only solution. In my view, it is simply an essential component in a whole set of solutions. I do not believe that eliminating debt can solve all our problems. I am thinking rather in terms of a conceptual break. To be quite honest, I really think that massive debt abolition is going to occur no matter what. For me the main issue is just how this is going to happen: openly, by virtue of a top-down decision designed to protect the interests of existing institutions, or under pressure from social movements. Most of the political and economic leaders to whom I have spoken acknowledge that some sort of debt abolition is required.

PIKETTY: That is precisely my problem: the bankers agree with you!

GRAEBER: Once we grant that debt cancellation is going to take place, the question becomes how we can control this process and ensure that its outcome is desirable. History offers many examples of debt elimination serving merely to preserve iniquitous social structures.

But debt abolition has also at times produced positive social change. Take the Athenian and Roman constitutions. At the origin of each was a debt crisis resolved in such a way that structural political reform ensued. The Roman republic and Athenian democracy were the offspring of debt crises. Indeed, there is a sense in which all great moments of political transformation have been precipitated by such crises. During the American Revolution, the annulment of debt by Great Britain was one of the revolutionaries' demands. I feel that we are now confronted by a similar situation and that it calls for political inventiveness.

Cancellation is not a solution in itself, because history records so many hopelessly regressive cases of it. Researchers at the Boston Consulting Group have written a paper entitled "Back to Mesopotamia?" on this issue. They roll out various models to see what might happen in the event of massive debt cancellation. Their conclusion is that great economic turbulence would result, but that failing to take such a course of action would create even more severe problems. In other words, the protection of prevailing economic structures requires debt cancellation. This is a typical case of reactionary calls for debt annulment.

As for capitalism, I have trouble imagining that it can last more than another fifty years, especially given the ecological issue. When the Occupy Wall Street movement was reproached for failing to frame concrete demands (even though it had in fact done so), I suggested—somewhat provocatively—that debts should be forgiven and the workday reduced to four hours. This would be beneficial from the ecological viewpoint and at the same time respond to our hypertrophied work time. (This means that we work a great deal at jobs whose sole purpose is to keep people occupied.) The present mode of production is based more on moral principles than on economic ones. The expansion of debt, of working hours, and of work discipline—all of them seem to be of a piece. If money is indeed a social relationship, founded on the assumption that everyone will assign the same value to the banknote that they have in their possession, shouldn't we think about what kind of assumptions we wish to embrace regarding future productivity and commitment to work?

That's why I say that the abolition of debt implies a conceptual break. My approach is intended to help us imagine other forms of social contract that could be democratically negotiated.

MODERATORS: Reading your work, Thomas Piketty, one gets the impression that for you the eradication of debt is not a "civilized" solution. What do you mean by this?

PIKETTY: The fact is, as I say, that the last creditors are not necessarily the ones who should be made to pay. What do you think, David, of the proposal that a progressive tax be imposed on wealth, which seems to me a more civilized way to arrive at the same result? I must repeat how perplexed I am by the fact that the most enthusiastic supporters of debt abolition, apart from you, are the partisans of "haircuts," to use an expression favored by the International Monetary Fund (IMF) and the Bundesbank. That proposal comes down to the idea that the holders of public debt took risks so now they must pay. So reduce the Greek debt by 50 percent or the Cypriot debt by 60 percent—hardly a progressive measure!

Forgive me, but I am very surprised that you attach so little importance to the question of what tools we should employ, what collective institutions we should create, the better to target those whom we wish to target. Part of our role as intellectuals is to say what collective institutions we want to construct. Taxation is part of this.

GRAEBER: Progressive taxation seems to me to epitomize the Keynesian era and redistributive mechanisms based on expectations of growth rates that no longer seem valid. This sort of redistributive mechanism relies on projections of the increased productivity, linked to rising wages, which historically accompanied the application of redistributive tax policies. But are such policies workable in the context of weak growth? And with what social impact?

PIKETTY: Well, weak growth actually makes those fiscal tools even more desirable. I am thinking not only of traditional income taxes, but also of a progressive tax on wealth and capital. People possess a certain quantity of capital, net of debt. If you impose a progressive tax rate on this, for those who possess very little that rate may be negative, which amounts to forgiving some of their debts. So this is a far cry from Keynesian income-tax policies.

Moreover, a weak growth rate makes both income taxes and wealth taxes even more desirable because it widens the gap between the rate of return on capital and the growth rate. For most of history, the growth rate was almost zero, whereas the return on capital was around 5 percent. So when the growth rate is around 5 percent, as it was in Europe after World War II, the gap between the two rates is minimal. But when the growth rate is 1 percent, or even negative, as in some European countries today, that gap is enormous. This is not a problem from a strictly economic point of view, but it certainly is in social terms, because it brings about great concentrations of wealth. In response to which, progressive wealth and inheritance taxes are of great utility.

GRAEBER: But shouldn't such a progressive tax on capital be international in scope?

PIKETTY: Yes, of course. I am an internationalist, and so are you, so we have no differences on that score.

GRAEBER: All the same, it is an interesting question, because historically whenever an era of expensive credit begins, some kind of overarching means is generally found for protecting debtors and giving creditors free rein—even going so far on occasion as to actively favor debtors. Such mechanisms for constraining creditors' power over debtors have taken many forms, including a monarchy based on divine right in Mesopotamia, the biblical Law of Jubilee, medieval canon law, Buddhism, Confucianism, and so on. In short, societies adopting such principles had institutional or moral structures designed to maintain some form of control over lending practices.

Today we are in a period in which lending is decisive, but we do things the other way around. We already have the overarching institutions, which are almost religious in character inasmuch as neoliberalism may be seen as a kind of faith. But instead of protecting debtors from creditors, these institutions do just the opposite.

For thirty years a combination of the IMF, the World Trade Organization (WTO), the financial institutions that came out of Bretton Woods, the investment banks, the multinationals, and the international NGOs has constituted an international bureaucracy of global scope. And unlike the United Nations, this bureaucracy has the means to enforce its decisions. Since this whole structure was explicitly put in place in order to defend the interests of financiers and creditors, how might it be politically possible to transform it in such a way as to have it do the exact opposite of what it was designed to do?

PIKETTY: All I can say is that a lot of people would need to be convinced! But it is important to know exactly where we want to get to. What bothers me here is the fact that for the large institutions you are talking about, it is far more natural than you think to forgive debt. Why do you think they like the word *haircut* so much? Your prescription is trapped in the moral universe of the market. The culprit is the party that owns the debt. The danger I see is that the financial institutions move in exactly the direction you describe.

Typically enough, in the case of the Cypriot crisis, after entertaining the idea of a (slightly) progressive tax on capital assets, the IMF and the European Central Bank eventually opted for "haircuts," along with a flat-level tax.

In the France of 1945–46, the public debt was enormous. Two means were used to deal with the problem. The first was high inflation, which is the main way, historically, of getting rid of debt. But this reduced the worth of those who had very little: poor old people, for example, who lost everything. As a result, in 1956, a national consensus supported the introduction of an old-age pension, a form of guaranteed minimum income for retirees so affected.

The rich, meanwhile, had been untouched by the inflation. Inflation did not reduce their wealth because their investments were in real capital, which sheltered them. What did lose them money was the second measure, adopted in 1945—namely, an uncustomary progressive tax imposed on wealth and capital. Today, seventy years later, the IMF would have us believe that it is technically impossible to establish a graduated tax on capital. I really am afraid that the institutions you mention have powerful ideological reasons for favoring haircuts.

MODERATORS: What about the risk of tax evasion? Isn't it easier for the owners of capital to avoid taxes than to avoid the impact of debt cancellation?

PIKETTY: No, it is very easy to avoid the effects of debt forgiveness, just as it is easy to protect oneself against inflation. The big portfolios do not hold letters of credit—they are composed of real capital. Is it possible to fight tax evasion? Yes, if you want to, you can. When modern governments really want their decisions to be respected, they succeed in getting them respected.

When Western governments want to send a million soldiers to Kuwait to prevent Kuwaiti oil from being seized by Iraq, they do it. Let's be serious: If they are not afraid of an Iraq, they have no reason to fear the Bahamas or New Jersey. Levying progressive taxes on wealth and capital poses no technical problems. It is a matter of political will.

PART III   BEYOND POWER

Culture as Creative Refusal

What I would like to do in this essay is to talk about cultural comparison as an active force in history. That is, I want to address the degree to which cultures are not just conceptions of what the world is like, not just ways of being and acting in the world, but active political projects which often operate by the explicit rejection of other ones.

The idea of cultural comparison is familiar enough. This is, after all, what anthropologists largely do. Most of us acknowledge that even the most careful, descriptive ethnography is ultimately the product of an endless stream of explicit, or not-so-explicit, back-and-forth comparisons between the observer's more familiar social surroundings and those observed.

As Marilyn Strathern has pointed out, this is equally true of anthropological theory. It is not just that we hone our own commonsense understandings of kinship, exchange, or politics with those that prevail in some particular village or urban neighborhood in Melanesia, Polynesia, or Africa—we also create the imaginary spaces of "Melanesia,"

Originally published in *Cambridge Anthropology*, vol. 31, no. 2, Autumn 2013.

"Polynesia," or "Africa" themselves by showing how what seem to be commonplace understandings in each area could be seen as inversions or negations of commonplace understandings in the other.[1] African kinship systems center on descent; Melanesian on alliance. Zande magic centers on objects; Trobriand magic on verbal performance. It is from these comparisons that we develop our theories of what kinship or magic could be said to be.

Such comparisons, however, are rarely, if ever, carried out directly: *kinship*, like *magic*, is neither a Melanesian nor an African term. We have to use our own conceptual language as a medium for conversations between them. This seems to be an unfortunate necessity considering the way global intellectual life is currently set up. One would really prefer, Strathern notes, to allow Melanesians, Polynesians, and Africans to carry out the conversation directly; but for the time being, the anthropologist is forced instead to play a very difficult three-sided game.

Obviously, on a local level, such conversations do happen all the time. No culture exists in isolation; self-definition is always necessarily a process of comparison. Inevitably, most of this sort of everyday comparison has tended to happen on the local level; the units have tended to be much smaller than "Polynesia" or "Africa." But I think there is reason to believe that it is rarely limited to that, and that large-scale projects of mutual self-definition have played a far more important role in human history than either anthropologists or historians have usually imagined. That is, many of the cultural forms we still, at least tacitly, treat as primordial could equally well be seen, in their origins and to a large degree in their maintenance, as self-conscious political projects.

The essay that follows is not a fully developed argument. It lays out a potential project of investigation more than proposing any full-fledged analysis. The first section, accordingly, brings together several streams of analysis that I believe could allow us to look at global historical processes in a new light, focusing in particular on the case of what have been called "heroic societies." The second section attempts to apply some of these insights, in a very preliminary manner, to the problem of Malagasy origins.

PART I: WORLD HISTORY

To make my case here I will draw, first, on an unlikely set of sources: Marcel Mauss's notion of civilizations; a peculiar essay written by the American anarchist thinker Peter Lamborn Wilson (perhaps better known by his sometime pseudonym, Hakim Bey); and finally, the work of the British archaeologist David Wengrow.

Most of us have forgotten Mauss's conception of civilization, partly because it is based on his rather extreme position in now-antiquated debates about diffusionism.[2] In the late nineteenth and early twentieth centuries, of course, one of the main endeavors of ethnology was to trace the supposed migration patterns of certain ideas, technologies, or cultural forms. Mauss felt the entire enterprise was misconceived, but not for the same reasons we have come to dismiss it today, but because it assumed a series of bounded, "primitive" societies in relative isolation. Such "primitive societies" do not exist, he argued, or do not exist except in Australia. Human societies are in constant contact. Mauss was, for example, convinced that the entire Pacific could be considered a single zone of cultural exchange, and on first viewing the famous Kwakiutl canoe in the American Museum of Natural History, he is said to have remarked that this is precisely what ancient Chinese canoes must have looked like. The real question is therefore why certain traits are *not* diffused.

Mauss noted dramatic examples of nondiffusion of even extremely practical technologies by neighboring peoples. Algonkians in Alaska refuse to adopt Inuit kayaks, despite their being self-evidently more suited to the environment than their own boats; Inuit, similarly, refuse to adopt Algonkian snowshoes. Since almost any existing style, form, or technique has always been available to almost anyone, he concluded, cultures—or civilizations—are based on conscious refusal.

Mauss is notorious for his rather scattershot style of exposition, but Peter Lamborn Wilson's work is much more so—so much so that he has never been taken seriously in the academy at all.[3] Still, the essay of his that I am interested in does have a certain anthropological pedigree, having emerged from an "anarchism and shamanism" seminar conducted by the author with Michael Taussig in the mid-1990s. Called "The Shamanic Trace," it skates through half a dozen different themes, but the heart of it has to do with a series of peculiar earth sculptures called "effigy mounds," built between roughly 750 and 1600 CE in a region centering on southern Wisconsin, just to the north of the northernmost enclave of the great Mississippian civilization. Building them required enormous amounts of labor, but they were not the focus of permanent settlement. In fact, they appear to have been created by a scattered population with no signs of social hierarchy or even systematic farming, much unlike the caste-stratified "mound builders" to their south, but evidently in reaction to them. The peculiar thing about these effigy mounds is that they seemed to be self-conscious celebrations of natural forms. In conjunction with the rejection of hierarchy, war, and farming, they might even be seen as a kind of utopian, self-conscious primitivism, an enchanted landscape fashioned into a self-conscious work of art. And all this was a reaction to the urban values of the Hopewell civilization to the south:

> The Effigy Mound culture was preceded, surrounded, invaded, and superseded by "advanced" societies which practiced agriculture, metallurgy, warfare and social hierarchy, and yet the Effigy Mound culture rejected all of these. It apparently "reverted" to hunting/gathering; its archaeological remains offer no evidence of social violence or class structure; it largely refused the use of metal; and it apparently did all these things consciously and by choice. It deliberately refused the "death cult," human sacrifice, cannibalism, warfare, kingship, aristocracy, and "high culture" of the Adena, Hopewell, and Temple Mound traditions which surrounded it in time and space. It chose an economy/technology which (according to the prejudices of social evolution and "progress") represents a step backward in human development. It took this step, apparently, because it considered this the right thing to do.[4]

Is it possible, Wilson asks, that the much-vaunted ecological conscious-ness of so many Northeast Woodlands societies might not be, as almost everyone assumes, simply a cultural given, but bear traces of a similar conscious rejection of urbanization?

In fact, one could take this much further. The first European set-tlers in North America encountered societies that were often both far more egalitarian and, at the same time, far more individualistic than anything they would have imagined possible. Accounts of these socie-ties had enormous impact on reshaping horizons of political possibility for many in Europe and ultimately around the world. Yet to this day, we tend to assume that such attitudes were somehow primordial or, at best, the product of some deep but ultimately arbitrary cultural matrix, but certainly not a self-conscious political project on the part of actors just as mature and sophisticated as the Europeans themselves. In all of this, the existence of a populous and apparently very hierarchical urban civilization that mysteriously vanished some generations immediately before somehow never seems to be considered relevant. We don't know why the cities collapsed. Probably we never will. But it is hard to imagine that popular resistance, internal or external, played no role at all. While it would no doubt be overstating things to argue that what the settlers encountered was the self-conscious revolutionary ideology originally developed by those who fled or overthrew that civilization, framing it that way is still less deceptive than imagining it took shape without ref-erence to any larger political context whatsoever.

The idea that at least some egalitarian societies were shaping their ideals and institutions in conscious reaction to hierarchical ones is not new. In recent years, we have even seen a small emerging literature on the "anarchist" societies of Southeast Asia, such societies being seen as deliberate rejections of the governing principles of nearby states, or even as societies that had defined themselves against those states in much the same way as Wilson has argued for the North American societies above; that is, through a process of schizmogenesis.[5]

This work has revolutionized the whole conversation about the na-ture of egalitarian societies, at least within the academy. But I think it runs the danger of leaving us with the unfortunate impression that these reactions and refusals cut only one way. In fact, I think reality is far more complex. Acts of creative refusal can lead to new ideals of equality, new forms of hierarchy, or often, a complicated mix of both. Whatever happened in the American Northeast led to a great deal of power and autonomy for women, but similar processes in Amazonia appear to have had the opposite effect. The case of ancient Western Asia seems if anything even more dramatic. As I argued in *Debt*, there is good reason to believe that biblical patriarchy itself, and many of the more defiant populist themes of patriarchal religions, are in large part the product of a dynamic of resistance against Mesopotamian temple elites, and the product of the complex intersection of debt peonage, temple prostitution, and strategies of exodus to the seminomadic fringes that had the result, over the course of two millennia, of driving women almost completely from political life.[6] By the early Iron Age, institutions had been created such as veiling, the sequestration of women, and obsessions with premarital virginity, that had never existed before.

One of the most fascinating, and ambivalent, of these movements of refusal overlapped with the rise of patriarchy both in time and roughly in space: the rise of what I will, after Hector Munro Chadwick, call "heroic societies."[7] Here let me turn to my third source of inspiration, the work of David Wengrow—in my view the most creative archaeological thinker alive today—on the Bronze Age potlatch.[8] Wengrow is addressing a long-standing puzzle: the existence, scattered across a band of territory that runs from roughly the Danube to the Ganges, of treasure troves full of large amounts of extremely valuable metalware that appear to have been self-consciously abandoned or even systematically destroyed. The remarkable thing is that such troves never occur within the great urban civilizations themselves, but always in the surrounding hill country, or similar marginal zones that were closely connected to the commercial-bureaucratic centers by trade but were in no sense incorporated. Hence the comparison with potlatches. Most of the great, extravagant feasting cycles of the seventeenth-century Huron or Great Lakes region, or the nineteenth-century Northwest Coast, or twentieth-century Melanesia, occurred in exactly this sort of context: societies being drawn into the trading orbit of other commercial-bureaucratic civilizations, and thus accumulating vast quantities of new material goods, while at the same time rejecting the ultimate values of the societies with which they were in contact. The difference is that the societies we know about historically, outgunned and outnumbered, were quickly overwhelmed. The Bronze Age barbarians, in contrast, often won. In fact, they left an enduring legacy, for it was exactly these potlatch zones that eventually produced the great epic traditions and ultimately the great philosophical traditions and world religions: Homer, the Rig Veda, Avesta, and even, in a more attenuated sense, the Bible. Here is where Chadwick comes in, since he, too, saw the great epics as having been written by people in contact with, and often employed as mercenaries by, the urban civilizations of their day, but who ultimately rejected the values of these civilizations.

For a long time, the notion of "heroic societies" fell into a certain disfavor: there was a widespread assumption that such societies did not really exist but were, like the society represented in Homer's *Iliad*, retroactively reconstructed in epic literature—even, as Georges Dumézil famously argued, largely a matter of rewriting onetime cosmic myths into the form of national histories.[9] But as archaeologists like Paul Treherne have more recently demonstrated, there is a very real pattern of heroic burials, indicating a newfound cultural emphasis on feasting, drinking, the beauty and fame of the individual male warrior—on what he calls the "lifestyle of an emergent warrior elite."[10] This appears across the area Wengrow identified in a strikingly similar form over the course of the Bronze Age. Mycenaean society might not have much resembled Homer's representation of it, but many of those in the hinterlands surrounding it certainly did. What's more, as Marshall Sahlins notes, clear ethnographic parallels exist as well.[11]

What are the common features of such heroic societies? Drawing on the epic literature, one finds a fairly consistent list (and one that applies just as well, in most of its features, to the potlatch societies of the Northwest coast):

- All are decentralized aristocracies, without any centralized authority or principle of sovereignty (or perhaps some largely symbolic, formal one). Instead of a single center, we find numerous heroic figures competing fiercely with one another for retainers and slaves, and no centralized authority; politics is composed of a history of personal debts of loyalty or vengeance between heroic individuals. There's also a huge amount of room to move up or down; the aristocracy usually pretends to be eternal but generally, in practice, it is possible to rise or fall far from one's initial station.
- All focus on gamelike contests as the primary business of ritual, indeed political, life. Often massive amounts of loot or wealth are squandered, sacrificed, or given away; gift-giving competitions are commonplace; animal sacrifice is a central religious ritual; there is a resistance to accumulation for its own sake.
- All are profoundly theatrical, and both boasting and lying are highly developed and appreciated arts.
- All explicitly resist certain features of nearby urban civilizations: above all, writing (for which they tend to substitute poets or priests who engage in rote memorization or elaborate techniques of oral composition) and commerce; hence money, either in physical or credit forms, tends to be eschewed and the focus instead is on unique material treasures.

The question we cannot answer is whether *all* these features are reactions to the life of the cities, or whether this is more a matter of preexisting features that began to take on much more elaborated form when societies organized around them encountered urban commercial-bureaucratic civilizations. After all, there are only so many ways a political system *can* be organized. Nonetheless it is clear that schizmogenetic processes of some kind were going on, and probably on both sides, as urbanites learned simultaneously to admire and revile the "barbarians" surrounding them.

However this may be, the heroic complex, if one might call it that, had an enduring impact. The city-states and empires of the classical Mediterranean, to take one vivid example, could well be seen as a kind of fusion of heroic principles into a standard of urban life drawn from the far older civilizations to its east—hardly surprising, perhaps, in a place where all literary education began with Homer. The most obvious aspect is the religious emphasis on sacrifice. On a deeper level, we find what Alvin Gouldner called "the Greek contest system," the tendency to turn absolutely everything, from art to politics to athletic achievement to tragic drama, into a game where there must be winners and losers.[12] The same spirit appears in a different way in the "games" and spirit of aristocratic competition in Rome. In fact, I would hazard to suggest that our own political culture, with its politicians and elections, traces back to heroic sensibilities. We tend to forget that for most of European history, election was considered the aristocratic mode of selecting officials, not the democratic one (the democratic mode was sortition).[13] What is unusual about our own political systems is rather the fusion of the heroic mode with the principle of sovereignty—a principle with its own peculiar history, which originally stood entirely apart from governance, and which has quite different implications—but one that cannot be more than alluded to here.

PART II: MADAGASCAR

The idea of heroic politics originating in acts of cultural refusal struck me as particularly intriguing considering that my own fieldwork in Madagascar had led me to conclude that politics there was largely an apparently calculated rejection of heroic principles. Malagasy origins are still shrouded in mystery and it is difficult to know precisely how this came about, how much this sort of rejection really does pervade Malagasy culture as a whole, or how much these political sensibilities are peculiar to contemporary rural Imerina.

The story of Malagasy origins itself is a beautiful illustration of the lingering evolutionist bias that continues to make it difficult for us to see early Indian Ocean voyagers (for example) as mature political actors.

The conventional story for most of this century has run roughly as follows: a group of swidden agriculturalists from the Barito valley in Borneo began engaging in long, Polynesian-style expeditions of migration
in outrigger canoes, till eventually, around 50 CE, they found a huge
uninhabited island[14]; they then began a process of "adaptive radiation"
whereby they spread out into different micro-environments, becoming
pastoralists, fishermen, irrigated rice cultivators, and gradually creating
chiefdoms and states and coming into contact with world religions like
Islam.[15] In the process, African elements were incorporated into an essentially Indonesian culture; the Africans are often assumed, tacitly or
explicitly, to have been brought in as slaves.

This picture was always highly implausible, but more recent archaeological and linguistic research has shown that, rather than being
innocent of states and world religions, the early settlers of Madagascar
appear to have known all about both, and to have actively decided they
wanted nothing to do with them. The main settlement did begin around
600 CE. Recent biological evidence suggests the ancestors of the current
Malagasy population were likely to have been a group of roughly thirty
Southeast Asian women who arrived on the island about this time.[16] But
linguistics also gives us reason to believe that even this was not a completely uniform population: the Austronesian colonists were not simply
from the Barito valley, but a collection of people largely from southeast
Borneo mixed with others from smaller islands like Sulawesi. What is
more, navigational and other technical terms in the language they spoke
were derived from Malay.[17] The linguist who has done the most systematic work on the topic, Alexander Adelaar, concludes:

> Southeast Barito speakers constituted only a part of the various
> groups of immigrants to Madagascar. They may have constituted
> the majority of these, but may also have been only a small first
> nuclear group, whose language was adopted by later immigrants
> who gradually arrived. Such a course of events would account for
> the fact that, although Malagasy is a Southeast Barito language,
> there is little anthropological or historical evidence that points

to a specifically Bornean origin of the Malagasy. I also propose that it was not speakers of Southeast Barito languages themselves who organized passages to East Africa and established colonies in Madagascar and possibly other places. The autochthonous peoples of Borneo are no seafarers, and there is little evidence that they had a seafaring tradition twelve centuries ago (a large part of the maritime vocabulary in Malagasy is borrowed from Malay). The people who were actively involved in sailing to East Africa must have been Malays.[18]

In fact, we know that merchants from Malay city-states were trading in gold and ivory in the Zambezi Valley opposite Madagascar at this time; it is easy to see how establishing a permanent trading post a safe distance away, on a large uninhabited island, might have seemed advantageous. But it leads one to ask: If Malay merchants brought a group of people, including at least thirty women, drawn from a variety of largely non-nautical people on other Indonesian islands, to such a place—what sort of people might those have been? Later history provides us with a pretty clear idea.[19] Borneo and islands such as Sulawesi were precisely the places from which later Malay city-states imported their slaves. By all accounts, such slaves made up a very large proportion of the populations of such cities. And what would be the likely result had a group of such merchants established a trading post populated largely by slaves on a giant uninhabited island? If any substantial number escaped to the interior, it would have been impossible to recover them.

Archaeology is beginning to give us at least a rough picture of Madagascar in the first centuries of its human habitation. The early picture is one of striking heterogeneity. There does not seem to be any sense in which we can talk about a "Malagasy" people. For at least the first five centuries, we find instead evidence for a collection of populations of very diverse origins, just about all of them, however, engaged in some form of trade with the wider world (even the earliest sites usually contain pottery from the Persian Gulf and/or China), and most of them not straying too far from the coast. Linguistic scholarship suggests that aside from an Austronesian population that probably arrived in several waves, and brought with it rice, yams, coconuts, and other Southeast Asian crops, there were also populations of East African origin in the north and west of Madagascar from quite early on, who brought with them zebu cattle, sorghum, and other African crops.[20] By the time we have evidence for actual port towns, they were connected culturally not with Indonesia but with the emerging Swahili civilization of the Comoros and East African coast, replete with mosques and mansions made of stone.

The historical origins of the Swahili remain slightly murky, but what happened seems in many ways analogous to the processes that led to the earlier emergence of the Malay city-states themselves. We have the creation of a cosmopolitan, mercantile elite of African origin, speaking a single African language with a great deal of imported vocabulary (in the Malay case, from Sanskrit, and in the Swahili case, from Arabic), and with these people identifying themselves with the cosmopolitan world of the Indian Ocean ecumene, and inhabiting a chain of city-states (some petty monarchies, some mercantile republics) ranging along the coast from what is now Kenya to Mozambique.[21]

As the early trading posts attest, these emerging networks did extend to Madagascar from very early times. Between c. 1000 and 1350 CE, for instance, a time when most of the island was still very sparsely populated, northern Madagascar was dominated by a small, apparently Swahili-speaking city-state that has come to be known by its site's later Malagasy name of Mahilaka. Archaeological reports describe it as a small city, similar to others in the Comoro Islands to the north, with evidence of sharp class divisions: the city centered on a series of magnificent stone houses and a central mosque, surrounded by smaller and flimsier structures, and attendant workshops, presumably inhabited by ordinary townsfolk and the poor.[22] According to Dewar, "Mahilaka probably served as a trading centre where island products such as tortoise shell, chlorite schist, gold, crystal, quartz and possibly wood, tree gum, and iron were exchanged for ceramics, glass vessels, trade beads and possibly cloth."[23]

According to the standard accounts, Mahilaka eventually declined owing to a fall in the demand for chlorite schist—a locally quarried green stone, used to make bowls that were for a while popular tableware in the region. However, the Malagasy archaeologist Chantal Radimilahy has managed to turn up what seems to be the one known literary reference to Mahilaka, from the eleventh-century Arab traveler al-Idrisi, which suggests that here, too, the story was probably a bit more complicated. It refers to the island of "Andjebeh":

> whose principal town is called El-Anfoudja in the language of Zanzibar, and whose inhabitants, although mixed, are actually mostly Muslims. The distance from it to Banas on the Zanj coast is a day and a half. The island is 400 miles round; bananas are the chief food . . .
>
> The island is traversed by a mountain called Wabra. The vagabonds who are expelled from the town flee there, and form a brave and numerous company which frequently infests the region surrounding the town, and who live at the top of the mountain in a state of defence against the ruler of the island. They are courageous, and feared for their arms and their number.[24]

Of course, one cannot be absolutely certain the passage really does refer to Mahilaka—or even to Madagascar. But it may well; and even if it doesn't, it suggests the kind of social process one is likely to have encountered in the hinterlands of such trade emporia at the time: extreme hierarchy at the center, with a servile or socially marginalized population escaping their merchant overlords and forming defiant communities in the interior. Nor is the violence likely to have been simply one-way. While gold, ivory, and various exotic products were still being traded up and down the coast, the focus of the East African trading economy increasingly shifted to the movement of slaves, captured largely from those same rebel communities.

One of the fascinating questions is how, amid all this diversity, the relatively uniform Malagasy culture of the present day emerged. It did so unevenly—there were populations speaking African languages on the west coast, for instance, as late as the eighteenth century—but at some point, what archaeologists have called a moment of "synthesis" occurred around one language, certain stylistic elements, and presumably, certain social and cosmological principles that came to dominate the island. This Malagasy cultural matrix has been remarkably effective in absorbing and incorporating almost any other population that later came to settle on the island.

Opinions vary about when this happened—perhaps it was around the period of the height of Mahilaka, perhaps that of its decline. The intriguing question for me is the degree to which it was itself part of a process of cultural refusal and schizmogenesis: that is, what came to be considered Malagasy culture itself coalesced in opposition to Mahilaka, which was, at the time, the principal outpost of the larger Indian Ocean world-system, with all the forms of religious, economic, and political power it entailed. Or it arose in opposition to that larger system itself. To give just one example: the existence of great stone mansions in Mahilaka, and in other, later medieval and early modern port cities, is quite striking in the light of the general, later Malagasy *fady*, or taboo, against building stone houses for the living, rather than for the dead.

To say that nowadays, Malagasy are in the habit of defining their culture against the ways of powerful, cosmopolitan outsiders is a commonplace and entirely unremarkable statement. When Maurice Bloch was doing his fieldwork in central Madagascar in the 1960s, he observed a popular tendency to classify everything, from customs and technologies to chickens and vegetables, into two varieties: one considered Malagasy (*gasy*), the other *vazaha*—a term that can, according to context, mean "foreign," "white," or "French."[25] This tendency to dichotomize has been observed since colonial times. This is usually assumed to have been a result of colonization. Frantz Fanon famously argued that before the arrival of white colonialists, one could not speak of Malagasy as a self-conscious identity, rather than simply as a way of being, at all.[26] The very category is born of relations of violent subordination and degradation. All I am suggesting is that this relationship might go back much further than we think. Even after the decline of Mahilaka, Islamic port towns continued to exist, often on islands just offshore from the Malagasy coast, and to carry out trade with the interior. The towns were regularly visited by clerics, merchants, and adventurers from as far as India, Egypt, and Arabia; they were very much a part of the Indian Ocean trading world that stopped abruptly in Madagascar proper. Most of their inhabitants showed nothing but disdain for the island's inhabitants, whom they regularly exported as slaves. Randy Pouwels provides us some telling examples from sixteenth-century Portuguese sources:

> In the words of one [Portuguese] friar around 1630: "ships come to this Island of Pate which go to the Island of Madagascar with sharifs, who are their qadis [judges], who go to spread their faith and transport many Madagascarenes, the lowliest [of] Gentiles, to Mecca and to make them into Moors."[27]

Or even:

> As maintained by Faria y Sousa and other Portuguese sources, the "Moors" of the coast and Mecca came annually to the towns of Manzalage and Lulungani . . . in northwest Madagascar, to trade in sandalwood, sweet woods, ebony and tortoise shell, and to buy boys "whom they send to Arabia to serve their lust," as well as to convert to Islam.[28]

The explicitly racial terms Fanon was addressing clearly came later: terms like *black* and *white* would have meant nothing for descendants of Indonesian and African slaves making common cause against medieval Arab and Swahili traders. Still, it is hard to imagine that if something like a common Malagasy identity did emerge, it could have been in anything but self-conscious opposition to all that was considered *silamo* (Muslim), in much the same way as everything *gasy* is now opposed to everything *vazaha*.

What I am suggesting, then, is that what we now think of as Malagasy culture has its origins in a rebel ideology of escaped slaves, and that the moment of "synthesis" in which it came together can best be thought of as a self-conscious movement of collective refusal directed against representatives of a larger world-system.

If this is the case, then, if nothing else, a lot of otherwise peculiar features of the actual content of the pan-Malagasy culture that emerged around that time would make a great deal of sense. Consider myths. As a student of Marshall Sahlins, I found it rather frustrating to try to carry out a "cosmological analysis" of Malagasy culture because most of the stories that looked like cosmological myths were, effectively, jokes. The traditional tagline used at the end of myths is "it is not I who lie, these lies come from ancient times." There is usually a high god, a Jovian figure, but other gods can be improvised as the plot requires; there is no pantheon; even in ritual, the approach to divine powers seems oddly improvisational: new ones can be discovered, created, cast out, or destroyed.

The closest there is to a core Malagasy cycle is what has been called the "Zatovo cycle," which appears in endless variations in every part of the island.[29] This is the story of a young man who declares that he was "not created by God," who then challenges God to some kind of contest to force him to acknowledge this, and, with the aid of some powerful magic, is ultimately successful. (He may also make off with a daughter of God, or rice, fire, or other essential elements of human civilization.) Let me give an example of one such story, collected around the turn of the last century in the Tanala region in the southeast:

> A man named Andrianonibe, they say, married a young woman and before long she became pregnant. Now, the child could already speak in his mother's womb; at the moment of his birth, he pierced his mother's navel, and it was through there that he came out into the world. He then spoke to the people assembled in the house: "I have not been made by God, because at the moment my mother gave birth to me, I came out of her navel; thus I will bear the name Andriamamakimpoetra, Andriana-who-breaks-the-navel."

Then he convoked the people, bid them follow him, and set out to climb a tall mountain. At the summit, he gathered together a pile of firewood; he also had an ox brought to sacrifice. Then he set the wood on fire and ordered his assistants to roast the quarters of the ox on them: an intense column of black smoke rose to heaven; after a few moments they had blinded the children of God, so he sent his messenger, named Yellow Eagle, to see what had happened. Once he was in the presence of Andriamamakimpoetra the messenger entreated him, on God's part, to put out the fire as soon as possible, but the man refused, crying out angrily, "Go find your master and tell him that I will not obey his orders, because it was not he who made me. So I will not put out the fire, because it was me who came out of the navel of my mother, and I am called Andriamamakimpoetra. Have you, God, ever anywhere seen another man bearing that name?"

"If that's how it is," said Yellow Eagle, "I shall carry your words to God." Then it left Andriamamakimpoetra and flew back to heaven, and told God everything that Andriana had said. God became very angry, and sent his messenger back to earth once more. This time Yellow Eagle carried a large ox bone; when he came before the great fire, still burning, he spoke as follows: "O Andriamamakimpoetra, you claim to have come out of the womb by breaking through your mother's navel. If it is true that you have not been created by God, then you must turn this bone into a living beast."

"As you like," declared the other. He took the bone, put it to cooking in a large rice pot, with which he had mixed some ody [magical charms]. As soon as the rice began to boil, the bone transformed into a little calf that lowed, and by the time the rice was cooked, it had become a great bull that set about roaring toward the cattle pen. Yellow Eagle, after having observed what happened, returned to his master. God, growing angrier and angrier, sent him back with a chicken bone and a banana leaf, and demanded Andriana turn it into a rooster and a banana tree full of ripe fruit.

Then Andriana made a new pot of rice, in which he had placed some ody. When the rice was at the point of boiling over, the bone had become a young chick, and the leaf, a young banana plant shoot. By the time it was done the chick had become a great rooster, and the shoot, a whole range of banana trees. The messenger once again returned to report what had happened.[30]

In most stories the hero is faced with a series of tests, which he passes with the aid of an ody, which is often personified, and plays the classic fairy-tale helper role. Here the power and knowledge seem entirely in the protagonist himself, and the charms are simply extensions. They are also about as powerful as it is possible to be.

God, stupefied and confounded, told Yellow Eagle to present Andriamamakimpoetra with a golden cane, and demand he determine which is the top, and which is the bottom. Now, the cane was of exactly the same size, top and bottom. When Andriamamakimpoetra had it within his hands, he threw it up in the air and allowed it to fall, and thus correctly identified the two ends.

This time God didn't know what to do, so, very confused, he left heaven to come meet Andriamamakimpoetra himself. The moment he arrived he made everything around Andriamamakimpoetra's village turn pitch black, so that the villagers, even in the middle of the day, could not see a thing. Then he brought forth great flashes of lightning and terrible crashes of thunder, so that everyone was left astounded. Only Andriana had no fear of anything, but delighted in the noise. He happily strode out of his house despite all the menacing lightning bolts, and carried in his hand an ody that he turned toward each of the cardinal points, so that the lightning turned away from him harmlessly. Finally, he called out, "O God, come down to earth if you like, but stop frightening the inhabitants of this country."

Then God came down before Andriamamakimpoetra's house and told him, "Let us go forth together, if you like, to a country far from your home; we shall have a contest of wits, since you deny ever having been created by me."

"Agreed!" replied Andriana. "Let's go, then!" And the two set forth upon their route.

After a little while, God advanced ahead, and once out of sight, he transformed himself into a great flowing spring, beside which grew a large number of fruit trees bearing many fine fruits. Everyone who passed stopped to drink the water from the spring, and to taste some of the delicious fruits, hanging so thickly on the branches of the trees. Like the others, Andriamamakimpoetra approached the place and stopped to rest, but then he recognized it was really God, and said, "Cut it out, God, I know what you're up to! Come on! Let's get on with our journey, because I'm never going to drink from you."

Then, in his turn, Andriana went off ahead, and as soon as he was out of sight he turned into a great wild orange tree full of fruits. God, when he saw the tree, started to gather the fruit, but then he saw that it was really Andriamamakimpoetra, who had changed into that form, and he cried out, "Come on! Let's get back on the road! Don't even dream that you can disguise yourself from me, because I can see perfectly well that the orange tree is really you."

Next, God went in advance, and at a certain distance he became a great plain, with enough rice growing from it that a great army of men could cultivate it for the rest of their lives. On this plain there were also many cattle and chickens. And it is from this time that human beings have known of rice and orange trees, and have raised cattle and chickens as domestic animals. But Andriamamakimpoetra recognized God; and in his turn, he went out in advance, and turned himself into a large village, with numerous houses occupied by rich inhabitants; and in this village, there lived three beautiful women. And God started searching for Andriana, but couldn't find him. Now, after a month's time, he came up to the beautiful village, and stopped, and married one of the three women. And after a certain time she became pregnant. She developed the desire to eat rat meat, so she begged her husband to go and find her some. He turned himself into a cat and went beneath the floorboards to find some, and it didn't take more than a few minutes before he'd caught four rats to bring back to his wife. She burned the hair off the four rats over the hearth, and when they'd been cleaned, chopped the meat into small pieces and cooked them. But she didn't eat any of them herself, she gave them all to God to eat. Some months later, she gave birth to a child. God was extremely happy, but at the very moment of his birth, the newborn began to speak: "I am called Fanihy [a bird], because I am not the son of God. No, it is I, Andriamamakimpoetra, for whom God has been so long searching, without being able to find."

Then the infant rose and began to walk, and mocked God, saying, "I made you eat rats, and you ate them! Is this not sufficient proof that I was not created by you?"

And so God, completely confounded, returned sadly home. But to this day he continues to think about Andriana, and whenever he becomes angry, he thunders and makes it rain, and this is a sign of his anger toward Andriamamakimpoetra. Whereas, for him, they say, he truly was never made by God. He created himself.[31]

Much could be said about this story. The building of a fire that chokes the inhabitants of heaven, which recurs in many similar stories, is always a kind of inversion of a sacrifice, and this is made explicit in this case. In Malagasy sacrifices, as in ancient Greek ones, the scent of roasting flesh is said to ascend to heaven to please the gods. Here, instead, it torments them. The entire story might appear as a playfully perverse variation on a familiar Austronesian cosmological theme regularly invoked in such sacrificial rituals as well: that fertility, creativity, the giving of life, is something we can ultimately acquire only from the gods, and therefore, that the gods have to be brought into the world, but then somehow removed again so humans can enjoy the fruits of their creations. The myth seems to deny this by allowing the hero to bring dead bones to life at the beginning of the story. He can create life himself; he created his own existence. But in fact we know this is not quite true, for he was conceived and given birth to like anyone else, even if—as he proudly points out—very unconventionally. And in the end, the hero does come to be created by God, because he is born again with God as his father; in a way he does accept that God created him, but only (from God's perspective) in the most outrageous and humiliating conceivable way.

This version is, admittedly, unusually triumphalist. In most, the stories do at least note that God has his revenge in the end: we are mortal, he is not. Still, these are essentially Prometheus stories where Prometheus defies the gods and wins. They also appear to be uniquely Malagasy. I have been unable to find, either in Africa or Southeast Asia, any other example of a heroic figure that claims not to be created by God, let alone that ends up successfully challenging God in order to prove it. But it makes sense that where we do find it, it would be in a population of runaways from pious city-states (Malay or Swahili) who suddenly find themselves on a vast uninhabited island where new lives and communities can, indeed, be created out of nothing.

Now, the cosmologies of heroic societies, from the Greeks to the Maori, do tend to give large place to transgressive figures ready to defy even the gods but, generally speaking, they ultimately come to a very bad end. It is difficult to build a structure of authority—even one as fluid as a heroic aristocracy—on this kind of foundation. This is not to say that Madagascar did not see its share of aristocracies and kingdoms. But it is telling that whenever we do see the rise of kingdoms in Madagascar, the story begins to transform: as in the Ikongo kingdom of the east coast, where Zatovo marries the daughter of God and founds a line of kings, or even more strikingly, within the Merina kingdom of the central highlands, where "Zatovo who was not created by God" is replaced by a character named "Ibonia who was not created by men," thus marked by an identical miraculous birth, in what is considered the only absolutely bona fide Malagasy heroic epic.[32]

It is possible, in other words, to build an ideology of rule on the basis of what seems like a fundamentally anti-authoritarian cultural grid. But the resulting arrangements are likely to remain unstable: and the history of Madagascar is indeed full of uprisings and the overthrow of aristocracies and kingdoms, because the basis for rejecting such arrangements is always readily at hand.

During the nineteenth century, for instance, foreign observers universally insisted that whatever the typical Merina farmer might have thought of court officials, no one would think to question the legitimacy of the monarchy, or their absolute personal devotion to the queen. Yet when I was in Imerina, a mere century later, I could not find a single person in the countryside who had not been through the higher education system who had anything good to say about the Merina monarchy. The only ancient kings who were remembered fondly were those said to have voluntarily abandoned their power. This was not a rejection of authority of every kind. The authority of elders and ancestors, for example, was treated as absolutely legitimate. But anything that smacked of individual, let alone heroic, forms of power was at the very least treated with suspicion by most or, more likely, openly mocked and rejected. Even at the time I labeled it an "anti-heroic society,"[33] since I appeared to be in the presence of an ideology that seemed to take every principle of heroic society and explicitly reject it, as summarized below:

- Rather than politics being composed of a history of personal debts of loyalty or vengeance between heroic individuals, all oral histories represented such figures as foolish, egotistical, and, therefore, as having imposed ridiculous, unjustifiable restrictions on their followers or descendants. A typical story would relate how two ancestors quarreled over land, agreed to have a fight between their dogs, both cheated, both caught each other, and thus ended up cursing their descendants never to marry.

"What a bunch of idiots," narrators would remark. Similarly, the quintessential exercise of the legitimate authority of elders—in a sense, the only completely legitimate way of exercising authority over others—was not to create projects or initiatives (these should rise spontaneously through the whole of the group) but to stop headstrong individuals from acting in ways that might produce such results.

- As the previous example suggests, it was felt that public and political life should definitely not consist of a series of gamelike contests. Decisions were made by consensus.
- Similarly, theatricality, boasting, and self-aggrandizing lying were at the very center of moral disapproval; public figures made dramatic displays of self-effacement.
- Curiously, despite the egalitarian emphasis, money and writing were the two features of urban civilization that were embraced and appreciated: everyone was involved in petty commerce in some form or another, and the literacy rate was extraordinarily high.

How did this happen, historically? One might well ask: Were there, in fact, heroic societies that rural Malagasy were even aware of, to define themselves against? Or was this again the product of a certain play of limited possibilities?

Presumably there were no classic heroic societies of the sort familiar from the Bronze Age in Madagascar, but there were certainly heroic elements aplenty in the self-aggrandizing stories of the Merina monarchy— and not just in their Ibonia epics and their defiance of tradition by building their palaces of stone. What really happened is a question that can be unraveled only with much further research, but the broad outlines can be made out. The port enclaves continued to exist, especially in the north of Madagascar, and by the sixteenth century were doing a brisk business supplying weapons to local Malagasy warrior elites, or would-be warrior elites, in exchange for a continual supply of slaves.[34] Most of what are now considered "ethnic groups" in Madagascar correspond to kingdoms created by these elites. But the warrior aristocrats never considered themselves part of those groups: in fact, they almost invariably insisted that they were not really Malagasy at all. So, for example, when the first Portuguese observers appeared in the sixteenth and seventeenth centuries, they reported that the rulers of the Antemoro and Antanosy kingdoms of southeast Madagascar claimed to be Muslims originally from Mangalore and Mecca—although they spoke only Malagasy and were unfamiliar with the Qur'an. Much of what we know of early Malagasy history comes from the heroic stories of their various battles and intrigues, preserved in Malagasy texts written in Arabic script. These dynasties have since disappeared (the Antemoro aristocracy was overthrown in a popular insurrection in the nineteenth century) but the descendants of their subjects still think of themselves as Antemoro and Antanosy. Similarly, the heroic rulers of the Sakalava kingdoms of the west coast in the eighteenth and nineteenth centuries claimed to be descended from the Antemoro, and worked closely with Arab and Swahili merchants. Those they conquered still consider themselves Sakalava, even though their rulers insisted they were neither this nor even Malagasy. Even the Betsimisaraka, who now dominate the east coast and are considered among the most doggedly egalitarian peoples of Madagascar, first came into being as the followers of a warrior elite called the Zana-Malata, made up of the half-Malagasy children of Euro-American pirates who settled the region at the beginning of the eighteenth century, and whose descendants remain a self-identified group in the region, separate from the Betsimisaraka, to this day. In other words, each ethnic group emerges in opposition to its own particular group of heroic semi-outsiders, who in turn mediate, for better or worse, between the Malagasy population itself and the temptations and depredations of the outside world. By such arrangements, the original schizmogenetic gesture of definition over and against the values of port cities such as Mahilaka could become, for each new emergent group, a permanent process of definition against their own specific collection of permanent heroic outsiders.

I have tried to outline in this essay, somewhat schematically, a cas-

cading series of gestures of refusal, reincorporation, and renewed refusal. Heroic societies emerge as a rejection of commercial bureaucratic
ones. Some of the logic of heroic society becomes recovered and reincor-
porated into urban civilizations, leading to a new round of schizmogenesis whereby they are rejected and social orders created around the very
rejection of those heroic elements. It would be interesting indeed to see,
if we were to reexamine world history as a series of such acts of creative
refusal, just how far such an approach could ultimately go.

Hatred Has Become a Political Taboo

By the end of the twentieth and beginning of the twenty-first century, it is the one emotion that is considered intrinsically illegitimate. We have legal categories such as "hate speech," "hate crimes." For a public figure, to profess or even publicly acknowledge feelings of hatred toward anyone—even their bitterest rival—would be to instantly place themselves outside the pale of acceptable political behavior. "Haters" are bad people. In no sense can it ever be legitimate to base a political or social policy on hatred, of any kind. It has come to such a pass that one can barely encourage hatred even against abstractions. Christians used to be encouraged to "love the sinner, hate the sin." Such language would never have been coined today. Even to encourage others to feel hatred for envy, pride, or gluttony might be considered slightly problematic.

This was not always so. There was a time when hatred was assumed to form part of the essential fabric—even, to constitute the essential fabric—of social and political life. Consider the following quotations:

Originally published in *Bad Feelings*, by Art Against Cuts, published by Book Works, 2015.

[The Emperor] Commodus had now attained the summit of vice and infamy. Amidst the acclamations of a flattering court, he was unable to disguise, from himself, that he had deserved the contempt and hatred of every man of sense and virtue in his empire. His ferocious spirit was irritated by the consciousness of that hatred, by the envy of every kind of merit, by the just apprehension of danger, and by the habit of slaughter, which he contracted in his daily amusements.

The honest labours of Papinian served only to inflame the hatred which Caracalla had already conceived against his father's minister . . .

The Persian monarchs adorned their new conquest with magnificent buildings; but these monuments had been erected at the expense of the people, and were abhorred as badges of slavery. The apprehension of a revolt had inspired the most rigorous precautions: oppression had been aggravated by insult, and the consciousness of the public hatred had been productive of every measure that could render it still more implacable . . . The hatred of Maximin towards the Senate was declared and implacable . . . The leaders of the conspiracy . . . rested their hopes on the hatred of mankind against Maximin.

The empire was afflicted by five civil wars; and the remainder of the time was not so much a state of tranquility as a suspension of arms between several hostile monarchs, who, viewing each other with an eye of fear and hatred, strove to increase their respective forces at the expense of their subjects.

The emperor [Constantine] had now imbibed the spirit of controversy, and the angry sarcastic style of his edicts was designed to inspire his subjects with the hatred which he had conceived against the enemies of Christ.

What jumps out about these passages—they are all drawn from Gibbon's *Decline and Fall of the Roman Empire*—is, first of all, just how normal hatred was assumed to be. It was only to be expected that kings and politicians should hate their rivals. Conquered people hated their conquerors, unjust rulers were detested, emperors hated the senate, senators loathed the common people, and imperial advisors and members of the emperor's family were detested by the urban mob, which would periodically try to burn their palaces. Even more remarkably to the contemporary ear, there is no sense, in the works of ancient historians or ancient moralists, that such hatreds were in principle illegitimate. They might be. But many were entirely justified. Indeed, hatred for a cruel and unjust ruler could even be considered a civic virtue. In Medieval times feelings of ill will between prominent families, neighborhoods, and guilds were often institutionalized in relations of formal "hatred," considered simply the inverse form of friendship; one could also be transformed into the other by appropriate rituals. In England, for instance, it was assumed that, in the ordinary course of events, the common people would detest the king, royalty in most places being seen as foreigners, and there would often be public celebrations at the failure of some royal project. Hatred for men of the cloth was inveterate. (As late as 1736, Jonathan Swift wrote an essay entitled "Concerning That Universal Hatred That Prevails Against the Clergy.") Different branches of the clergy hated one another: the schoolmen hated members of the monastic orders, the lay clergy detested the priests. According to Thomas Aquinas, even the hatred of God himself was preferable to unbelief or indifference, since it was, in its own way, a form of intense engagement with the Divine.

Hatred, then, was part of the very fabric of social life. Neither did anyone really imagine things could be otherwise. Nor was this a peculiarly European phenomenon. Similar passages could easily be assembled for China, India, the Valley of Mexico, or almost any society that existed under monarchical or aristocratic rule.

So: When did hatred begin to fall into such disfavor? One might argue that there was always a strain of disapproval in Christian literature, but even the phrase "love the sinner, hate the sin" implies that it is legitimate to hate a sin, and nowadays, things have got to such a pass that even that is likely to be considered problematic. Still, the evocation of Christian love, and the feeling that political hatred is a violation of Christian principles, only really appears in the nineteenth century, in Britain, in appeals against the "class hatred" of the Chartists, which—it was held by elite politicians, middle-class reformers, and Christian socialists alike—would lead only to the violent envy and paroxysms of revenge that characterized the French Revolution. The essentially reactionary impulse here can be seen even more clearly in the common reaction at the time to any assertion of the rights of women: early feminists were invariably denounced as "man-haters."

All this is important to bear in mind because nowadays we tend to assume the phrase "politics of hate" has necessarily right-wing implications (since the phrase is normally applied to racism, ethnic hatred, or homophobia), and as a result, that the taboo on expression of political hatred is a triumph of essentially left-wing sensibilities. In fact, the history suggests this is far from the case.

First of all, even in the case of racism, anti-Semitism, or ethnic chauvinism, to frame these things in terms of "hatred" almost necessarily means focusing on followers, and not leaders. The great murderers of the twentieth century were not men driven by terrible passions, they were cynics who fomented and exploited the passions of others. It is utterly unclear if Hitler personally hated Jews (or for that matter whether Stalin personally hated Kulaks). There are indeed many indications they were emotionally incapable of any such deep feelings. What's more, the passions they manipulated were from every part of the emotional spectrum, their followers murdered just as much from love of humanity, or at least love of nation, family, community, than from hatred. To treat the lesson of all this as that one should be against "hate," and create a category of "hate crimes," is tacitly placing the blame on the dupes and simply informing would-be mass manipulators that their craft is perfectly legitimate, just that there are certain levers that they really shouldn't push.

In fact, if you really think about it, the universal taboo over any expression of hatred in political life actually has the effect of validating this sort of manipulation. As I mentioned, politicians nowadays (unlike those in the past) are expected to pretend that they feel no personal hatred for anyone. But what sort of person can exist within a world of constant rivalry, scheming, and betrayal, and not hate anyone? There are only two real possibilities: one would either have to be a saint, or an utter cynic. No one really imagines politicians are saints. Rather, by maintaining the superficial pretense of sainthood, they simply prove the depths of their cynicism.

One could go further. The outlawing of hatred could be seen as the opening move toward a world where the cynical pursuit of self-interest is the only legitimate political motive. Note how the very idea of a "hate crime" inverts the familiar legal principle that a crime of passion should always be punished less severely than one driven by cold, self-interested calculation. It's probably no coincidence that a wave of legislation against hate crime, in the '90s, was soon followed by "anti-terrorism" legislation, which, similarly, stipulated that penalties on crimes driven by political passions (and the way the laws are generally phrased, these passions could include the most benevolent idealism and love of humanity or nature) be more severe than those that would have been imposed on the same crimes had they been committed for economic profit or personal self-interest.

It's significant that this logic applies only on the political level. After all, the very idea of a "crime of passion" largely exists to justify male violence against women in domestic situations. Any realistic analysis of the way that power works in our society would have to begin by acknowledging that such passions, and the fear and terror they create in their victims, are the very foundation of those larger systems of structural violence that uphold inequalities of all kinds (including those ostensibly covered by "hate crimes"). Yet domestic violence is never, itself, considered a "hate crime."

Passions make crimes worse only when they take place in an explicitly political context. At home, they are an exonerating circumstance.

It would seem there are only two universally recognized exceptions to the taboo on hatred.

These are telling in themselves.

The first is what might be termed "consumer hatred." It is acceptable to express hatred, even passionate hatred, for things that others consider desirable, but you do not: for boy bands, UGG shoes, the films of the Coen brothers, for mushrooms or anchovies on pizza. This of course is entirely in keeping with the general principle that passions are to be confined to domestic affairs and not to politics. The second is more ambiguous: the hatred of criminals. It is permissible to hate those who cause pain and suffering by violations of the law. But even here, perhaps because we are in an ambiguous zone moving from the personal to public sphere, it is rarely explicitly framed as "hatred." There often seems to be a kind of coy flirting with forbidden emotions here: as in the villains in so many pulp fiction genres, whether cowboy or spy movies, superhero comic books, or, above all, the endless true-crime, serial-killer literature, where the whole idea seems to be to try to imagine a human being so extraordinarily detestable that one could be forgiven for hating them after all. In America, for instance, crime victims are granted a particular license in this regard, since they are allowed—indeed, encouraged—to express the most hateful emotions conceivable toward criminals, including sadistic desires for the suffering of others that could never be acceptable under any other circumstance. But this itself can be extended to a form of license. It might seem odd to watch TV interviewers gush with sympathy as some crime victim expresses the comfort they take in the despair and misery of their daughter's killer ("perhaps it's better he think he has a possibility of being freed, because then being locked up again will make him suffer even more!"); until, that is, one realizes that we are dealing with a kind of pornography of hatred, where the moral virtue of empathizing with one who has suffered provides an alibi for the vicarious experience of feelings one would otherwise have to treat as profoundly reprehensible.

We would do well, I think, to learn a little from the ancient world. Hatred of injustice can be a form of virtue. Aquinas wrote that hatred for God, in the face of unjust structures of power, is at the very least superior to either indifference or disbelief. We need to acknowledge that many forms of hatred can be a positive social force: hatred for work, hatred for wealth, hatred for bureaucracy, hatred for militarism, nationalism, cynicism, and the arrogance of power. And that in many circumstances, this will also mean hatred for individual bosses, tycoons, bureaucrats, generals, and politicians, and a rich feeling of accomplishment when one knows one has earned their hatred. To absolutely exclude hatred from politics is to rip the fiber out, to deny the main motor of social transformation, ultimately, to reduce it to a flat plane of hopeless cynicism.

It is also to exclude any real possibility for a politics of redemption.

Without the existence of hatred, love is meaningless. It is just insipid idealization: idealization simultaneously of the self, and of the object of one's devotion. As such it is fundamentally sterile. Real love, the only kind genuinely worthy of the name, is a kind of dialectical overcoming. It only becomes possible at the point where one comes to understand the full reality of one's beloved, which necessarily, means encountering even those qualities one finds infuriating, loathsome, or detestable. For surely, if you know enough about anyone, you will find something in them that you hate. But it's only when one encounters that, and decides nonetheless to love them anyway, that we can talk of love as an active, redemptive, and powerful force. And some element of hatred, however small, must always remain there for this to continue to be true. Real love can be love only if it conquers hatred, not by annihilating but by containing and transcending it, and not just once, but forever.

I should add that this is not just true of romantic love—it's equally true within families, friendships, even, if in perhaps more attenuated form, within communities, political associations. There are profound lessons here, I think, for the practice of solidarity, mutual aid, and direct democracy. Traditional communities, we are often told, can come to collective decisions by consensus, or engage in forms of mutual support and cooperation, because they are relatively small, intimate groups with common sensibilities; this would not be possible, supposedly, for larger, impersonal bodies assembled in contemporary metropolises. But anyone who has spent any time in such a small, intimate community knows that they are also riven with deep and abiding hatred. If you think about it, how could it be otherwise? Coming to a public meeting in a village means trying to come to a common decision in a group that contains everyone who has ever insulted one's mother, seduced one's spouse or lover, stolen one's cattle, or made one look ridiculous in front of one's friends. Yet they are, generally speaking, able to do it anyway. This overcoming of communal hatred is the concrete manifestation of collective love. It is far, far more difficult to achieve than an impersonal decision among those who know little about one another, beyond the fact that they are united in opposition to something else. A true geography of revolutionary groups, then, would begin, not by imagining groups based on some perfect, idealized solidarity (and then bewailing the fact that they don't really exist), but rather, by mapping out the lines within which such webs of hatred have been, and continue to be, actively overcome, through practices of solidarity, and across which (justifiable) hatreds cannot be overcome without transforming their fundamental institutional basis—whether those be the organization of workplace, government bureaus, or patriarchal families. Once we stop seeing hatred as something to be ashamed of, it will simply become obvious that even the deepest, most personal hatreds can be overcome within relations of solidarity—in fact, are overcome, on a daily basis, in any social group that isn't entirely dysfunctional—which, in turn, will make it obvious that once those institutional structures are destroyed, no human being will remain beyond redemption.

Dead Zones of the Imagination

On Violence, Bureaucracy, and Interpretive Labor

I

This essay is an exploration of certain areas of human life that have tended to make anthropologists uncomfortable: those areas of starkness, simplicity, obliviousness, and outright stupidity in our lives made possible by violence.[1] By "violence" here, I am not referring to the kind of occasional, spectacular acts of violence that we tend to think of first when the word is invoked, but again, the boring, humdrum, yet omnipresent forms of structural violence that define the very conditions of our existence, the subtle or not-so-subtle threats of physical force that lie behind everything from enforcing rules about where one is allowed to sit or stand or eat or drink in parks or other public places, to the threats

Originally published in *HAU: Journal of Ethnographic Theory*, vol. 2, no. 2, Fall 2012, pp. 105–28; based on the Malinowski Memorial Lecture, 2006.

or physical intimidations or attacks that underpin the enforcement of tacit gender norms.

Let us call these *areas of violent simplification*. They affect us in almost every aspect of our lives. Yet no one likes to talk about them very much. Indeed, one might argue that social theorists seem to have a particular aversion to dealing with the subject because it raises profound issues of the status of social theory itself, and anthropologists dislike talking about them most of all, because anthropologists are drawn, above all, to what might be called *areas of symbolic richness or density of meaning*, where "thick description" becomes possible. The preference is understandable. But it tends to warp our perceptions of what power actually is, and how it operates, in ways that are both decidedly self-serving and, in overlooking structural blindness, effectively become forms of structural blindness themselves.

*   *   *

Let me begin with a brief story about bureaucracy.

Over the last year my mother had a series of strokes. It soon became obvious that she would eventually be incapable of living at home without assistance; since her insurance would not cover home care, a series of social workers advised us to put in for Medicaid. To qualify for Medicaid, however, one's total worth can amount to only six thousand dollars. We arranged to transfer her savings—this was, I suppose, technically a scam, though it's a peculiar sort of scam since the government employs thousands of social workers whose main work seems to be telling citizens how to do it—but shortly thereafter, she had another very serious stroke, and found herself in a nursing home undergoing long-term rehabilitation. When she emerged from there she would definitely need home care, but there was a problem: her Social Security check was being deposited directly, she was barely able to sign her name, so unless I acquired power of attorney over her account and was thus able to pay her monthly rent bills for her, the money would immediately build up and disqualify her, even after I filled out the enormous raft of Medicaid documents I needed to file to qualify her for pending status.

I went to her bank, picked up the requisite forms, and brought them to the nursing home. The documents needed to be notarized. The nurse on the floor informed me there was an in-house notary, but I needed to make an appointment; she picked up the phone and put me through to a disembodied voice who then transferred me to the notary. The notary proceeded to inform me that I first had to get authorization from the head of social work, and hung up. So I acquired his name and room number and duly took the elevator downstairs, appeared at his office—only to discover he was, in fact, the disembodied voice on the phone. The head of social work picked up the phone, said, "Marjorie, that was me, you're driving this man crazy with this nonsense and you're driving me crazy too," and proceeded to secure me an appointment for early the next week.

The next week the notary duly appeared, accompanied me upstairs, made sure I'd filled out my side of the form (as had been repeatedly emphasized to me), and then, in my mother's presence, proceeded to fill out her own. I was a little puzzled that she didn't ask my mother to sign anything, only me, but I figured she must know what she was doing. The next day I took it to the bank, where the woman at the desk took one look, asked why my mother hadn't signed it, and showed it to her manager, who told me to take it back and do it right. Apparently the notary had no idea what she was doing. So I got new forms, filled out my side of each, and made a new appointment. On the appointed day the notary duly appeared, and after some awkward remarks about the difficulties caused by each bank having its own, completely different power of attorney form, we proceeded upstairs. I signed, my mother signed—with some difficulty—and the next day I returned to the bank. Another woman at a different desk examined the forms and asked why I had signed the line where it said to write my name and printed my name on the line where it said to sign.

"I did? Well, I just did exactly what the notary told me to do."

"But it says clearly 'signature' here."

"Oh, yes, it does, doesn't it? I guess she told me wrong. Again. Well . . . all the information is still there, isn't it? It's just those two bits that are reversed. So is it really a problem? It's kind of pressing and I'd really rather not have to wait to make another appointment."

"Well, normally we don't even accept these forms without all the signatories being here in person."

"My mother had a stroke. She's bedridden. That's why I need power of attorney in the first place."

She said she'd check with the manager, and after ten minutes returned (with the manager hanging just within earshot in the background) to announce the bank could not accept the forms in their present state—and in addition, even if they were filled out correctly, I would still need a letter from my mother's doctor certifying that she was mentally competent to sign such a document.

I pointed out that no one had mentioned any such letter previously.

"What?" the manager suddenly interjected. "Who gave you those forms and didn't tell you about the letter?"

Since the culprit was one of the more sympathetic bank employees, I dodged the question, noting instead that in the bankbook it was printed, quite clearly, "in trust for David Graeber." He of course replied that would only matter if she was dead.

As it happened, the whole problem soon became academic: my mother did indeed die a few weeks later.

At the time, I found this experience extremely disconcerting. Having led an existence comparatively insulated from this sort of thing, I found myself continually asking my friends: Is this what ordinary life, for most people, is really like? Most were inclined to suspect it was. Obviously, the notary was unusually incompetent. Still, I had to spend over a month, not long after, dealing with the ramifying consequences of the act of an anonymous clerk in the New York Department of Motor Vehicles who inscribed my given name as "Daid"—not to mention the Verizon clerk who spelled my surname "Grueber." Bureaucracies public and private appear—for whatever historical reasons—to be organized in such a way as to guarantee that a significant proportion of actors will not be able to perform their tasks as expected. It also exemplifies what I have come to think of as the defining feature of certain utopian forms of practice: that is, ones where those maintaining the system, on discovering that it will regularly produce such failures, conclude that the problem is not with the system itself but with the inadequacy of the human beings involved—or, indeed, of human beings in general.

As an intellectual, probably the most disturbing thing was how dealing with these forms somehow rendered me stupid too. How could I not have noticed that I was printing my name on the line that said "signature" and this despite the fact that I had been investing a great deal of mental and emotional energy in the whole affair? The problem, I realized, was that most of this energy was going into a continual attempt to try to understand and influence whoever, at any moment, seemed to have some kind of bureaucratic power over me—when all that was required was the accurate interpretation of one or two Latin words, and a correct performance of certain purely mechanical functions. Spending so much of my time worrying about how not to seem like I was rubbing the notary's face in her incompetence, or imagining what might make me seem sympathetic to various bank officials, made me less inclined to notice when they told me to do something foolish. It was an obviously misplaced strategy, since insofar as anyone had the power to bend the rules they were usually not the people I was talking to; moreover, if I did encounter them, I was constantly being reminded that if I did complain, even about a purely structural absurdity, the only possible result would be to get some junior functionary in trouble.

As an anthropologist, probably the most curious thing for me was how little trace any of this tends to leave in the ethnographic literature. After all, we anthropologists have made something of a specialty out of dealing with the rituals surrounding birth, marriage, death, and similar rites of passage. We are particularly concerned with ritual gestures that are socially efficacious: where the mere act of saying or doing something makes it socially true. Yet in most existing societies at this point, it is precisely paperwork, rather than any other forms of ritual, that is socially efficacious. My mother, for example, wished to be cremated without ceremony; my main memory of the funeral home, though, was of the plump, good-natured clerk who walked me through a fourteen-page document he had to file in order to obtain a death certificate, written in ballpoint on carbon paper so it came out in triplicate. "How many hours a day do you spend filling out forms like that?" I asked. He sighed. "It's all I do," he said, holding up a hand bandaged from some kind of incipient carpal tunnel syndrome. But without those forms, my mother would not be legally—hence socially—dead.

Why, then, are there not vast ethnographic tomes about American or British rites of passage, with long chapters about forms and paperwork? There is an obvious answer. Paperwork is boring. One can describe the ritual surrounding it. One can observe how people talk about or react to it. But when it comes to the paperwork itself, there just aren't that many interesting things one can say about it.

Anthropologists are drawn to areas of density. The interpretive tools we have at our disposal are best suited to wend our way through complex webs of meaning or signification: to understand intricate ritual symbolism, social dramas, poetic forms, or kinship networks. What all these have in common is that they tend to be both infinitely rich and, at the same time, open-ended. If one sets out to exhaust every meaning, motive, or association packed into a single Swazi Ncwala ritual, Balinese cockfight, Zande witchcraft accusation, or Mexican family saga, one could easily spend a lifetime; and quite a number of them, if one also sought to trace the fan of relations with other elements in the larger social or symbolic fields such work invariably opens up. Paperwork in contrast is designed to be maximally simple and self-contained. Even when forms are complex, even bafflingly complex, it's by an endless accretion of very simple yet apparently contradictory components, like a maze made out of the endless juxtaposition of two or three very simple geometrical elements. And like a maze, it doesn't really open on anything outside itself. As a result, there just isn't very much to interpret. A Geertzian "thick description" of a mortgage application, for example, would not really be possible, no matter how dense the document. Even if some defiant soul set out to write one just to prove it could be done, it would be even harder to imagine anyone actually reading it.

II

Novelists often do manage to make great literature out of the apparent circularity and emptiness, not to mention idiocy, of bureaucracy—but largely by embracing it, and producing literary works that partake of something like the same mazelike, senseless form. As a result, almost all great literature on the subject takes the form of horror-comedy. Franz Kafka's *The Trial* (1925) is of course the paradigm, but one can cite any number of others: from Stanisław Lem's *Memoirs Found in a Bathtub* (1961), which is pretty much straight Kafka, to Ismail Kadare's *Palace of Dreams* (1980), José Saramago's *All the Names* (1999), or work that's simply informed by the bureaucratic spirit (e.g., almost anything by Jorge Luis Borges). Joseph Heller's *Catch-22* (1961), which takes on military bureaucracies, and *Something Happened* (1974), about corporate bureaucracies, are considered latter-day masterworks in this genre. As is David Foster Wallace's *The Pale King* (2011), an imaginative meditation on the nature of boredom set in a Midwestern office of the Internal Revenue Service. It's interesting that just about all these works of fiction not only emphasize the comic senselessness of bureaucratic life, but mix it with at least undertones of violence. That is to say, they emphasize the very aspects most likely to be sidestepped in the social scientific literature.

Now, it's true there are works of anthropology that echo some of these themes: one thinks, for instance, of Jack Goody's reflection on the idea of the list in *The Domestication of the Savage Mind* (1977), which is just as much about the birth of self-enclosing bureaucratic systems of classification as Roland Barthes's *Sade, Fourier, Loyola* (1971) is about the moment such logic came to be applied—at least imaginatively—to absolutely every corporeal aspect of human life: passions, sexual acts, or religious devotion. But most are not explicitly about bureaucracy at all. Within the anthropological literature on bureaucracy itself, in turn, there are works that echo something of the absurdist mode so prevalent in literature: Matthew Hull's work on paperwork as ritual, Akhil Gupta's recent *Red Tape* (2012), which directly takes on the failures of Indian bureaucracies to alleviate poverty, or Andrew Mathews's work on the

Mexican forestry service. But these are somewhat exceptional. The real core of the anthropological literature on bureaucracy, even at the height of the "literary turn," took the completely opposite direction, asking not why bureaucracy produces absurdity, but rather, why so many people believe this is the case. The single best-known anthropological work on bureaucracy is Michael Herzfeld's *The Social Production of Indifference* (1992), which begins by framing the question thusly:

> [I]n most industrial democracies—where the state is supposed to be a respecter of persons—people rail in quite predictable ways against the evils of bureaucracy. It does not matter that their outrage is often unjustified; what counts is their ability to draw on a predictable image of malfunction. If one could not grumble about "bureaucracy," bureaucracy itself could not easily exist: both bureaucracy and the stereotypical complaints about it are parts of a larger universe that we might call, quite simply, the ideology and practice of accountability.[2]

To understand the system in cultural terms—that is, to find the areas of symbolic richness, rife for anthropological analysis, where its victims can represent themselves as Christlike, for example, and imagine local officials as embodiments of Oriental Despotism—one has to move out of the offices entirely and into the cafés.

> The symbolic roots of Western bureaucracy are not to be sought, in the first instance, in the official forms of bureaucracy itself, although significant traces may be discovered there. They subsist above all in popular reactions to bureaucracy—in the ways in which ordinary people actually manage and conceptualize bureaucratic relations.[3]

This is not to say Herzfeld and others who have followed in his wake[4] explicitly deny that immersion in bureaucratic codes and regulations can, in fact, cause people to act in ways that in any other context would be considered idiotic. Just about anyone is aware from personal experiences that they regularly do. Yet for purposes of cultural analysis, truth is rarely considered an adequate explanation. At best one can expect a "yes, but . . ."—with the assumption that the "but" introduces everything that's really interesting and important: for instance, the way that complaints about that idiocy subtly act to reinscribe the complainers as subjects within the same moral field of accountability that bureaucrats inhabit, the way this creates a certain conception of the nation, and so on.

When we move away from ethnography and enter more rarified domains of social theory, even that "yes, but" has been known to disappear. In fact, one often finds a remarkable sympathy—dare one say, sense of affinity?—between scholars, who generally double as academic bureaucrats, and the bureaucrats they study. Consider the hegemonic role, in U.S. social theory, of Max Weber in the 1950s and 1960s, and of Michel Foucault since the 1970s. Their popularity, no doubt, had much to do with the ease with which each could be adopted as a kind of anti-Marx, their theories put forth (usually in crudely simplified form) to argue that power is not simply or primarily a matter of the control of production but rather a pervasive, multifaceted, and unavoidable feature of any social life. I also think it is no coincidence that these sometimes appear to be the only two intelligent people in human history who honestly believed that bureaucracy is characterized primarily by its effectiveness. Weber saw bureaucratic forms of organization—public and private—as the very embodiment of impersonal rationality, and as such, so obviously superior to all other possible forms of organization that they threatened to engulf everything, locking humanity in a joyless "iron cage," bereft of spirit and charisma.[5] Foucault was more subversive, but in a way that made bureaucratic power more effective, not less. In his work on asylums, clinics, prisons, and the rest, bodies, subjects—even truth itself—all become the products of administrative discourses. Through concepts like governmentality and biopower, state bureaucracies end up shaping the parameters of human existence in ways far more intimate than anything Weber might have imagined.

It's hard to avoid the conclusion that, in either case, their popularity owed much to the fact that the American university system during this period had itself become increasingly an institution dedicated to producing functionaries for an imperial administrative apparatus on a global scale. During the Cold War, this was often fairly explicit, especially in the early years when both Boasians such as Mead and Benedict and Weberians such as Geertz often found themselves operating within the military-intelligence apparatus, or even funded by CIA fronts.[6] Gradually, over the course of the campus mobilizations of the Vietnam War, this kind of complicity was made an issue. Max Weber—or, to be more accurate, that version of Weber promoted by sociologists such as Parsons and Shils, which gradually became the basis for State Department "modernization theory"—came to be seen as the embodiment of everything radicals wished to reject.[7] But it wasn't long before Foucault, who had been whisked out of his retreat in Tunisia and placed in the Collège de France after the uprising of May 1968, began to fill the gap. One might even speak here of the gradual emergence of a kind of division of labor within American universities, with the optimistic side of Weber reinvented (in even more simplified form) for the actual training of bureaucrats under the name of "rational choice theory," while his pessimistic side was relegated to the Foucauldians. Foucault's ascendancy, in turn, was precisely within those fields of academic endeavor that both became the haven for former radicals, and were almost completely divorced from any access to political power—or, increasingly, from any influence on social movements as well. This gave Foucault's emphasis on the "power/knowledge" nexus—the assertion that forms of knowledge are always also forms of social power, indeed, the most important forms of social power—a particular appeal.

No doubt, any such pocket historical summary can only be a bit caricaturish and unfair. Still, I think there is a profound truth here. It is not just that we are drawn to areas of density, where our skills at interpretation are best deployed. We also have an increasing tendency to identify what's interesting with what's important, and to assume that places of density are also places of power. The power of bureaucracy shows just how much this is often not the case.

This essay is not, however, primarily about bureaucracy—or even about the reasons for its neglect in anthropology and related disciplines. It is really about violence. What I would like to argue is that situations created by violence—particularly structural violence, by which I mean forms of pervasive social inequality that are ultimately backed up by the threat of physical harm—invariably tend to create the kinds of willful blindness we normally associate with bureaucratic procedures. To put it crudely: it is not so much that bureaucratic procedures are inherently stupid, or even that they tend to produce behavior that they themselves define as stupid, but rather, that they are invariably ways of managing social situations that are already stupid because they are founded on structural violence. I think this approach allows potential insights into matters that are, in fact, both interesting and important: for instance, the actual relationship between those forms of simplification typical of social theory, and those typical of administrative procedures.

III

We are not used to thinking of nursing homes or banks or even HMOs as violent institutions—except perhaps in the most abstract and metaphorical sense. But the violence I'm referring to here is not epistemic. It's quite concrete. All of these are institutions involved in the allocation of resources within a system of property rights regulated and guaranteed by governments in a system that ultimately rests on the threat of force. "Force," in turn, is just a euphemistic way to refer to violence.

All of this is obvious enough. What's of ethnographic interest, perhaps, is how rarely citizens in industrial democracies actually think about this fact, or how instinctively we try to discount its importance. This is what makes it possible, for example, for graduate students to be able to spend days in the stacks of university libraries poring over theoretical tracts about the declining importance of coercion as a factor in modern life, without ever reflecting on that fact that, had they insisted on their right to enter the stacks without showing a properly stamped and validated ID, armed men would indeed be summoned to physically remove them, using whatever force might be required. It's almost as if the more we allow aspects of our everyday existence to fall under the purview of bureaucratic regulations, the more everyone concerned colludes to downplay the fact (perfectly obvious to those actually running the system) that all of it ultimately depends on the threat of physical harm.

Actually, one could make the same argument about the way that the term "structural violence" itself is deployed in contemporary social theory—because the way I am using it here is quite decidedly unconventional. The term itself traces back to debates within Peace Studies in the 1960s; it was coined by Johann Galtung to meet the charge that to define "peace" as the mere absence of acts of physical assault is to overlook the prevalence of much more insidious structures of human exploitation.[8] Galtung felt the term *exploitation* was too loaded, owing to its identification with Marxism, and proposed as an alternative "structural violence"—i.e., any institutional arrangement that, by its very operation, regularly causes physical or psychological harm to a certain portion of the population, or imposes limits on their freedom. Structural violence could thus be distinguished from both "personal violence" (violence by an identifiable human agent) and "cultural violence" (those beliefs and assumptions about the world that justify the infliction of harm). This is the how the term has mainly been taken up in the anthropological literature as well.[9] Paul Farmer, for instance, writes that he found the term apt in describing the suffering and early death of so many of the poor Haitian farmers among whom he worked and treated,

> because such suffering is "structured" by historically given (and often economically driven) processes and forces that conspire— whether through routine, ritual, or, as is more commonly the case, the hard surfaces of life—to constrain agency. For many, including most of my patients and informants, choices both large and small are limited by racism, sexism, political violence, and grinding poverty.[10]

In all these formulations, "structural violence" is treated as structures that have violent effects, whether or not actual physical violence is involved. This is actually quite different from my own formulation, more consonant with the feminist tradition,[11] which sees these more as structures of violence—since it is only the constant fear of physical violence that makes them possible, and allows them to have violent effects. Racism, sexism, poverty: these cannot exist except in an environment defined by the ultimate threat of actual physical force. To insist on a distinction makes sense only if one wishes, for some reason, to also insist that there could be, for example, a system of patriarchy that operated in the total absence of domestic violence, or sexual assault—despite the fact that, to my knowledge, no such system has ever been observed.

Given the world as it actually exists, this clearly makes no sense. If, say, there is a place where women are excluded from certain spaces for fear of physical or sexual assault, what precisely is achieved by making a distinction between actual attacks, the fear those attacks inspire, the assumptions that motivate men to carry out such assaults or police to feel the victim "had it coming," and the resultant feeling on the part of most women that these are not the kind of spaces women really ought to be in? Or, for that matter, to distinguish all of these, in turn, from the "economic" consequences of women who cannot be hired for certain jobs as a result. They all form a single structure of violence.[12]

The ultimate problem with Galtung's approach, as Catia Confortini notes, is that it views "structures" as abstract, free-floating entities; when what we are really referring to here are material processes, in which violence, and the threat of violence, play a crucial, constitutive role.[13] In fact, one could argue it's this very tendency toward abstraction that makes it possible for everyone involved to imagine that the violence upholding the system is somehow not responsible for its violent effects.

Anthropologists would do well not to make the same mistake.

All this becomes even clearer when one looks at the role of government. In many of the rural communities anthropologists are most familiar with, where modern administrative techniques are explicitly seen as alien impositions, many of these connections are much easier to see. In the part of rural Madagascar where I did my fieldwork, for example, that governments operate primarily by inspiring fear was seen as obvious. At the same time, in the absence of any significant government interference in the minutiae of daily life (via building codes, open container laws, the mandatory licensing and insurance of vehicles, and so on), it became all the more apparent that the main business of government bureaucracy was the registration of taxable property. One curious result was that it was precisely the sort of information that was available from the Malagasy archives for the nineteenth and early twentieth centuries for the community I was studying—precise figures about the size of each family and its holdings in land and cattle (and in the earlier period, slaves)—that I was least able to attain for the time I was there, simply because that was precisely what most people assumed an outsider coming from the capital would likely be asking about, and therefore, that which they were least inclined to tell them.

What's more, one result of the colonial experience was that which might be called "relations of command"—basically, any ongoing relationship in which one adult renders another an extension of his or her will—had become identified with slavery, and slavery with the essential nature of the state. In the community I studied, such associations were most likely to come to the fore when people were talking about the great slave-holding families of the nineteenth century whose children went on to become the core of the colonial-era administration, largely (it was always remarked) by dint of their devotion to education and skill with paperwork. In other contexts, relations of command— particularly in bureaucratic contexts—were linguistically coded. They were firmly identified with French; Malagasy, in contrast, was seen as the language appropriate to deliberation, explanation, and consensus-based decision-making. Minor functionaries, when they wished to impose arbitrary dictates, would almost invariably switch to French. I particularly remember one occasion when an official who had had many conversations with me in Malagasy, and had no idea I even understood French, was flustered one day to discover me dropping by at exactly the moment everyone had decided to go home early. "The office is closed," he announced, in French, "if you have any business you must return tomorrow at eight a.m." When I pretended confusion and claimed, in

Malagasy, not to understand French, he proved utterly incapable of re-peating the sentence in the vernacular, but just kept repeating the French over and over. Others later confirmed what I suspected: that if he had switched to Malagasy, he would at the very least have had to explain why the office had closed at such an unusual time. French is actually referred to in Malagasy as "the language of command"—it was characteristic of contexts where explanations, deliberation, and ultimately, consent was not really required, since they were in the final analysis premised on the threat of violence.[14]

In Madagascar, bureaucratic power was somewhat redeemed in most people's minds by its tie to education, which was held in near-universal esteem. Comparative analysis suggests there is a direct rela-tion, however, between the level of violence employed in a bureaucratic system, and the level of absurdity it is seen to produce. Keith Breck-enridge, for example, has documented at some length the regimes of "power without knowledge," typical of colonial South Africa, where coercion and paperwork largely substituted for the need to understand African subjects.[15] The actual installation of apartheid in the 1950s, for example, was heralded by a new pass system designed to simplify earlier rules that obliged African workers to carry extensive documentation of labor contracts, substituting a single identity booklet, marked with their "names, locale, fingerprints, tax status, and their officially prescribed 'rights' to live and work in the towns and cities," and nothing else.[16] Government functionaries appreciated it for streamlining administra-tion, police for relieving them of the responsibility of having to actually talk to African workers—the latter universally referred to as the dompas (or "stupid pass"), for precisely that reason. Andrew Mathews's brilliant ethnography of the Mexican forestry service in Oaxaca likewise dem-onstrates that it is precisely the structural inequality of power between government officials and local farmers that allows foresters to remain in a kind of ideological bubble, maintaining simple black-and-white ideas about forest fires (for instance) that allow them to remain pretty much the only people in Oaxaca who don't understand what effects their regu-lations actually have.[17]

There are traces of the link between coercion and absurdity even in the way we talk about bureaucracy in English. Note, for example, how most of the colloquial terms that specifically refer to bureaucratic foolishness—*SNAFU*, *catch-22*, and the like—derive from military slang. More generally, political scientists have long observed a "negative correlation," as David Apter put it, between coercion and information: that is, while relatively democratic regimes tend to be awash in too much information, as everyone bombards political authorities with explanations and demands, the more authoritarian and repressive a regime, the less reason people have to tell it anything—which is why such regimes are forced to rely so heavily on spies, intelligence agencies, and secret police.[18]

IV

Violence's capacity to allow arbitrary decisions, and thus to avoid the kind of debate, clarification, and renegotiation typical of more egalitarian social relations, is obviously what allows its victims to see procedures created on the basis of violence as stupid or unreasonable. One might say those relying on the fear of force are not obliged to engage in a lot of interpretative labor, and thus, generally speaking, do not.

This is not an aspect of violence that has received much attention in the burgeoning "anthropology of violence" literature. The latter has tended instead to move in exactly the opposite direction, emphasizing the ways that acts of violence are meaningful and communicative. Neil Whitehead, for instance, in a recent collection entitled simply *Violence*, goes so far as to insist that anthropologists need to examine why people are ever wont to speak of "meaningless violence" at all.[19] Violence, he suggests, is best understood as analogous with poetry:

> Violent actions, no less than any other kind of behavioral expression, are deeply infused with cultural meaning and are the moment for individual agency within historically embedded patterns of behavior. Individual agency, utilizing extant cultural

forms, symbols, and icons, may thus be considered "poetic" for the rule-governed substrate that underlies it, and for how this substrate is deployed, through which new meanings and forms of cultural expression emerge.[20]

When I object to this emphasis on the meaningful nature of violence, I'm not trying to suggest that the fundamental point is in any way untrue. It would be absurd to deny that acts of violence are, typically, meant as acts of communication, or that they tend to be surrounded by symbols and generate myths. Yet it seems to me that, just as in the case of bureaucracy, this is an area where anthropologists are particularly inclined to confuse interpretive depth with social significance: that is, to assume that the most interesting aspect of violence is also, necessarily, the most important. Yes, violent acts tend to have a communicative element. But this is true of any other form of human action as well. It strikes me that what is really important about violence is that it is perhaps the only form of human action that holds out even the possibility of having social effects *without* being communicative.

To be more precise: violence may well be the only form of human action by which it is possible to have relatively predictable effects on the actions of a person about whom you understand nothing. Pretty much any other way one might try to influence another's actions, one at least has to have some idea of who they think they are, who they think you are, what they might want out of the situation, and what their aversions and proclivities are. Hit them over the head hard enough and all of this becomes irrelevant.

It is true that the effects one can have by disabling or killing someone are very limited, but they are real enough—and critically, it is possible to know in advance exactly what they will be. Any alternative form of action cannot, without some sort of appeal to shared meanings or understandings, have any predictable effects at all. What's more, while attempts to influence others by the threat of violence do require some level of shared understanding, these can be pretty minimal. Most human relations—particularly ongoing ones, whether between long-standing friends or long-standing enemies—are extremely complicated, dense with experience and meaning. Maintaining them requires a constant and often subtle work of interpretation, of endlessly imagining others' points of view. Threatening others with physical harm allows the possibility of cutting through all this. It makes possible relations of a far more schematic kind (i.e., "cross this line and I will shoot you"). This is, of course, why violence is so often the preferred weapon of the stupid. Indeed, one might say it is one of the tragedies of human existence that this is the one form of stupidity to which it is most difficult to come up with an intelligent response.

I do need to introduce one crucial qualification here. If two parties are engaged in a relatively equal contest of violence—say, generals commanding opposing armies—they have good reason to try to get inside each other's head. It is really only when one side has an overwhelming advantage in their capacity to cause physical harm that they no longer need to do so. But this has very profound effects, because it means that the most characteristic effect of violence—its ability to obviate the need for what I would call "interpretive labor"—becomes most salient when the violence itself is least visible, in fact, where acts of spectacular physical violence are least likely to occur. These are situations of what I've referred to as structural violence, on the assumption that systematic inequalities backed up by the threat of force can be treated as forms of violence in themselves. For this reason, situations of structural violence invariably produce extreme lopsided structures of imaginative identifications.

These effects are often most visible when the structures of inequality take the most deeply internalized forms. A constant staple of 1950s American situation comedies, for example, was jokes about the impossibility of understanding women. The jokes (always, of course, told by men) represented women's logic as fundamentally alien and incomprehensible. One never had the impression the women in question had any trouble understanding men. The reasons are obvious: women had no choice but to understand men; this was the heyday of a certain image of the patriarchal family, and women with no access to their own income or resources had little choice but to spend a great deal of time and energy understanding what their menfolk thought was going on. Hopefully, at this point, I do not have to point out that patriarchal arrangements of this sort are prima facie examples of structural violence; they are norms sanctioned by the threat of physical harm in endless subtle and not-so-subtle ways. And this kind of rhetoric about the mysteries of woman-kind appears to be a perennial feature of them. Generations of women novelists—Virginia Woolf comes most immediately to mind—have also documented the other side of such arrangements: the constant efforts women end up having to expend in managing, maintaining, and adjust-ing the egos of oblivious and self-important men involve a continual work of imaginative identification, or what I've called "interpretive la-bor." This carries over on every level. Women are always expected to imagine what things look like from a male point of view. Men are al-most never expected to reciprocate. So deeply internalized is this pat-tern of behavior that many men react to the suggestion that they might do otherwise as if it were an act of violence in itself. A popular exercise among high school creative writing teachers in America, for example, is to ask students to imagine they have been transformed, for a day, into someone of the opposite sex, and describe what that day might be like. The results, apparently, are uncannily uniform. The girls all write long and detailed essays that clearly show they have spent a great deal of time thinking about the subject. Usually, a good proportion of the boys refuse to write the essay entirely. Those who do make it clear they have not the slightest conception what being a teenage girl might be like, and deeply resent having to think about it.[21]

Nothing I am saying here is particularly new to anyone familiar with Feminist Standpoint Theory or Critical Race Studies. Indeed, I was originally inspired to these broader reflections by a passage by bell hooks:

> Although there has never been any official body of black people in the United States who have gathered as anthropologists and/ or ethnographers to study whiteness, black folks have, from

slavery on, shared in conversations with one another "special" knowledge of whiteness gleaned from close scrutiny of white people. Deemed special because it is not a way of knowing that has been recorded fully in written material, its purpose was to help black folks cope and survive in a white supremacist society. For years black domestic servants, working in white homes, acted as informants who brought knowledge back to segregated communities—details, facts, psychoanalytic readings of the white "Other."[22]

If there is a flaw in the feminist literature, I would say it's that it can be, if anything, too generous, tending to emphasize the insights of the oppressed over the blindness or foolishness of their oppressors.[23]

Could it be possible to develop a general theory of interpretive labor? We'd probably have to begin by recognizing that there are two critical elements here that, while linked, need to be formally distinguished. The first is the process of imaginative identification as a form of knowledge, the fact that within relations of domination, it is generally the subordinates who are effectively relegated to the work of understanding how the social relations in question really work. Anyone who has ever worked in a restaurant kitchen, for example, knows that if something goes terribly wrong and an angry boss appears to size things up, he is unlikely to carry out a detailed investigation, or even to pay serious attention to the workers all scrambling to explain their version of what happened. He is much more likely to tell them all to shut up and arbitrarily impose a story that allows instant judgment: i.e., "you're the new guy, you messed up—if you do it again, you're fired." It's those who do not have the power to hire and fire who are left with the work of figuring out what actually did go wrong so as to make sure it doesn't happen again. The same thing usually happens with ongoing relations: everyone knows that servants tend to know a great deal about their employers' families, but the opposite almost never occurs. The second element is the resultant pattern of sympathetic identification. Curiously, it was Adam Smith, in his *Theory of Moral Sentiments* (1762), who first observed the phenomenon we now

refer to as "compassion fatigue." Human beings, he proposed, are normally inclined not only to imaginatively identify with their fellows, but
as a result, to spontaneously feel one another's joys and sorrows. The
poor, however, are so consistently miserable that otherwise sympathetic
observers face a tacit choice between being entirely overwhelmed and
simply blotting out their existence. The result is that while those on the
bottom of a social ladder spend a great deal of time imagining the perspectives of, and genuinely caring about, those on the top, it almost
never happens the other way around.

Whether one is dealing with masters and servants, men and women,
employers and employees, rich and poor, structural inequality—what
I've been calling structural violence—invariably creates highly lopsided structures of the imagination. Since I think Smith was right to
observe that imagination tends to bring with it sympathy, the result is
that victims of structural violence tend to care about its beneficiaries
far more than those beneficiaries care about them. This might well be,
after the violence itself, the single most powerful force preserving such
relations.

V

All this, I think, has some interesting theoretical implications.

Now, in contemporary industrialized democracies, the legitimate
administration of violence is turned over to what is euphemistically referred to as "law enforcement"—particularly, to police officers, whose
real role, as police sociologists have repeatedly emphasized,[24] has much
less to do with enforcing criminal law than with the scientific application of physical force to aid in the resolution of administrative problems.
Police are, essentially, bureaucrats with weapons. At the same time, they
have significantly, over the last fifty years or so, become the almost ob-
sessive objects of imaginative identification in popular culture. It has
come to the point that it's not at all unusual for a citizen in a contemporary industrialized democracy to spend several hours a day reading
books, watching movies, or viewing TV shows that invite them to look
at the world from a police point of view, and to vicariously participate in

their exploits. If nothing else, all this throws an odd wrinkle in Weber's dire prophecies about the iron cage: as it turns out, faceless bureaucracies do seem inclined to throw up charismatic heroes of a sort, in the form of an endless assortment of mythic detectives, spies, and police officers—all, significantly, figures whose job is to operate precisely where the bureaucratic structures for ordering information encounter, and appeal to, genuine physical violence.

Even more striking, I think, are the implications for the status of theory itself.

Bureaucratic knowledge is all about schematization. In practice, bureaucratic procedure invariably means ignoring all the subtleties of real social existence and reducing everything to preconceived mechanical or statistical formulae. Whether it's a matter of forms, rules, statistics, or questionnaires, it is always a matter of simplification. Usually it's not so different than the boss who walks into the kitchen to make arbitrary snap decisions as to what went wrong: in either case it is a matter of applying very simple preexisting templates to complex and often ambiguous situations. The result often leaves those forced to deal with bureaucratic administration with the impression that they are dealing with people who have, for some arbitrary reason, decided to put on a set of glasses that allows them to see only 2 percent of what's in front of them. But doesn't something very similar happen in social theory? An ethnographic description, even a very good one, captures at best 2 percent of what's happening in any particular Nuer feud or Balinese cockfight. A theoretical work will normally focus on only a tiny part of that, plucking perhaps one or two strands out of an endlessly complex fabric of human circumstance, and using them as the basis on which to make generalizations: say, about the dynamics of social conflict, the nature of performance, or the principle of hierarchy. I am not trying to say there's anything wrong in this kind of theoretical reduction. To the contrary, I am convinced some such process is necessary if one wishes to say something dramatically new about the world.

Consider the role of structural analysis, so famously endorsed by Edmund Leach in the first Malinowski Memorial Lecture almost half a century ago.[25] Nowadays structural analysis is considered definitively passé, and Claude Lévi-Strauss's corpus vaguely ridiculous. This strikes me as unfortunate. Certainly the idea that structuralism provides some kind of genetic key to unlock the mysteries of human culture has been justifiably abandoned; but to likewise abandon even the practice of structural analysis, it seems to me, robs us of one of our most ingenious tools. Because the great merit of structural analysis is that it provides a well-nigh foolproof technique for doing what any good theory should do, namely simplifying and schematizing complex material in such a way as to be able to say something unexpected. This is incidentally how I came up with the point about Weber and heroes of bureaucracy three paragraphs above. It all came from an experiment demonstrating structural analysis to students at a seminar in Yale; I had just laid out how vampires could be conceived as structural inversions of werewolves (and Frankenstein of the Mummy), and someone suggested we try the same thing on other genres. I quickly established, to my own satisfaction at least, that James Bond was a structural inversion of Sherlock Holmes (see figure 1). It was in mapping out the field that became visible once we set out that initial opposition that I came to realize that everything here was organized precisely around the relation between information and violence—just as one would expect for heroes of a bureaucratic age.

For my own part, I prefer to see someone like Lévi-Strauss as a heroic figure, a man with the sheer intellectual courage to pursue his model as far as it would go, no matter how obviously absurd the results could sometimes be—or, if you prefer, how much violence he thus did to reality.

As long as one remains within the domain of theory, then, I would argue that simplification can be a form of intelligence. The problems arise when the violence is no longer metaphorical. Here let me turn from imaginary cops to real ones. A former LAPD officer turned sociologist observed that the overwhelming majority of those beaten by police turn out not to be guilty of any crime.[26] "Cops don't beat up burglars," he observed. The reason, he explained, is simple: the one thing most guaranteed to evoke a violent reaction from police is to challenge their right to "define the situation." If what I've been saying is true, then this is just what we'd expect. The police truncheon is precisely the point where the state's bureaucratic imperative for imposing simple administrative schema, and its monopoly of coercive force, come together. It only makes sense, then, that bureaucratic violence should consist first and foremost of attacks on those who insist on alternative schemas or interpretations. At the same time, if one accepts Piaget's famous definition of mature intelligence as the ability to coordinate among multiple perspectives (or possible perspectives), one can see, here, precisely how bureaucratic power, at the moment it turns to violence, becomes literally a form of infantile stupidity.[27]

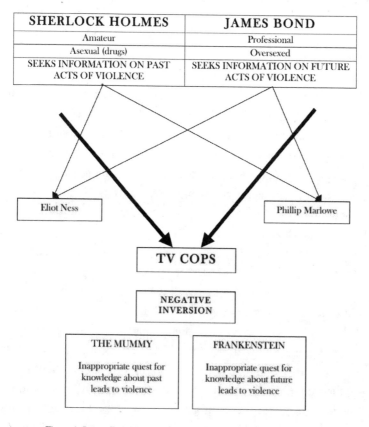

Figure 1. James Bond as a Structural Inversion of Sherlock Holmes.

If I had more time I would suggest why I feel this approach could suggest new ways to consider old problems. From a Marxian perspective, for example, one might note that my notion of "interpretive labor" that keeps social life running smoothly implies a fundamental distinction between the domain of social production (the production of persons and social relations), where the imaginative labor is relegated to those on the bottom, and a domain of commodity production, where the imaginative aspects of work are relegated to those on the top. In either case, though, structures of inequality produce lopsided structures of the imagination. I would also propose that what we are used to calling "alienation" is largely the subjective experience of living inside such lopsided structures. This in turn has implications for any liberatory politics.[28] For present purposes, though, let me just draw attention to some of the implications for anthropology.

One is that many of the interpretive techniques we employ have, historically, served as weapons of the weak far more often than as instruments of power. In an essay in *Writing Culture*, Renato Rosaldo made a famous argument that when Evans-Pritchard, annoyed that no one would speak to him, ended up gazing at a Nuer camp of Muot Dit "from the door of his tent," he rendered it equivalent to a Foucauldian Panopticon.[29] The logic seems to be that any knowledge gathered under unequal conditions serves a disciplinary function. To me, this is absurd. Bentham's Panopticon was a prison. There were guards. Prisoners endured the gaze, and internalized its dictates, because if they tried to escape, or resist, they could be punished, even killed.[30] Absent the apparatus of coercion, such an observer is reduced to the equivalent of a neighborhood gossip, deprived even of the sanction of public opinion.

Underlying the analogy, I think, is the assumption that comprehensive knowledge of this sort is an inherent part of any imperial project. Even the briefest examination of the historical record, though, makes clear that empires tend to have little or no interest in documenting ethnographic material. They tend to be interested instead in questions of law and administration. For information on exotic marriage customs or mortuary ritual, one almost invariably has to fall back on travelers' accounts—on the likes of Herodotus, Ibn Battuta, or Zhang Qian—that is, on descriptions of those lands which fell outside the jurisdiction of whatever state the traveler belonged to.[31]

Historical research reveals that the inhabitants of Muot Dit were, in fact, largely former followers of a prophet named Gwek who had been victims of RAF bombing and forced displacement the year before—the whole affair being occasioned by fairly typical bureaucratic foolishness (basic misunderstandings about the nature of power in Nuer society, attempts to separate Nuer and Dinka populations that had been entangled for generations, and so forth).[32] When Evans-Pritchard was there they were still subject to punitive raids from the British authorities. Evans-Pritchard was asked to go to Nuerland basically as a spy. At first he refused, then finally agreed; he later said it was because he "felt sorry for them." He appears to have carefully avoided gathering the specific information the authorities were really after (mainly, about the prophets whom they saw as leaders of resistance), while, at the same time, doing his best to use his more general insights into the workings of Nuer society to discourage some of their more idiotic abuses, as he put it, to "humanize" the authorities.[33] As an ethnographer, then, he ended up doing something very much like traditional women's work: keeping the system from disaster by tactful interventions meant to protect the oblivious and self-important men in charge from the consequences of their blindness.

Would it have been better to have kept one's hands clean? These strike me as questions of personal conscience. I suspect the greater moral dangers lie on an entirely different level. The question for me is whether our theoretical work is ultimately directed at undoing or dismantling some of the effects of these lopsided structures of imagination, or whether—as can so easily happen when even our best ideas come to be backed up by bureaucratically administered violence—we end up reinforcing them.

VI

Social theory itself could be seen as a kind of radical simplification, a form of calculated ignorance, meant to reveal patterns one could never otherwise be able to see. This is as true of this essay as of any other. If this essay has largely sidestepped the existing anthropological literature on bureaucracy, violence, or even ignorance,[34] it is not because I don't believe this literature offers insight, but rather because I wanted to see what different insights could be gained by looking through a different lens—or, one might even say, a different set of blinders.

Still, some blinders have different effects than others. I began the essay as I did—about the paperwork surrounding my mother's illness and death—to make a point. There are dead zones that riddle our lives, areas so devoid of any possibility of interpretive depth that they seem to repel any attempt to give them value or meaning. They are spaces, as I discovered, where interpretive labor no longer works. It's hardly surprising that we don't like to talk about them. They repel the imagination. But if we ignore them entirely, we risk becoming complicit in the very violence that creates them.

It is one thing to say that, when a master whips a slave, he is engaging in a form of meaningful, communicative action, conveying the need for unquestioning obedience, and at the same time trying to create a terrifying mythic image of absolute and arbitrary power. All of this is true. It is quite another to insist that is all that is happening, or all that we need to talk about. After all, if we do not go on to explore what "unquestioning" actually means—the master's ability to remain completely unaware of the slave's understanding of any situation, the slave's inability to say anything even when she becomes aware of some dire practical flaw in the master's reasoning, the forms of blindness or stupidity that result, the fact that these oblige the slave to devote even more energy trying to understand and anticipate the master's confused perceptions—are we not, in however small a way, doing the same work as the whip? There is a reason Elaine Scarry called torture a form of "stupidity."[35] It's not really about making its victims talk. Ultimately, it's about the very opposite.

There is another reason I began with that story. As my apparently inexplicable confusion over the signatures makes clear, such dead zones can, temporarily at least, render anybody stupid—in the same way, ultimately, that my position as a male academic could make it possible for me to write a first draft of this essay entirely oblivious to the fact that many of its arguments were simply reproducing commonplace feminist ideas. All of these forms of blindness ultimately stem from trying to navigate our way through situations made possible by structural violence. It will take an enormous amount of work to begin to clear away these dead zones. But recognizing their existence is a necessary first step.

The Bully's Pulpit

On the Elementary Structure of Domination

In late February and early March 1991, during the first Gulf War, U.S. forces bombed, shelled, and otherwise set fire to thousands of young Iraqi men who were trying to flee Kuwait. There were a series of such incidents—the "Highway of Death," "Highway 8," the "Battle of Rumaila"—in which U.S. air power cut off columns of retreating Iraqis and engaged in what the military refers to as a "turkey shoot," where trapped soldiers are simply slaughtered in their vehicles. Images of charred bodies trying desperately to crawl from their trucks became iconic symbols of the war.

I have never understood why this mass slaughter of Iraqi men isn't considered a war crime. It's clear that, at the time, the U.S. command feared it might be. President George H. W. Bush quickly announced a temporary cessation of hostilities, and the military has deployed enormous efforts since then to minimize the casualty count, obscure the

Originally published in *The Baffler*, no. 28, July 2015, thebaffler.com.

circumstances, defame the victims ("a bunch of rapists, murderers, and thugs," General Norman Schwarzkopf later insisted), and prevent the most graphic images from appearing on U.S. television. It's rumored that there are videos from cameras mounted on helicopter gunships of panicked Iraqis, which will never be released.

It makes sense that the elites were worried. These were, after all, mostly young men who'd been drafted and who, when thrown into combat, made precisely the decision one would wish all young men in such a situation would make: saying to hell with this, packing up their things, and going home. For this, they should be burned alive? When ISIS burned a Jordanian pilot alive last winter, it was universally denounced as unspeakably barbaric—which it was, of course. Still, ISIS at least could point out that the pilot had been dropping bombs on them. The retreating Iraqis on the "Highway of Death" and other main drags of American carnage were just kids who didn't want to fight.

But maybe it was this very refusal that's prevented the Iraqi soldiers from garnering more sympathy, not only in elite circles, where you wouldn't expect much, but also in the court of public opinion. On some level, let's face it: these men were cowards. They got what they deserved.

There seems, indeed, a decided lack of sympathy for noncombatant men in war zones. Even reports by international human rights organizations speak of massacres as being directed almost exclusively against women, children, and, perhaps, the elderly. The implication, almost never stated outright, is that adult males are either combatants or have something wrong with them. ("You mean to say there were people out there slaughtering women and children and you weren't out there defending them? What are you? Chicken?") Those who carry out massacres have been known to cynically manipulate this tacit conscription: most famously, the Bosnian Serb commanders who calculated they could avoid charges of genocide if, instead of exterminating the entire population of conquered towns and villages, they merely exterminated all males between ages fifteen and fifty-five.

But there is something more at work in circumscribing our empathy for the fleeing Iraqi massacre victims. U.S. news consumers were bombarded with accusations that they were actually a bunch of criminals who'd been personally raping and pillaging and tossing newborn babies out of incubators (unlike that Jordanian pilot, who'd merely been dropping bombs on cities full of women and children from a safe, or so he thought, altitude). We are all taught that bullies are really cowards, so we easily accept that the reverse must naturally be true as well. For most of us, the primordial experience of bullying and being bullied lurks in the background whenever crimes and atrocities are discussed. It shapes our sensibilities and our capacities for empathy in deep and pernicious ways.

COWARDICE IS A CAUSE TOO

Most people dislike wars and feel the world would be a better place without them. Yet contempt for cowardice seems to move them on a far deeper level. After all, desertion—the tendency of conscripts called up for their first experience of military glory to duck out of the line of march and hide in the nearest forest, gulch, or empty farmhouse and then, when the column has safely passed, figure out a way to return home—is probably the greatest threat to wars of conquest. Napoleon's armies, for instance, lost far more troops to desertion than to combat. Conscript armies often have to deploy a significant percentage of their conscripts behind the lines with orders to shoot any of their fellow conscripts who try to run away. Yet even those who claim to hate war often feel uncomfortable celebrating desertion.

About the only real exception I know of is Germany, which has erected a series of monuments labeled "To the Unknown Deserter." The first and most famous, in Potsdam, is inscribed: TO A MAN WHO REFUSED TO KILL HIS FELLOW MAN. Yet even here, when I tell friends about this monument, I often encounter a sort of instinctive wince. I guess what people will ask is: "Did they really desert because they didn't want to kill others, or because they didn't want to die themselves?" As if there's something wrong with that.

In militaristic societies like the United States, it is almost axiomatic

that our enemies must be cowards—especially if the enemy can be labeled a "terrorist" (i.e., someone accused of wishing to create fear in us,
to turn us, of all people, into cowards). It is then necessary to ritually
turn matters around and insist that no, it is they who are actually fear-
ful. All attacks on U.S. citizens are by definition "cowardly attacks." The
second George Bush was referring to the 9/11 attacks as "cowardly acts"
the very next morning. On the face of it, this is odd. After all, there's no
lack of bad things one can find to say about Mohammed Atta and his
confederates—take your pick, really—but surely "coward" isn't one of
them. Blowing up a wedding party using an unmanned drone might
be considered an act of cowardice. Personally flying an airplane into a
skyscraper takes guts. Nevertheless, the idea that one can be courageous
in a bad cause seems to somehow fall outside the domain of acceptable
public discourse, despite the fact that much of what passes for world
history consists of endless accounts of courageous people doing awful
things.

ON FUNDAMENTAL FLAWS

Sooner or later, every project for human freedom will have to compre-
hend why we accept societies being ranked and ordered by violence and
domination to begin with. And it strikes me that our visceral reaction to
weakness and cowardice, our strange reluctance to identify with even the
most justifiable forms of fear, might provide a clue. The problem is that
debate so far has been dominated by proponents of two equally absurd
positions. On the one side, there are those who deny that it's possible to
say anything about humans as a species; on the other, there are those
who assume that the goal is to explain why it is that some humans seem
to take pleasure in pushing other ones around. The latter camp almost
invariably ends up spinning stories about baboons and chimps, usually
to introduce the proposition that humans—or at least those of us with
sufficient quantities of testosterone—inherit from our primate ancestors
an inbuilt tendency toward self-aggrandizing aggression that manifests
itself in war, which cannot be gotten rid of, but may be diverted into

competitive market activity. On the basis of these assumptions, the cowards are those who lack a fundamental biological impulse, and it's hardly surprising that we would hold them in contempt.

There are a lot of problems with this story, but the most obvious is that it simply isn't true. The prospect of going to war does not automatically set off a biological trigger in the human male. Just consider what Andrew Bard Schmookler has referred to as "the parable of the tribes." Five societies share the same river valley. They can all live in peace only if every one of them remains peaceful. The moment one "bad apple" is introduced—say, the young men in one tribe decide that an appropriate way of handling the loss of a loved one is to go bring back some foreigner's head, or that their God has chosen them to be the scourge of unbelievers—well, the other tribes, if they don't want to be exterminated, have only three options: flee, submit, or reorganize their own societies around effectiveness in war. The logic seems hard to fault. Nevertheless, as anyone familiar with the history of, say, Oceania, Amazonia, or Africa would be aware, a great many societies simply refused to organize themselves on military lines. Again and again, we encounter descriptions of relatively peaceful communities who just accepted that every few years, they'd have to take to the hills as some raiding party of local bad boys arrived to torch their villages, rape, pillage, and carry off trophy parts from hapless stragglers. The vast majority of human males have refused to spend their time training for war, even when it was in their immediate practical interest to do so. To me, this is proof positive that human beings are not a particularly bellicose species.[1]

No one would deny, of course, that humans are flawed creatures. Just about every human language has some analogue of the English *humane* or expressions like "to treat someone like a human being," implying that simply recognizing another creature as a fellow human entails a responsibility to treat them with a certain minimum of kindness, consideration, and respect. It is obvious, however, that nowhere do humans consistently live up to that responsibility. And when we fail, we shrug and say we're "only human." To be human, then, is both to have ideals and to fail to live up to them.

If this is how humans tend to think of themselves, then it's hardly surprising that when we try to understand what makes structures of violent domination possible, we tend to look at the existence of antisocial impulses and ask: Why are some people cruel? Why do they desire to dominate others? These, however, are exactly the wrong questions to ask. Humans have an endless variety of urges. Usually, they're pulling us in any number of different directions at once. Their mere existence implies nothing.

The question we should be asking is not why people are sometimes cruel, or even why a few people are usually cruel (all evidence suggests true sadists are an extremely small proportion of the population overall), but how we have come to create institutions that encourage such behavior and that suggest cruel people are in some ways admirable—or at least as deserving of sympathy as those they push around.

Here I think it's important to look carefully at how institutions organize the reactions of the audience. Usually, when we try to imagine the primordial scene of domination, we see some kind of Hegelian master-slave dialectic in which two parties are vying for recognition from each other, leading to one being permanently trampled underfoot. We should imagine instead a three-way relation of aggressor, victim, and witness, one in which both contending parties are appealing for recognition (validation, sympathy, etc.) from someone else. The Hegelian battle for supremacy, after all, is just an abstraction. A just-so story. Few of us have witnessed two grown men duel to the death in order to get the other to recognize him as truly human. The three-way scenario, in which one party pummels another while both appeal to those around them to recognize their humanity, we've all witnessed and participated in, taking one role or the other, a thousand times since grade school.

ELEMENTARY (SCHOOL) STRUCTURES OF DOMINATION

I am speaking, of course, about schoolyard bullying. Bullying, I propose, represents a kind of elementary structure of human domination. If we want to understand how everything goes wrong, this is where we should begin.

In this case, too, provisos must be introduced. It would be very easy to slip back into crude evolutionary arguments. There is a tradition of thought—the *Lord of the Flies* tradition, we might call it—that interprets schoolyard bullies as a modern incarnation of the ancestral "killer ape," the primordial alpha male who instantly restores the law of the jungle once no longer restrained by rational adult male authority. But this is clearly false. In fact, books like *Lord of the Flies* are better read as meditations on the kind of calculated techniques of terror and intimidation that British "public" schools employed to shape upper-class children into officials capable of running an empire. These techniques did not emerge in the absence of authority; they were techniques designed to create a certain sort of cold-blooded, calculating adult male authority to begin with.

Today, most schools are not like the Eton and Harrow of William Golding's day, but even at those that boast of their elaborate antibullying programs, schoolyard bullying happens in a way that's in no sense at odds with or in spite of the school's institutional authority. Bullying is more like a refraction of its authority. To begin with an obvious point: children in school can't leave. Normally, a child's first instinct upon being tormented or humiliated by someone much larger is to go someplace else. Schoolchildren, however, don't have that option. If they try persistently to flee to safety, the authorities will bring them back. This is one reason, I suspect, for the stereotype of the bully as teacher's pet or hall monitor: even when it's not true, it draws on the tacit knowledge that the bully does depend on the authority of the institution in at least that one way—the school is, effectively, holding the victims in place while their tormentors hit them. This dependency on authority is also why the most extreme and elaborate forms of bullying take place in prisons, where dominant inmates and prison guards fall into alliances.

Even more, bullies are usually aware that the system is likely to punish any victim who strikes back more harshly. Just as a woman, confronted by an abusive man who may well be twice her size, cannot afford to engage in a "fair fight," but must seize the opportune moment to inflict as much as damage as possible on the man who's been abusing her—since she cannot leave him in a position to retaliate—so, too, must the schoolyard bullying victim respond with disproportionate force, not to disable the opponent, in this case, but to deliver a blow so decisive that it makes the antagonist hesitate to engage again.

I learned this lesson firsthand. I was scrawny in grade school, younger than my peers—I'd skipped a grade—and thus a prime target for some of the bigger kids who seemed to have developed a quasi-scientific technique of jabbing runts like me sharp, hard, and quick enough to avoid being accused of "fighting." Hardly a day went by that I was not attacked. Finally, I decided enough was enough, found my moment, and sent one particularly noxious galoot sprawling across the corridor with a well-placed blow to the head. I think I might have cracked his lip. In a way, it worked exactly as intended: for a month or two, bullies largely stayed away. But the immediate result was that we were both taken to the office for fighting, and the fact that he had struck first was determined to be irrelevant. I was found to be the guilty party and expelled from the school's advanced math and science club. (Since he was a C student, there was nothing, really, for him to be expelled from.)

"It doesn't matter who started it" are probably six of the most insidious words in the English language. Of course it matters.

CROWDSOURCED CRUELTY

Very little of this focus on the role of institutional authority is reflected in the psychological literature on bullying, which, being largely written for school authorities, assumes that their role is entirely benign. Still, recent research—of which there has been an outpouring since Columbine—has yielded, I think, a number of surprising revelations about the elementary forms of domination. Let's go deeper.

The first thing this research reveals is that the overwhelming majority of bullying incidents take place in front of an audience. Lonely, private persecution is relatively rare. Much of bullying is about humiliation, and the effects cannot really be produced without someone to witness them. Sometimes, onlookers actively abet the bully, laughing, goading, or joining in. More often, the audience is passively acquiescent. Only rarely does anyone step in to defend a classmate being threatened, mocked, or physically attacked.

When researchers question children on why they do not intervene, a minority say they felt the victim got what he or she deserved, but the majority say they didn't like what happened, and certainly didn't much like the bully, but decided that getting involved might mean ending up on the receiving end of the same treatment—and that would only make things worse. Interestingly, this is not true. Studies also show that in general, if one or two onlookers object, then bullies back off. Yet somehow most onlookers are convinced the opposite will happen. Why?

For one thing, because nearly every genre of popular fiction they are likely to be exposed to tells them it will. Comic book superheroes routinely step in to say, "Hey, stop beating on that kid"—and invariably the culprit does indeed turn his wrath on them, resulting in all sorts of mayhem. (If there is a covert message in such fiction, it is surely along the lines of: "You had better not get involved in such matters unless you are capable of taking on some monster from another dimension who can shoot lightning from its eyes.") The "hero," as deployed in the U.S. media, is largely an alibi for passivity. This first occurred to me when watching a small-town TV newscaster praising some teenager who'd jumped into a river to save a drowning child. "When I asked him why he did it," the newscaster remarked, "he said what true heroes always say, 'I just did what anyone would do under the circumstances.'" The audience is supposed to understand that, of course, this isn't true. Anyone would not do that. And that's okay. Heroes are extraordinary. It's perfectly acceptable under the same circumstances for you to just stand there and wait for a professional rescue team.

It's also possible that audiences of grade schoolers react passively to bullying because they have caught on to how adult authority operates and mistakenly assume the same logic applies to interactions with their peers. If it is, say, a police officer who is pushing around some hapless adult, then yes, it is absolutely true that intervening is likely to land you in serious trouble—quite possibly, at the wrong end of a club. And we all know what happens to "whistleblowers." (Remember Secretary of State John Kerry calling on Edward Snowden to "man up" and submit himself to a lifetime of sadistic bullying at the hands of the U.S. criminal justice system? What is an innocent child supposed to make of this?) The fates of the Mannings or Snowdens of the world are high-profile advertisements for a cardinal principle of American culture: while abusing authority may be bad, openly pointing out that someone is abusing authority is much worse—and merits the severest punishment.

A second surprising finding from recent research: bullies do not, in fact, suffer from low self-esteem. Psychologists had long assumed that mean kids were taking out their insecurities on others. No. It turns out that most bullies act like self-satisfied little pricks not because they are tortured by self-doubt, but because they actually are self-satisfied little pricks. Indeed, such is their self-assurance that they create a moral universe in which their swagger and violence becomes the standard by which all others are to be judged; weakness, clumsiness, absentmindedness, or self-righteous whining are not just sins, but provocations that would be wrong to leave unaddressed.

Here, too, I can offer personal testimony. I keenly remember a conversation with a jock I knew in high school. He was a lunk, but a good-natured one. I think we'd even gotten stoned together once or twice. One day, after rehearsing some costume drama, I thought it would be fun to walk into the dorm in Renaissance garb. As soon as he saw me, he pounced as if about to pulverize. I was so indignant I forgot to be terrified. "Matt! What the hell are you doing? Why would you want to attack me?" Matt seemed so taken aback that he forgot to continue menacing me. "But . . . you came into the dorm wearing tights!" he protested. "I mean, what did you expect?" Was Matt enacting deep-seated insecurities about his own sexuality? I don't know. Probably so. But the real question is, why do we assume his troubled mind is so important? What really matters was that he genuinely felt he was defending a social code.

In this instance, the adolescent bully was deploying violence to enforce a code of homophobic masculinity that underpins adult authority as well. But with smaller children, this is often not the case. Here we come to a third surprising finding of the psychological literature—maybe the most telling of all. At first, it's not actually the fat girl, or the boy with glasses, who is most likely to be targeted. That comes later, as bullies (ever cognizant of power relations) learn to choose their victims according to adult standards. At first, the principal criterion is how the victim reacts. The ideal victim is not absolutely passive. No, the ideal victim is one who fights back in some way but does so ineffectively, by flailing about, say, or screaming or crying, threatening to tell their mother, pretending they're going to fight and then trying to run away. Doing so is precisely what makes it possible to create a moral drama in which the audience can tell itself the bully must be, in some sense, in the right.

This triangular dynamic among bully, victim, and audience is what I mean by the deep structure of bullying. It deserves to be analyzed in the textbooks. Actually, it deserves to be set in giant neon letters everywhere: Bullying creates a moral drama in which the manner of the victim's reaction to an act of aggression can be used as retrospective justification for the original act of aggression itself.

Not only does this drama appear at the very origins of bullying in early childhood; it is precisely the aspect that endures in adult life. I call it the "you two cut it out" fallacy. Anyone who frequents social media forums will recognize the pattern. Aggressor attacks. Target tries to rise above and do nothing. No one intervenes. Aggressor ramps up attack. Target tries to rise above and do nothing. No one intervenes. Aggressor further ramps up attack.

This can happen a dozen, fifty times, until finally, the target answers back. Then, and only then, a dozen voices immediately sound, crying "Fight! Fight! Look at those two idiots going at it!" or "Can't you two just calm down and learn to see the other's point of view?" The clever bully knows that this will happen—and that he will forfeit no points for being the aggressor. He also knows that if he tempers his aggression to just the right pitch, the victim's response can itself be represented as the problem.

>   NOB: You're a decent chap, Jeeves, but I must say, you're a bit of an
>   imbecile.
>   JEEVES: A bit of a . . . what?? What the hell do you mean by that?
>   NOB: See what I mean? Calm down! I said you were a decent chap.
>   And such language! Don't you realize there are ladies present?

And what is true of social class is also true of any other form of structural inequality: hence epithets such as "shrill women," "angry black men," and an endless variety of similar terms of dismissive contempt. But the essential logic of bullying is prior to such inequalities. It is the ur-stuff of which they are made.

STOP HITTING YOURSELF

And this, I propose, is the critical human flaw. It's not that as a species we're particularly aggressive. It's that we tend to respond to aggression very poorly. Our first instinct when we observe unprovoked aggression is either to pretend it isn't happening or, if that becomes impossible, to equate attacker and victim, placing both under a kind of contagion, which, it is hoped, can be prevented from spreading to everybody else. (Hence, the psychologists' finding that bullies and victims tend to be about equally disliked.) The feeling of guilt caused by the suspicion that this is a fundamentally cowardly way to behave—since it is a fundamentally cowardly way to behave—opens up a complex play of projections, in which the bully is seen simultaneously as an unconquerable supervillain and a pitiable, insecure blowhard, while the victim becomes both an aggressor (a violator of whatever social conventions the bully has invoked or invented) and a pathetic coward unwilling to defend himself.

Obviously, I am offering only the most minimal sketch of complex psychodynamics. But even so, these insights may help us understand why we find it so difficult to extend our sympathies to, among others, fleeing Iraqi conscripts gunned down in "turkey shoots" by U.S. war-riors. We apply the same logic we did when passively watching some childhood bully terrorizing his flailing victim: we equate aggressors and victims, insist that everyone is equally guilty (notice how, whenever one hears a report of an atrocity, some will immediately start insisting that the victims must have committed atrocities too), and just hope that by doing so, the contagion will not spread to us.

This is difficult stuff. I don't claim to understand it completely. But if we are ever going to move toward a genuinely free society, then we're going to have to recognize how the triangular and mutually constitu-tive relationship of bully, victim, and audience really works, and then develop ways to combat it. Remember, the situation isn't hopeless. If it were not possible to create structures—habits, sensibilities, forms of common wisdom—that do sometimes prevent the dynamic from click-ing in, then egalitarian societies of any sort would never have been pos-sible. Remember, too, how little courage is usually required to thwart bullies who are not backed up by any sort of institutional power. Most of all, remember that when the bullies really are backed up by such power, the heroes may be those who simply run away.

I Didn't Understand How Widespread Rape Was. Then the Penny Dropped

This is a very difficult column for me to write because it's about my mother.

A week or two after the then IMF director Dominique Strauss-Kahn was arrested for sexually assaulting a chambermaid in a posh New York hotel in 2011, there was another case when an Egyptian businessman was briefly arrested for a similar assault at another such New York hotel.

This first struck me as puzzling. It could hardly be a copycat crime; considering the drama surrounding the arrest and travails of DSK, it was inconceivable that anyone would see this and say: "Oh, good idea, I'll attack a chambermaid as well."

Then it dawned on me.

The only logical explanation was that businessmen, politicians, officials, and financiers rape, or attempt to rape, hotel workers all the time. It's just that normally, those assaulted know there's nothing they can do about it.

Originally published in *The Guardian*, November 5, 2017, theguardian.com.

In DSK's case, someone—for whatever complex political reasons—must have refused to make the usual phone call. There was a scandal. As a result, when the next assault took place, the survivor must have said to herself, "Oh, so does this mean we actually *are* allowed to call the cops now if a customer tries to rape us?" and acted accordingly. And sure enough this is precisely what turned out to have happened. (In the end, both women were silenced, and neither man convicted of any crime.)

What I really want to draw attention to here is my initial reaction of disbelief: "Sure things are bad; *but it can't be that bad.*" Even a lefty academic versed in feminist theory instinctively rebelled against the idea that rich and powerful men regularly rape or attempt to rape the women cleaning their rooms, that this happens all the time, that everyone in the hotel industry knows it happens (since they must know), and that those rich and powerful men in turn know they could get away with it because if any woman they attacked did protest too strenuously, everyone would move in lockstep to do whatever was required to make the problem go away.

It's of course this very disbelief that allows such things to happen. We are loath to accept people we know might practice pure, naked aggression. This is how bullies get away with what they do. I've written about this.

Bullying is not just a relation between bully and victim. It's really a three-way relation, between bully, victim and everyone who refuses to do anything about the aggression; all those people who say "boys will be boys" or pretend there's some equivalence between aggressor and aggressed. Who see a conflict and say "it doesn't matter who started it" even in cases where, in reality, nothing could possibly matter more.

It makes no difference if there's a real physical audience or if the audience just exists inside the victim's head. You know what will happen if you fight back. You know what people will say about you. You internalize it. Before long, even if nothing is said, you can't help wonder if these things they *would* say are actually true.

Sexual predation is a particular variety of bullying but like all forms of bullying it operates above all in precisely this way, by destroying the victim's sense of self.

I had another, similar, horrified moment of realization in reading Dame Emma Thompson's remarks about Harvey Weinstein. Not because of her observation that his predations were, as she said, "the tip of the iceberg"—this is surely true, but not entirely unknown; what startled me was one word. She described Weinstein's behavior as typical of "a system of harassment and belittling and bullying and interference" that women had faced from time immemorial.

The word that struck me was *belittling*.

This is where the story becomes personal.

Let me tell you about my mother. Mom was a prodigy. Arriving in America at age ten, speaking not a word of English, she skipped so many grades she was in college by sixteen. Then she dropped out of college to help the family (it was the Depression) by getting a factory job sewing brassieres.

The union had the crazy idea at that time to put on a musical comedy performed entirely by garment workers. The play (*Pins and Needles*) surprised everyone by becoming a smash hit on Broadway, with Mom (then Ruth Rubinstein) as female lead.

She was hailed as a comic genius, which I can attest she definitely was, was featured in *Life*, met FDR and Gypsy Rose Lee, and for three years hobnobbed with celebrities and was gossiped about in gossip columns. Then she went back to working in the factory again.

Eventually she met my father, then a sailor; he found work in offset lithography, she dedicated herself to raising me and my brother, along with a variety of local activist projects and occasional part-time jobs.

As a child it never occurred to me to ask why she never continued in the theater, even though she followed it avidly, or went back to college, even though she filled the house with books, or pursued her own career.

When I later asked she'd just say, "I lacked self-confidence." But once I remember the phrase "casting couch" came up and I asked her if such things had existed in her day. She threw her eyes up and said, "Well, why do you think I never pursued a career in show business? Some of us were willing to sleep with producers. I wasn't."

This is why I'd like to get my thumbs on the throat of Harvey Weinstein. It's not just that creeps like him drove my mother off the stage. It's that in the process, they broke something. I don't know what actually happened, or if any one specific thing even did happen; but the result was to leave her convinced she was unworthy; intellectually superficial; not genuinely talented; a lightweight; a fraud.

Because just as everyone associated with hotels falls into lockstep to tell chambermaids they are unworthy of protection from rapists, so did everything in my mother's environment conspire to tell her she had no grounds for complaint if someone told her she was unworthy to continue to perform on stage, whatever her attainments, without also performing in private as a part-time sex worker.

As a result, her sense of self collapsed.

All of us are heirs to a thousand forms of violence. Many shape our lives in ways we'll never know. My mother was an enormous human stuck in a tiny box. Late in her life she was still hilariously funny; but she also collected tea towels with inscriptions like "Don't expect miracles."

She raised me to assume I was destined for greatness (like her, I was considered something of a prodigy), then would fall into inexplicable depression for days that would invariably end with her lashing out at me as a terrible, selfish, uncaring person for not properly cleaning my room.

Only now do I understand she was really lashing out at even having to care about my room. Later she lived in part vicariously through me but also—I have to assume—was racked by guilt for any indignation she could not help but feel that this was the only way she could live the kind of life she should have had.

In endless ways, the violence of powerful men plays havoc with our souls. It makes us complicit in acts of mutual destruction. It's too late now for my mother. She died ten years ago, taking the details of what happened with her. But if we can do anything for her now, can't we at least break out of lockstep?

Let's stop pretending these things can't really be happening—and then, as soon as we learn it did happen, telling the person it happened to, "Well, what else did you expect?"

On the Phenomenology of Giant Puppets

Broken Windows, Imaginary Jars of Urine, and
the Cosmological Role of the Police in American Culture

What follows is an essay of interpretation. It is about direct action in North America, about the mass mobilizations organized by the so-called anti-globalization movement, and especially, about the war of images that has surrounded it. It begins with a simple observation. I think it's fair to say that if the average American knows just two things about these mobilizations, they are, first of all, that there are often people dressed in black who break windows; second, that they involve colorful giant puppets.

I want to start by asking why these images in particular appear to have so struck the popular imagination. I also want to ask why it is that of the two, American police seem to hate the puppets more. As many activists have observed, the forces of order in the United States seem to

Originally published in *Possibilities: Essays on Hierarchy, Rebellion, and Desire* (Oakland, CA: AK Press, 2007).

have a profound aversion to giant puppets. Often police strategies aim to destroy or capture them before they can even appear on the streets. As a result, a major concern for those planning actions soon became how to hide the puppets so they would not be destroyed in preemptive attacks. What's more, for many individual officers at least, the objection to puppets appeared to be not merely strategic, but personal, even visceral. Cops hate puppets. Activists are puzzled as to why.

To some degree this essay emerges from that puzzlement. It is written very much from the perspective of a participant. I have been involved in the global justice movement[1] for six years now, having helped to organize and taken part in actions small and large, and I have spent a good time wondering about such questions myself. If this were simply an essay on police psychology, of course, my involvement would put me at a significant disadvantage, since it makes it difficult to carry out detailed interviews with police. Granted, being active in the movement does afford frequent occasions for casual chats with cops. But such chats aren't always the most enlightening. The only extended conversation I ever had with police officers on the subject of puppets, on the other hand, was carried out while I was handcuffed—which if nothing else makes it very difficult to take notes. At any rate, this essay is not so much about the particulars of police, or activist, psychology as what the Annales school historians liked to call a "structure of the conjuncture": the peculiar—and endlessly shifting—symbolic interactions of state, capital, mass media, and oppositional movements that the globalization movement has sparked. Since any strategic planning must start from an understanding of such matters, those engaged in planning such actions end up endlessly discussing the current state of this conjuncture. I see this essay, therefore, as a contribution to an ongoing conversation—one that is necessarily aesthetic, critical, ethical, and political all at the same time. I also see it as ultimately pursuing the movements' aims and aspirations in another form. To ask these questions—Why puppets? Why windows? Why do these images seem to have such mythic power? Why do representatives of the state react the way they do? What is the public's perception? What is "the public," anyway? How would it be possible to transform "the public" into something else?—is to begin to try to piece together the tacit rules of the game of symbolic warfare, from its elementary assumptions to the details of how the terms of engagement are negotiated in any given action, ultimately, to understand the stakes in new forms of revolutionary politics. I am myself personally convinced that such understandings are themselves revolutionary in their implications.

Hence the unusual structure of this essay, in which an analysis of the symbolism of puppets leads to a discussion of police media strategies, to reflections on the very nature of violence and the state of international politics. It is an attempt to understand a historical moment from the perspective of someone situated inside it.

A PROBLEMATIC

There is a widespread perception that events surrounding the WTO ministerial in Seattle in November 1999 marked the birth of a new movement in North America. It would probably be better to say that Seattle marked the moment when a much larger, global movement—one that traces back at least to the Zapatista rebellion in 1994—made its first appearance on North American shores.

Nonetheless, the actions in Seattle were widely considered a spectacular victory. They were quickly followed in 2000 and 2001 by a series of similar mobilizations in Washington, Prague, Quebec City, and Genoa, growing in size but facing increasing levels of state repression. September 11 and the subsequent "war on terror" changed the nature of the playing field, enabling governments to step up this repression quite dramatically, as became clear in the United States with the extraordinary violence of police tactics when confronting protesters during the Free Trade Areas of the Americas summit in Miami in November 2003. Since then the movement has largely been in a process of regrouping, though at the time of writing (summer 2006) there are increasing signs of a second wind.

The movement's disarray was not simply due to heightened levels of repression. Another reason was, however paradoxical this may seem, that it reached so many of its immediate goals so quickly.

After Seattle, the WTO process froze in its tracks and has never really recovered. Most ambitious global trade schemes were scotched. The effects on political discourse were even more remarkable. In fact, the change was so dramatic that it has become difficult, for many, to even remember what public discourse in the years immediately before Seattle was actually like. In the late '90s, the "Washington consensus," as it was then called, simply had no significant challengers. In the United States itself, politicians and journalists appeared to have come to unanimous agreement that radical "free market reforms" were the only possible approach to economic development, anywhere and everywhere. In the mainstream media, anyone who challenged the basic tenets of this faith was likely to be treated as if they were almost literally insane. Speaking as someone who became active in the first months of 2000, I can attest that, however exhilarated by what had happened at Seattle, most of us still felt it would take five or ten years to shatter these assumptions. In fact it took less than two. By late 2001, it was commonplace to see even news journals that had just months before denounced protesters as so many ignorant children declaring that we had won the war of ideas. Much as the movement against nuclear power discovered in the '70s and early '80s, the direct action approach was so effective that short-term goals were reached almost immediately, forcing participants to have to scramble to redefine what the movement was actually about. Splits quickly developed between the "anticorporates" and the "anticapitalists."

As anarchist ideas and forms of organization became increasingly important, unions and NGOs began to draw back. What's critical for present purposes is that all this became a problem largely because the initial movement was so successful in getting its message out.

I must, however, introduce one crucial qualification. This success applied only to the movement's *negative* message—what we were against. That organizations such as the IMF, WTO, and World Bank were inherently unaccountable and undemocratic, that neoliberal policies were devastating the planet and throwing millions of human beings into death, poverty, hopelessness, and despair—all this, we found, was relatively easy to communicate. While mainstream media were never willing to quote our spokespeople or run the editorials we sent them, it wasn't long before accredited pundits and talking heads (encouraged by renegade economists like Joseph Stiglitz), began simply repeating the same things as if they'd made them up themselves. Admittedly, American newspaper columnists were not going to repeat the whole of the movement's arguments—they certainly were not willing to repeat anything that suggested these problems were ultimately rooted in the very nature of the state and capitalism. But the immediate message did get out.

Not so for what most in the movement were actually *for*. If there was one central inspiration to the global justice movement, it was the principle of direct action. This is a notion very much at the heart of the anarchist tradition and, in fact, most of the movement's central organizers—more and more in fact as time went on—considered themselves anarchists, or at least heavily influenced by anarchist ideas. They saw mass mobilizations not only as opportunities to expose the illegitimate, undemocratic nature of existing institutions, but as ways to do so in a form that itself demonstrated why such institutions were unnecessary, by providing a living example of genuine, direct democracy. The key word here is *process*—meaning decision-making process. When members of the Direct Action Network or similar groups are considering whether to work with some other group, the first question that's likely to be asked is "What sort of process do they use?"—that is: Do they practice internal democracy? Do they vote or use consensus? Is there a formal leadership? Such questions are usually considered of much more immediate importance than questions of ideology.[2] Similarly, if one talks to someone fresh from a major mobilization and asks what she found most new and exciting about the experience, one is most likely to hear long descriptions of the organization of affinity groups, clusters, blockades, flying squads, spokescouncils, network structures, or about the apparent miracle of consensus decision-making in which one can see thousands of people coordinate their actions without any formal leadership structure. There is a technical term for all this: "prefigurative politics." Direct action is a form of resistance that, in its structure, is meant to prefigure the genuinely free society one wishes to create. Revolutionary action is not a form of self-sacrifice, a grim dedication to doing whatever it takes to achieve a future world of freedom. It is the defiant insistence on acting as if one is already free.

The positive message, then, was a new vision of democracy. In its ability to get it out before a larger public, though, the movement has been strikingly unsuccessful. Groups like the Direct Action Network have been fairly effective in disseminating their models of decision-making within activist circles (since they do, in fact, work remarkably well), but beyond those circles, they have had very little luck. Early attempts to provoke a public debate about the nature of democracy were invariably brushed aside by the mainstream media. As for the new forms of organization: readers of mainstream newspapers or TV viewers, even those who followed stories about the movement fairly assiduously, would have had little way of knowing that they existed.

MEDIA IMAGES

I do not want to leave the reader with the impression that many of those involved in the global justice movement see their main task as getting a message out through the media. It is a somewhat unusual feature of this new movement that large elements of it are openly hostile to any attempt to influence what they called the "corporate media," or even, in many cases, to engage with it at all.

Companies like CNN or the Associated Press, they argue, are capitalist firms; it would be utterly naïve to imagine they would be willing to provide a friendly venue for anyone actively opposed to capitalism—let alone to carry anticapitalist messages to the public. Some argue that, as a key element in the structure of power, the media apparatus should itself be considered an appropriate target for direct action. One of the greatest accomplishments of the movement, in fact, has been to develop an entirely new, alternative media network—Independent Media, an international, participatory, activist-driven, largely internet-based media project that has, since Seattle, provided moment-to-moment coverage of large mobilizations in email, print, radio, and video forms.

All this is very much in the spirit of direct action. Nonetheless, there are always activists—even anarchists—who are willing to do more traditional media work. I myself can often be counted among them. During several mobilizations, I ended up spending much of my time preparing press conferences, attending meetings on daily spins and sound bites, and fielding calls from reporters. I have in fact been the object of severe opprobrium from certain hard-core anarchist circles as a result. Still, I think the anarchist critique is largely correct—especially in America. In my own experience, editors and most reporters in this country are inherently suspicious of protests, which they tend to see not as real news stories but as artificial events concocted to influence them.[3] They seem willing to cover artificial events only when constituted by proper authorities. When they do cover activist events, they are very self-conscious about the danger that they might be manipulated—particularly if they see protests as "violent." For journalists, there is an inherent dilemma here, because violence in itself is inherently newsworthy. A "violent" protest is far more likely to be covered; but for that reason, the last thing journalists would wish to think of themselves as doing is allowing violent protesters to "hijack" the media to convey a message. The matter is further complicated by the fact that journalists have a fairly idiosyncratic definition of *violence*: something like "damage to persons or property not authorized by properly constituted authorities." This has the effect that if even one protester damages a Starbucks window, one can speak of "violent protests," but if police then proceed to attack everyone present with Tasers, sticks, and plastic bullets, this cannot be described as violent. In these circumstances, it's hardly surprising that anarchist media teams mainly end up doing damage control.

One can now begin to understand the environment in which images of Black Bloc anarchists smashing windows, and colorful puppets, predominate media coverage. "Message" is largely off-limits. Almost every major mobilization has been accompanied by a day of public seminars in which radical intellectuals analyze the policies of the IMF, G8, and so on, and discuss possible alternatives. None to my knowledge have ever been covered by the corporate press. "Process" is complicated and difficult to capture visually; meetings are usually off-limits to reporters anyway. Still, the relative lack of attention to street blockades and street parties, lockdowns, banner drops, critical mass rides, and the like is harder to explain. All these are dramatic, public, and often quite visually striking. Admittedly since it is almost impossible to describe those engaged in such tactics as "violent," the fact that they frequently end up gassed, beaten, pepper-sprayed, shot at with plastic bullets, and otherwise manhandled by police provides narrative dilemmas most journalists would (apparently) prefer to avoid.[4] But this alone does not seem an adequate explanation.[5]

We return then to my initial observation: that there would seem to be something compelling about the paired images of masked window-breakers and giant puppets. Why?

Well, if nothing else the two do mark a kind of neat structural opposition. Anarchists in Black Bloc mean to render themselves anonymous and interchangeable, identifiable only by their political affinity, their willingness to engage in militant tactics, and their solidarity with one another. Hence the uniform black hooded sweatshirts and black bandannas worn as masks. The papier-mâché puppets used in actions are all unique and individual: they tend to be brightly painted, but otherwise to vary wildly in size, shape, and conception. So on the one hand one has faceless, black anonymous figures, all roughly the same; on the other polychrome goddesses and birds and pigs and politicians. One is a mass, anonymous, destructive, deadly serious; the other, a multiplicity of spectacular displays of whimsical creativity.

If the paired images seem somehow powerful, I would suggest, it is because their juxtaposition does, in fact, say something important about what direct action aims to achieve. Let me begin by considering property destruction. Such acts are anything but random. They tend to follow strict ethical guidelines: individual possessions are off-limits, for example, along with any commercial property that's the base of its owner's immediate livelihood. Every possible precaution is to be taken to avoid harming actual human beings. The targets—often carefully researched in advance—are corporate facades, banks and mass retail outlets, government buildings or other symbols of state power. When describing their strategic vision, anarchists tend to draw on Situationism (Debord and Vaneigem have always been the most popular French theorists in anarchist infoshops). Consumer capitalism renders us isolated passive spectators, our only relation to one another our shared fascination with an endless play of images that are, ultimately, representations of the very sense of wholeness and community we have thus lost. Property destruction, then, is an attempt to "break the spell," to divert and redefine. It is a direct assault upon the Spectacle. Consider here the words of the famous N30 Seattle Black Bloc communiqué, from the section entitled "On the Violence of Property":

When we smash a window, we aim to destroy the thin veneer of legitimacy that surrounds private property rights. At the same time, we exorcise that set of violent and destructive social relationships which has been imbued in almost everything around us. By "destroying" private property, we convert its limited exchange value into an expanded use value. A storefront window becomes a vent to let some fresh air into the oppressive atmosphere of a retail outlet (at least until the police decide to tear-gas a nearby road blockade). A newspaper box becomes a tool for creating such vents or a small blockade for the reclamation of public space or an object to improve one's vantage point by standing on it. A dumpster becomes an obstruction to a phalanx of rioting cops and a source of heat and light. A building facade becomes a message board to record brainstorm ideas for a better world.

After N30, many people will never see a shop window or a hammer the same way again. The potential uses of an entire cityscape have increased a thousand-fold. The number of broken windows pales in comparison to the number of broken spells— spells cast by a corporate hegemony to lull us into forgetfulness of all the violence committed in the name of private property rights and of all the potential of a society without them. Broken windows can be boarded up (with yet more waste of our forests) and eventually replaced, but the shattering of assumptions will hopefully persist for some time to come.[6]

Property destruction is a matter of taking an urban landscape full of endless corporate facades and flashing imagery that seems immutable, permanent, monumental—and demonstrating just how fragile it really is. It is a literal shattering of illusions.

What, then, of puppets?

Again, they seem the perfect complement. Giant papier-mâché puppets are created by taking the most ephemeral of material—ideas, paper, wire mesh—and transforming it into something very like a monument, even if they are, at the same time, somewhat ridiculous. A giant puppet is the mockery of the idea of a monument,[7] and of everything monuments represent: the inapproachability, monochrome solemnity, above all the implication of permanence, the state's (itself ultimately somewhat ridiculous) attempt to turn its principle and history into eternal verities. If one is meant to shatter the existing Spectacle, the other is, it seems to me, to suggest the permanent capacity to create new ones.

In fact, from the perspective of the activists, it is again process—in this case, the process of production—that is really the point. There are brainstorming sessions to come up with themes and visions, organizing meetings, but above all, the wires and frames lie on the floors of garages or yards or warehouses or similar quasi-industrial spaces for days, surrounded by buckets of paint and construction materials, almost never alone, with small teams in attendance, molding, painting, smoking, eating, playing music, arguing, wandering in and out. Everything is designed to be communal, egalitarian, expressive. The objects themselves are not expected to last. They are for the most part made of fairly delicate materials; few would withstand a heavy rainstorm; some are even self-consciously destroyed or set ablaze in the course of actions. Even otherwise, in the absence of permanent storage facilities, they usually quickly start to fall apart.

As for the images: these are clearly meant to encompass, and hence constitute, a kind of universe. Normally Puppetistas, as they sometimes call themselves, aim for a rough balance between positive and negative images. On the one hand, one might have the Giant Pig that represents the World Bank, on the other, a Giant Liberation Puppet whose arms can block an entire highway. Many of the most famous images identify marchers and the things they wear or carry: for instance, a giant bird puppet at A16 (the 2000 IMF/World Bank actions) was accompanied by hundreds of little birds on top of signs distributed to all and sundry. Similarly, Haymarket martyrs, Zapatistas, the Statue of Liberty, or a Liberation Monkeywrench might carry slogans identical to those carried on the signs, stickers, or T-shirts of those actually taking part in the action.

The most striking images, though, are often negative ones: the corporate-control puppet at the 2000 democratic convention, operating both Bush and Gore like marionettes, a giant riot policeman who shoots out pepper spray, and endless effigies to be encompassed and ridiculed.

The mocking and destruction of effigies is of course one of the oldest and most familiar gestures of political protest. Often such effigies are an explicit assault on monumentality. The fall of regimes are marked by the pulling down of statues; it was the (apparently staged) felling of the statue of Saddam Hussein in Baghdad that, in the minds of almost everyone, determined the moment of the actual end of his regime. Similarly, during George Bush's visit to Britain in 2004, protesters built innumerable mock statues of Bush, large and small, just in order to pull them down again.

Still, the positive images are often treated with little more respect than the effigies.

Here is an extract from my early reflections on the subject, jotted down shortly after spending time in the Puppet Warehouse in Philadelphia before the Republican Convention in 2000, somewhat reedited.

(FIELD NOTES EXTRACTS, JULY 31, 2000)

The question I keep asking myself is: Why are these things even called "puppets"?

Normally one thinks of "puppets" as figures that move in response to the motions of some puppeteer. Most of these have few if any moving parts. These are more light moving statues, sometimes worn, sometimes carried. So in what sense are they "puppets"?

Puppets are extremely visual, large, but also delicate and ephemeral. Usually they fall apart after a single action. This combination of huge size and lightness seems to me to make them a bridge between words and reality; they are the point of transition; they represent the ability to start to make ideas real and take on solid form, to make our view of the world into something of equal physical bulk and greater spectacular power even to the engines of state violence that stand against it. The idea that they are extensions of our minds, words, make help explain the use of the term "puppets." They may not move around as an extension of some individual's will. But if they did, this would somewhat contradict the emphasis on collective creativity.

Insofar as they are characters in a drama, it is a drama with a collective author; insofar as they are manipulated, it is in a sense by everyone, in processions, often passed around from one activist to the next. Above all, they are meant to be emanations of a collective imagination. As such, for them either to become fully solid or fully manipulable by a single individual would contradict the point.

Puppets can be worn like costumes, and in large actions, they are in fact continuous with costumes. Every major mobilization had its totem, or totems: the famous sea turtles at Seattle, the birds and sharks at A16, the Dancing Skeletons at R2K (the Republican Convention in Philly), the caribou at Bush's inauguration, or for that matter, the fragments of Picasso's *Guernica* designed for the protests against the upcoming Iraq invasion in 2003, designed so that they could each wander off and then all periodically combine together.

In fact, there are usually no clear lines between puppets, costumes, banners and symbols, and simple props. Everything is designed to overlap and reinforce one another. Puppets tend to be surrounded by a much larger "carnival bloc," replete with clowns, stilt walkers, jugglers, fire-breathers, unicyclists, Radical Cheerleaders, costumed kick lines, or often entire marching bands—such as the Infernal Noise Brigade of the Bay Area or Hungry March Band in New York—that usually specialize in klezmer or circus music, in addition to the ubiquitous drums and whistles. The circus metaphor seems to sit particularly well with anarchists, presumably because circuses are collections of extreme individuals (one can't get much more individualistic than a collection of circus freaks) nonetheless engaged in a purely cooperative enterprise that also involves transgressing ordinary boundaries. Tony Blair's famous comment in 2004 that he was not about to be swayed by "some traveling anarchist circus" was not taken, by many, as an insult. There are in fact quite a number of explicitly anarchist circus troupes, their numbers only matched, perhaps, by that of various phony preachers. The connection is significant; for now, the critical thing is that every action will normally have its circus fringe, a collection of flying squads that circulate through the large street blockades to lift spirits, perform street theater, and also, critically, to try to defuse moments of tension or potential conflict. This latter is crucial. Since direct actions, unlike permitted marches, scrupulously avoid marshals or formal peacekeepers (who police will always try to co-opt), the puppet/circus squads often end up serving some of the same functions.

Here is a firsthand account by members of one such affinity group from Chapel Hill (Paperhand Puppet Intervention) about how this might work itself out in practice.

Burger and Zimmerman brought puppets to the explosive protests of the World Trade Organization in Seattle two years ago, where they joined a group that was blockading the building in which talks were being held. "People had linked arms," Zimmerman says. "The police had beaten and pepper-sprayed them already, and they threatened that they were coming back in five minutes to attack them again." But the protesters held their line, linking arms and crying, blinded by the pepper spray.

Burger, Zimmerman, and their friends came along—on stilts, with clowns, a forty-foot puppet, and a belly dancer. They went up and down the line, leading the protesters in song. When the security van returned, they'd back the giant puppet up into its way. Somehow, this motley circus defused the situation. "They couldn't bring themselves to attack this bunch of people who were now singing songs," Zimmerman says. Injecting humor and celebration into a grim situation, he says, is the essence of a puppet intervention.[8]

For all the circus trappings, those most involved in making and deploying giant puppets will often insist that they are deeply serious. "Puppets are not cute, like Muppets," insists Peter Schumann, the director of Bread and Puppet Theater—the group historically most responsible for popularizing the use of papier-mâché figures in political protest in the '60s. "Puppets are effigies and gods and meaningful creatures."[9] Sometimes, they are literally so, as with the Maya gods that came to greet delegates at the WTO meetings in Cancun in September 2003. Always, they have a certain numinous quality.

Still, if giant puppets, generically, are gods, most are obviously foolish, silly, ridiculous gods. It is as if the process of producing and displaying puppets becomes a way to both seize the power to make gods and to make fun of it at the same time. Here one seems to be striking against a profoundly anarchist sensibility. Within anarchism, one encounters a similar impulse at every point where one approaches the mythic or deeply meaningful. It appears to be operative in the doctrines of Zerzanites and similar Primitivists, who go about self-consciously creating myths (their own version of the Garden of Eden, the Fall, the coming Apocalypse) that seem to imply they want to see millions perish in a worldwide industrial collapse, or that they seek to abolish agriculture or even language—then bridle at the suggestion that they really do. It's clearly present in the writings of theorists such as Peter Lamborn Wilson, whose meditations on the role of the sacred in revolutionary action are written under the persona of an insane Ismaili pederastic poet named Hakim Bey. It's even more clearly present among pagan anarchist groups like Reclaiming, who since the antinuclear movement of the '80s[10] have specialized in conducting what often seem like extravagant satires of pagan rituals that they nonetheless insist are real rituals which are really effective—even, that represent what they see as the deepest possible spiritual truths about the world.[11]

Puppets simply push this logic to a kind of extreme. The sacred here is, ultimately, the sheer power of creativity, of the imagination—or, perhaps more exactly, the power to bring the imagination into reality. This is, after all, the ultimate ideal of all revolutionary practice, to, as the '68 slogan put it, "give power to the imagination." But it is also as if the democratization of the sacred can be accomplished only through a kind of burlesque. Hence the constant self-mockery, which, however, is never meant to genuinely undercut the gravity and importance of what's being asserted, but rather, to imply the ultimate recognition that just because gods are human creations they are still gods, and that taking this fact too seriously might prove dangerous.

SYMBOLIC WARFARE ON THE PART OF THE POLICE

Anarchists, as I've said, avoid designing their strategies around the media. The same cannot be said of the police.

It's obvious that the events of N30 in Seattle came as a surprise to most in the U.S. government. The Seattle police were clearly unprepared for the sophisticated tactics adopted by the hundreds of affinity groups that surrounded the hotel and, at least for the first day, effectively shut down the meetings. The first impulse of many commanders appears to have been to respect the nonviolence of the actions.[12] It was only after 1 p.m. on the thirtieth, after Madeleine Albright's call to the governor from inside the hotel demanding that he tell them to do whatever they had to do to break the blockade,[13] that police began a full-blown assault with tear gas, pepper spray, and concussion grenades.

Even then many seemed to hesitate, while others, when they did enter the fray, descended into wild rampages, attacking and arresting scores of ordinary shoppers in Seattle's commercial district. In the end the governor was forced to call in the National Guard. While the media pitched in by representing police actions as a response to Black Bloc actions that began much later, having to bring in federal troops was an undeniable spectacular symbolic defeat.

In the immediate aftermath of Seattle, law enforcement officials—on the national and international level—appear to have begun a concerted effort to develop a new strategy. The details of such deliberations are, obviously, not available to the public. Nonetheless, judging by subsequent events, it seems that their conclusion (unsurprisingly enough) was that the Seattle police had not resorted to violence quickly or efficiently enough. The new strategy—soon put into practice during subsequent actions in Washington, Windsor, Philadelphia, Los Angeles, and Quebec—appears to have been one of aggressive preemption. The problem was how to justify this against a movement that was overwhelmingly nonviolent, engaged in actions that for the most part could not even be defined as criminal,[14] and whose message appeared to have at least potentially strong public appeal.

One might phrase it this way. The summits and other events targeted by the movement—trade summits, political conventions, IMF meetings—were largely symbolic events. They were not, for the most part, venues for formal political decision-making, but junkets, self-celebratory rituals, and networking occasions for some of the richest and most powerful people on earth. The effect of the actions is normally not to shut down the meetings, but to create a sense of siege. It might all be done in such a way as not to physically endanger anyone; the catapults might (as in Quebec) only be hurling stuffed animals, but the result is to produce meetings surrounded by mayhem, in which those attending have to be escorted about by heavily armed security, the cocktail parties are canceled, and the celebrations, effectively, ruined. Nothing could have been more effective in shattering the air of triumphant inevitability that had surrounded such meetings in the '90s. To imagine that the "forces of order" would not respond aggressively would be naïve indeed. For them, the nonviolence of the blockaders was simply irrelevant. Or: to be more precise, it was an issue only because it created potential problems of public perception. This problem, however, was quite serious. How was one to represent protesters as a threat to public safety, justifying extreme measures, if they did not actually do anyone physical harm?

Here one should probably let events speak for themselves. If one looks at what happened during the months immediately following Seattle, the first things one observes are a series of preemptive strikes, always aimed at threats that (not unlike Iraq's weapons of mass destruction) never quite materialized:

April 2000, Washington, D.C.

Hours before the protests against the IMF and World Bank are to begin on April 15, police round up six hundred marchers in a preemptive arrest and seize the protesters' Convergence Center. Police Chief Charles Ramsey loudly claims to have discovered a workshop for manufacturing Molotov cocktails and homemade pepper spray inside. D.C. police later admit no such workshop existed (really they'd found paint thinner used in art projects and peppers being used for the manufacture of gazpacho); however, the convergence center remains closed and much of the art and many of the puppets inside are appropriated.

July 2000, Minneapolis

Days before a scheduled protest against the International Society of Animal Geneticists, local police claim that activists had detonated a cyanide bomb at a local McDonald's and might have their hands on stolen explosives. The next day the DEA raids a house used by organizers, drags off the bloodied inhabitants, and appropriates their computers and boxes full of outreach materials. Police later admit there never actually was a cyanide bomb and they had no reason to believe activists were in possession of explosives.

August 2000, Philadelphia

Hours before the protests against the Republican Convention are to begin, police, claiming to be acting on a tip, seize the warehouse where the art, banners, and puppets used for the action are being prepared, arresting all of the at least seventy-five activists discovered inside. Police Chief John Timoney loudly claims to have discovered C4 explosives and water balloons full of hydrochloric acid in the building. Police later admit no explosives or acid were really found; the arrestees are however not released until well after the actions are over. All of the puppets, banners, art, and literature to be used in the protest are systematically destroyed.

While it is possible that we are dealing with a remarkable series of honest mistakes, this does look an awful lot like a series of attacks on the material activists were intending to use to get their message out to the public. Certainly that's how the activists interpreted them—especially after Philadelphia. Organizers planning the parallel protests against the Democratic Convention in L.A. managed to obtain a restraining order barring police from attacking their convergence center, but ever since, in the weeks before any major mobilization, a key issue is always how to hide and protect the puppets.

By Philadelphia, it became quite clear that the police had adopted a very self-conscious media strategy. Their spokesmen would pepper each daily press conference with wild accusations, well aware that the crime-desk reporters assigned to cover them (who usually relied on good working relations with police for their livelihood) would normally reproduce anything they said uncritically, and rarely considered it to merit a story if afterward the claims turned out to be false. I was working the phones for the activist media team during much of this time and can attest that a large part of what we ended up doing was coming up with responses to what we came to call the "lie of the day." The first day, police announced that they had seized a van full of poisonous snakes and reptiles that activists were intending to release in the city center (they were later forced to admit that it actually belonged to a pet store and had nothing to do with the protests). The second day they claimed that anarchists had splashed acid in an officer's face; this sent us scrambling to figure out what might have actually happened. (They dropped the story immediately thereafter, but it would appear that if anything was actually splashed on an officer, it was probably red paint that was actually directed at a wall.) On the third day we were accused of planting "dry ice bombs" throughout the city; this, again, sent the anarchist media teams scrambling to try to figure out precisely what dry ice bombs were (it turned out the police had apparently found the reference in a copy of *The Anarchist Cookbook*). Interestingly, this last story does not seem to have actually made the news: at this point, most reporters no longer were willing to reproduce the most dramatic claims by the authorities. The fact that the first two claims turned out to be false, however, along with the claims of acid and explosives in the puppet warehouse, or that Timoney appeared to have developed an intentional policy of lying to them, was never itself considered newsworthy. Neither, however, was the actual reason for the actions, which were meant to draw attention to the prison-industrial complex (a phrase that we repeated endlessly to reporters, but which never made it into a single news report)—presumably, on the grounds that it would be unethical for reporters to allow violent protesters to "hijack" the media.

This same period began to see increasingly outlandish accounts of what had happened at Seattle. During the WTO protests themselves, I must emphasize, no one, including the Seattle police, had claimed anarchists had done anything more militant than break windows. That was the end of November 1999. In March 2000, less than three months later, a story in the *Boston Herald* reported that, in the weeks before an upcoming biotech conference, officers from Seattle had come to brief the local police on how to deal with "Seattle tactics," such as attacking police with "chunks of concrete, BB guns, wrist rockets and large capacity squirt guns loaded with bleach and urine."[15] In June, a *New York Times* reporter, apparently relying on police sources in Detroit preparing for a trade protest across the Canadian border in Windsor, claimed that Seattle demonstrators had "hurled Molotov cocktails, rocks and excrement at delegates and police officers." On this occasion, after the New York Direct Action Network picketed its offices, the *Times* ended up having to run a retraction, admitting that according to Seattle authorities, no objects had been thrown at human beings.[16] Nonetheless, the retracted account appears to have become canonical. Each time there is a new mobilization, stories invariably surface in local newspapers with the same list of "Seattle tactics"—a list that also appears to have become enshrined in training manuals distributed to street cops. Before the Miami Summit of the Americas in 2003, for example, circulars distributed to local businessmen and civic groups listed every one of these "Seattle tactics" as what they should expect to see on the streets once anarchists arrived:

> **Wrist Rockets**—larger hunter-type sling shots that they use to shoot steel ball bearings or large bolts. A very dangerous and deadly weapon.
>
> **Molotov Cocktails**—many were thrown in Seattle and Quebec and caused extensive damage.
>
> **Crow Bars**—to smash windows, cars, etc. They also pry up curbs, then break the cement into pieces that they can throw at police officers. This was done extensively in Seattle.
>
> **Squirt guns**—filled with acid or urine.[17]

Again, according to local police's own accounts, none of these weapons or tactics had been used in Seattle and no one has produced any evidence they've been used in any subsequent U.S. mobilization.[18]

In Miami, the predictable result was that, by the time the first marches began, most of downtown lay shuttered and abandoned.

Miami, as the first major convergence in the new security climate after September 11, might be said to mark the full culmination of this approach, combining aggressive disinformation and preemptive attacks on activists. During the actions, the police chief—John Timoney again—had officers pouring out an endless series of accusations of activists hurling rocks, bottles, urine, and bags of feces at police. (As usual, despite ubiquitous video cameras and hundreds of arrests, no one was ever charged, let alone convicted, of assaulting an officer with any such substance, and no reporter managed to produce an image of an activist doing so.) Police strategy consisted almost entirely of raids and preemptive attacks on protesters employing the full arsenal of old and newly developed "nonlethal" weaponry: Tasers, pepper spray, plastic and rubber and wooden bullets, bean-bag bullets soaked in pepper spray, tear gas, and so on—and rules of engagement that allowed them to pretty much fire on anyone at will.

Here, too, puppets were singled out. In the months before the summit, the Miami city council actually attempted to pass a law making the display of puppets illegal, on the grounds that they could be used to conceal bombs or other weapons.[19] It failed, since it was patently unconstitutional, but the message got out. As a result, the Black Bloc in Miami actually ended up spending most of their time and energy on protecting the puppets. Miami also provides a vivid example of the peculiar personal animus many police seem to have against large figures made of papier-mâché. According to one eyewitness report, after police routed protesters from Seaside Plaza, forcing them to abandon their puppets, officers spent the next half hour or so systematically attacking and destroying them: shooting, kicking, and ripping the remains; one even putting a giant puppet in his squad car with the head sticking out and driving so as to smash it against every sign and street post available.

RALLYING THE TROOPS

The Boston example is particularly striking because it indicates that there were elements in the Seattle police actually training other police in how to deal with violent tactics that official Seattle spokesmen were, simultaneously, denying had actually been employed. While it's very difficult to know exactly what's going on here—even, really, to figure out precisely who these endlessly cited "police intelligence" sources actually are (we seem to be entering a murky zone involving information being collected, concocted, and passed back and forth among a variety of federal police task forces, private security agencies, and allied right-wing think tanks, in such a way that the images become self-reinforcing and, presumably, no one is quite sure what is and isn't true)—it is easy to see how one of the main concerns in the wake of Seattle would be to ensure the reliability of one's troops. As commanders discovered in Seattle, officers used to considering themselves guardians of public safety frequently balk, or at least waver, when given orders to make a baton charge against a collection of nonviolent sixteen-year-old white girls. These were, after all, the very sort of people they are ordinarily expected to protect. At least some of the imagery, then, appears to be designed specifically to appeal to the sensibility of ordinary street cops.

This at least would help to explain the otherwise peculiar emphasis on bodily fluids: the water pistols full of bleach and urine, for example, or claims that officers were pelted with urine and excrement. This appears to be very much a police obsession. Certainly it has next to nothing to do with anarchist sensibilities. When I've asked activists where they think such stories come from, most confess themselves deeply puzzled. One or two suggested that, when defending a besieged squat, sometimes buckets of human waste is one of the few things one has to throw. But none have ever heard of anyone actually transporting human waste to an action in order to hurl or shoot at police, or could suggest why anyone might want to. A brick, some point out, is unlikely to injure an officer in full riot gear; but it will certainly slow him down. But what would be the point of shooting urine at him? Yet images like this reemerge almost every time police attempt to justify a preemptive strike. In press conferences, they have been known to actually produce jars of urine and bags of feces that they claim to have discovered hidden in backpacks or activist convergence sites.[20]

It is hard to see these claims as making sense except within the peculiar economy of personal honor typical of any institution that, like the police, operates on an essentially military ethos. For police officers, the most legitimate justification for violence is an assault on one's personal dignity. To cover another person in shit and piss is obviously about as powerful an assault on one's personal dignity as one can possibly make. We also seem to be dealing here with a self-conscious allusion to the famous image of '60s protesters "spitting on soldiers in uniform" when they returned from Vietnam—one whose mythic power continues to resonate, not just in right-wing circles, to this day, despite the fact that there's little evidence that it ever happened.[21] It's almost as if someone decided to ratchet the image up a notch: "if spitting on a uniform is such an insult, what would be even worse?"

That there might have been some kind of coordination in this effort could be gleaned, too, from the fact that it was precisely around the time of the Democratic and Republican conventions in the summer of 2000 that mayors and police chiefs around the United States began regularly declaring, often in strikingly similar terms (and based on no evidence whatsoever), that anarchists were actually a bunch of "trust fund babies" who disguised their faces while breaking things so their wealthy parents wouldn't recognize them on TV—an accusation that soon became received wisdom among right-wing talk show hosts and law enforcement professionals across America.[22] The obvious message to the officer on the street appeared to be: "Do not think of your assignment as having to protect a bunch of bankers and politicians who have contempt for you against protesters whose actual positions on economic issues you might well agree with; think of it, rather, as a chance to beat up on those bankers' and politicians' children." In a sense, one might say the message was perfectly calibrated to the level of repression required, since it suggests that while force was appropriate, deadly force was not: if one were to actually maim or kill a protester one might well be killing the son or daughter of a senator or CEO, which would be likely to provoke a scandal.

Police are also apparently regularly warned that puppets might be used to conceal bombs or weapons.[23] If questioned on their attitudes toward puppets, this is how they are likely to respond. However, it's hard to imagine this alone could explain the level of personal vindictiveness witnessed in Miami and other actions—especially since police hacking puppets to pieces must have been aware that there was nothing hidden inside them. The antipathy seems to run far deeper. Many activists have speculated on the reasons.

David Corston-Knowles's opinion: You have to bear in mind these are people who are trained to be paranoid. They really do have to ask themselves whether something so big and inscrutable might contain explosives, however absurd that might seem from a nonviolent protester's perspective. Police view their jobs not just as law enforcement, but also as maintaining order. And they take that job very personally. Giant demonstrations and giant puppets aren't orderly. They are about creating something— a different society, a different way of looking at things—and creativity is fundamentally at odds with the status quo.

Daniel Lang's opinion: Well, one theory is that the cops just don't like being upstaged by someone putting on a bigger show. After all, normally *they're* the spectacle: they've got the blue uniforms, they've got the helicopters and horses and rows of shiny motorcycles. So maybe they just resent it when someone steals the show by coming up with something even bigger and even more visually striking. They want to take out the competition.

Yvonne Liu's opinion: It's because they're so big. Cops don't like things that tower over them. That's why they like to be on horses. Plus, puppets are silly and round and misshapen. Notice how much cops always have to maintain straight lines? They stand in straight lines, they always try to make you stand in straight lines . . . I think round misshapen things somehow offend them.

Max Uhlenbeck's opinion: Obviously, they hate to be reminded that they're puppets themselves.

I will return to this question shortly.

ANALYSIS I: THE HOLLYWOOD MOVIE PRINCIPLE

From the point of view of security officials during this period, rallying the troops was presumably the easy part. The stickier problem was what to do with the fact that the bulk of the American public refused to see the global justice movement as a threat. The only survey I am aware of taken at the time that addressed the question—a Zogby America poll taken of TV viewers during the Republican convention in 2000—found that about a third claimed to feel "pride" when they saw images of protesters on TV, and less than 16 percent had an unqualified negative reaction.[24] This was especially striking in a poll of television viewers, since TV coverage during the convention was unremittingly hostile, treating the events almost exclusively as potential security threats.

There is, I think, a simple explanation. I would propose to call it the Hollywood movie principle. Most Americans, in watching a dramatic confrontation on TV, effectively ask themselves: "If this were a Hollywood movie, who would be the good guys?" Presented with a contest between what appear to be a collection of idealistic kids who do not actually injure anyone, and a collection of heavily armed riot cops protecting trade bureaucrats and corporate CEOs, the answer is pretty obvious.

Individual maverick cops can be movie heroes. Riot cops never are. In fact, in Hollywood movies, riot cops almost never appear; about the closest one can find to them are the imperial stormtroopers in *Star Wars*, who, like their leader Darth Vader, stand in American popular culture as one of the most familiar archetypes of evil. This point is not lost on the anarchists, who have since A16 taken to regularly bringing recordings of the imperial stormtrooper music from *Star Wars* to blast from their ranks as soon as a line of riot cops starts advancing.

If so, the key problem for the forces of order became: What would it take to reverse this perception? How to cast protesters in the role of the villain?

In the immediate aftermath of Seattle the focus was all on broken windows. As we've seen, this imagery certainly did strike some sort of chord. But in terms of creating a sense that decisive measures were required, efforts to make a national issue out of property destruction came to surprisingly little effect. In the terms of my analysis this makes perfect sense. After all, in the moral economy of Hollywood, property destruction is at best a very minor peccadillo. In fact, if the popularity of the various *Terminators*, *Lethal Weapons*, or *Die Hards* and the like reveal anything, it is that most Americans seem to rather like the idea of property destruction. If they did not themselves harbor a certain hidden glee at the idea of someone smashing a branch of their local bank, or a McDonald's (not to mention police cars, shopping malls, and complex construction machinery), it's hard to imagine why they would so regularly pay money to watch idealistic do-gooders smashing and blowing them up for hours on end, always in ways that, through the magic of the movies—but also like the practice of the Black Bloc—tend to leave innocent bystanders entirely unharmed. Certainly, it's unlikely that there are significant numbers of Americans who have not, at some time or another, had a fantasy about smashing up their bank. In the land of demolition derbies and monster trucks, Black Bloc anarchists might be said to be living a hidden aspect of the American dream.

Obviously, these are just fantasies. Most working-class Americans do not overtly approve of destroying a Starbucks facade; but unlike the talking classes, neither do they see such activity as a threat to the nation, let alone anything requiring military-style repression.

ANALYSIS II: CREATIVE DESTRUCTION AND THE PRIVATIZATION OF DESIRE

One could even say that in a sense, the Black Bloc appear to be the latest avatars of an artistic/revolutionary tradition that runs at least through the Dadaists, Surrealists, and Situationists (the latter by far the most popular theorists in American anarchist bookshops): one that tries to play off the contradictions of capitalism by turning its own destructive, leveling forces against it. Capitalist societies—and the United States in particular—are, in essence, potlatch societies. That is, they are built around the spectacular destruction of consumer goods.[25] They are societies that imagine themselves as built on something they call "the economy," which in turn is imagined as a nexus between "production" and "consumption," endlessly spitting out products and then destroying them again. Since it is all based on the principle of infinite expansion of industrial production—the very principle that the Black Bloc anarchists, mostly being highly ecologically conscious anticapitalists, most vehemently oppose—all that stuff has to be constantly destroyed to make way for new products. But this, in turn, means inculcating a certain passion for or delight in the smashing and destruction of property that can very easily slip into a delight in the shattering of those structures of relation which make capitalism possible.

It is a system that can renew itself only by cultivating a hidden pleasure at the prospect of its own destruction.[26]

Actually, one could well argue that there have been two strains in twentieth-century artistic/revolutionary thought, and that both have been entangled in the—endlessly ambivalent—image of the potlatch. In the 1930s, for example, Georges Bataille became fascinated by Marcel Mauss's description of the spectacular destruction of property in Kwakiutl potlatches; it ultimately became the basis for his famous theory of "expenditure," of the creation of meaning through destruction, that he felt was ultimately lacking under modern capitalism. There are endless ironies here. First of all, what Bataille and subsequent authors seized on was not, in fact, the "potlatch" at all, but a small number of very unusual potlatches held around the turn of the century, at a time marked both by a rapid decline in Kwakiutl population and a minor economic boom that had left the region awash in an unprecedented number of consumer goods. Ordinary potlatches did not normally involve the destruction of property at all; they were simply occasions for aristocrats to lavish wealth on the community. If the image of Indians setting fire to thousands of blankets or other consumer goods proved captivating, in other words, it was not because it represented some fundamental truth about human society that consumer capitalism had forgotten, but rather because it reflected the ultimate truth of consumer capitalism itself.

In 1937, Bataille teamed up with Roger Caillois to found a reading group called the College of Sociology, which expanded his insights into a general theory of the revolutionary festival: arguing that it was only by reclaiming the principle of the sacred, and the power of myth embodied in popular festivals, that effective revolutionary action would be possible. Similar ideas were developed in the '50s by Henri Lefebvre, and within the Letterist International, whose journal, edited by Guy Debord, was, significantly, entitled *Potlatch*.[27] Here there is of course a direct line from the Situationists, with their promulgation of art as a form of revolutionary direct action, to the punk movement and contemporary anarchism.

If Black Blocs embody one side of this tradition—capitalism's encouragement of a kind of fascination with consumerist destruction that can, ultimately, be turned back against capitalism itself—the puppets surely represent the other one, the recuperation of the sacred and unalienated experience in the collective festival. Radical puppeteers tend to be keenly aware that their art harkens back to the wickerwork giants and dragons, Gargantuas and Pantagruels of Medieval festivals. Even those who have not themselves read Rabelais or Bakhtin are likely to be familiar with the notion of the carnivalesque.[28] Convergences are regularly framed as "carnivals against capitalism" or "festivals of resistance." The baseline reference seems to be the late Medieval world immediately before the emergence of capitalism, particularly the period after the Black Death when the sudden decline in population had the effect of putting unprecedented amounts of money into the hands of the laboring classes. Most of it ended up being poured into popular festivals of one sort or another, which themselves began to multiply until they took up large parts of the calendar year; what nowadays might be called events of "collective consumption," celebrations of carnality and rowdy pleasures and—if Bakhtin is to be believed—tacit attacks on the very principle of hierarchy. One might say that the first wave of capitalism, the Puritan Moment as it's sometimes called, had to begin with a concerted assault on this world, which was condemned by improving landlords and nascent capitalists as pagan, immoral, and utterly unconducive to the maintenance of labor discipline. Of course a movement to abolish all moments of public festivity could not last forever; Cromwell's reign in England is reviled to this day on the grounds that he outlawed Christmas. More important, once moments of festive, collective consumption were eliminated, the nascent capitalism would be left with the obvious problem of how to sell its products, particularly in light of the need to constantly expand production. The end result was what I like to call a process of the privatization of desire; the creation of endless individual, familial, or semi-furtive forms of consumption; none of which, as we are so often reminded, could really be fully satisfying or else the whole logic of endless expansion wouldn't work. While one should hardly imagine that police strategists are fully cognizant of all this, the very existence of police is tied to a political cosmology that sees such forms of collective consumption as inherently disorderly, and (much like a Medieval carnival) always brimming with the possibility of violent insurrection. "Order" means that citizens should go home and watch TV.[29]

For police, then, what revolutionaries see as an eruption of the sacred through a re-creation of the popular festival is a "disorderly assembly"—and exactly the sort of thing they exist to disperse.

However, since this sense of festival as threatening does not appear to resonate with large sectors of the TV audience, the police were forced to, as it were, change the script. What we've seen is a very calculated campaign of symbolic warfare, an attempt to eliminate images of colorful floats and puppets, and substitute images of bombs and hydrochloric acid—the very substances that, in police fantasies, are likely to actually lurk beneath the papier-mâché facade.

ANALYSIS III: THE LAWS OF WAR

To fully understand the place of puppets, though, I think one has to grapple with the question of rules of engagement.

I already touched on this question obliquely earlier when I suggested that when politicians informed street cops that protesters were "trust fund babies," what they really meant to suggest was that they could be brutalized, but not maimed or killed, and that police tactics should be designed accordingly. From an ethnographer's perspective, one of the most puzzling things about direct action is to understand how these rules are actually negotiated. Certainly, rules exist. There are lines that cannot be crossed by the police without risk of major scandal; there are endless lines that cannot be crossed by activists. Yet each side acts as if it is playing a game whose rules it had worked out exclusively through its own internal processes, without any consultation with the other players.

This could not ultimately be the case. I first began thinking about these questions after my experience in Philly during the Republican Convention in the summer of 2000. I had been working mainly with an activist media team. During the day of action, however, my job was to go out into the streets with a cell phone to report back to them what was actually happening. I ended up accompanying a column of Black Blockers whose actions were originally meant as a diversion, to lure police away from street blockades in a different part of town. The police appear to have decided not to take the bait, and as a result, the Bloc briefly had their run of a wide stretch of downtown Philadelphia:

(BASED ON FIELD NOTES, PHILADELPHIA,
AUGUST 1, 2000)

faced with a rapidly moving column of several hundred anarchists appearing out of nowhere, small groups of police would often abandon their cars, which the anarchists would then proceed to trash and spray-paint. A couple dozen police cars, one stretch limo, and numerous official buildings were hit in the course of the next hour or so. Eventually, reinforcements, in the form of police bicycle squads, began to appear and before long there was a rough balance of forces. What followed at this point could only be described as an episode of some kind of nonviolent warfare. A few Black Bloc kids would try to shut down a bus by playing with valves in the back; a squad of bike cops would swoop in and grab a few, cuffing them and locking their bikes together to create tiny fortresses in which to hold them. Once, a large mass of protesters appeared from another direction and the cops ended up besieged in their little bike fort, with Black Blockers surrounding them, screaming insults, throwing paint bombs above their heads, doing everything but actually attacking them. On that occasion the Bloc wasn't quite able to snatch back their arrested comrades before police vans with reinforcements appeared to take them away; elsewhere, there were rumors of successful "unarrests." The police even suffered a casualty in that particular confrontation: one overweight cop, overwhelmed by the tension and stifling heat, collapsed and had to be carried off or revived with smelling salts.

It was obvious that both sides had carefully worked out rules of engagement. Activists tended to work out their principles carefully in advance, and while there were certainly differences, say, between those who adopted classic nonviolent civil disobedience rules (who had, for example, undergone nonviolence trainings) and the more militant anarchists I was with, all agreed at least on the need to avoid directly causing harm to other human beings, or damaging personal property or owner-operated "mom and pop" stores. The police of course could attack protesters more or less at will, but at this point at least, they seemed to feel they had to do so in such a way as to be fairly sure that none would be killed or more than a handful require hospitalization—which, in the absence of very specific training and technologies, required a fair amount of constraint.

These basic rules applied throughout; however, over the course of the day, the tenor of events was constantly shifting. The Black Bloc confrontations were tense and angry; other areas were placid or somber ritual, drum circles or pagan spiral dances; others, full of music or ridiculous carnival. The Black Bloc column I was accompanying, for example, eventually converged with a series of others until there were almost a thousand anarchists rampaging through the center of the city. The district attorney's office was thoroughly paint-bombed.

More police cars were destroyed. However, it was all done quickly on the move, and larger and larger bike squads started following our columns, splitting the Bloc and threatening to isolate smaller groups that could, then, be arrested. We were running faster and faster, dodging through alleys and parking lots.

Finally, the largest group descended on a plaza where a permitted rally was being held; this was assumed to be a safe space.

In fact, it wasn't quite. Riot police soon began surrounding the plaza and cutting off routes of escape; it seemed like they were preparing for a mass arrest.

Such matters usually simply come down to numbers: it takes something like two officers in the field for every protester to carry off a mass arrest, probably three if the victims are trying to resist, and have some idea of how to go about it (i.e., know enough to link arms and try to keep a continuous line.) In this situation the Black Bloc kids could be expected to know exactly what to do; the others, who thought they were attending a safe, permanent event, were mostly entirely unprepared but could nonetheless be assumed to follow their lead; on the other hand, they were trapped, they had no way to receive reinforcements, while the police were getting a constant flow of them. The mood was extremely tense. Activists who had earlier been conducting a teach-in and small rally against the prison-industrial complex milled about uncomfortably around a giant poster board as the Bloc, now reduced to a couple hundred black figures in bandannas and gas masks, formed a mini-spokescouncil, then faced off against the police lines at two different points where it seemed there might be a break in their lines (there usually is, when the police first begin to deploy); but to no avail.

I lingered on the plaza, chatting with a friend, Brad, who was complaining that he had lost his backpack and most of his worldly goods in the police raid on the puppet space that morning. We munched on apples—none of us had eaten all day—and watched as four performance artists on bicycles with papier-mâché goat heads, carrying a little sign saying "Goats with a Vote," began wading into the police lines to perform an a capella rap song. "You see what you can do with puppets?" laughed Brad. "No one else would ever be able to get away with that."

The Goats, as it turned out, were just the first wave. They were followed, ten minutes later, by a kind of "puppet intervention." Not with real puppets—the puppets had all been destroyed, and the musicians all arrested, at the warehouse earlier that morning. Instead, the Revolutionary Anarchist Clown Bloc appeared; led by two figures on high bicycles, blowing horns and kazoos, spreading streamers and confetti everywhere; alongside a large contingent of "Billionaires for Bush (or Gore)", dressed in high-camp tuxedos and evening gowns. There were probably not more than thirty or forty of them in all but among them they immediately managed to change the tenor of the whole event, and to throw everything into confusion. The Billionaires started handing fake money to the police ("to thank them for suppressing dissent"), the clowns attacked the Billionaires with squeaky mallets. Unicycles appeared, and fire jugglers. In the ensuing confusion, cracks did appear in the police lines and just about everyone on the plaza took advantage to form a wedge and burst out and to safety, with the Black Bloc leading the way.

Let's consider for a moment this idea of nonviolent warfare. How much of a metaphor is it really?

One could well make the argument that it is not a metaphor at all. Clausewitz notwithstanding, war has never been a pure contest of force with no rules. Just about all armed conflicts have had very complex and detailed sets of mutual understandings between the warring parties. When total war does occur, its practitioners—Attila, Cortés—tend to be remembered a thousand years later for this very reason. There are always rules. As the Israeli military theorist Martin Van Creveld observes, if nothing else, in any armed conflict there will normally be:

- rules for parlays and truces (this would include, for example, the sanctity of negotiators)
- rules for how to surrender and how captives are to be treated
- rules for how to identify and deal with noncombatants (normally including medics)
- rules for levels and types of force allowable between combatants— which weapons or tactics are dishonorable or illegal (i.e., even when Hitler and Stalin were going at it neither tried to assassinate each other or used chemical weapons)[30]

Van Creveld emphasizes that such rules are actually necessary for any effective use of force, because to maintain an effective army, one needs to maintain a certain sense of honor and discipline, a sense of being the good guys. Without the rules, in other words, it would be impossible to maintain any real morale or command structure. An army that does not obey rules degenerates into a marauding band, and faced with a real army, marauding bands invariably lose. Van Creveld suggests there are probably other reasons why there must be rules: for instance, that violence is so intrinsically frightening that humans always immediately surround it with regulation . . . But one of the most interesting, because it brings home how much the battlefield is an extension of a larger political field, is that, without rules, it is impossible to know when you have won—since ultimately one needs to have both sides agree on this question.

Now consider the police. Police certainly see themselves soldiers of a sort. But insofar as they see themselves as fighting a war (the "war on crime"), they also know they are involved in a conflict in which victory is by definition impossible.

How does this affect the rules of engagement? On one level the answer is obvious. When it comes to levels of force, what sort of weapons or tactics one can use in what circumstances, police operate under enormous constraints—far more than any army. Some of these constraints remain tacit.

Others are quite legal and explicit. Certainly, every time a policeman fires a gun, there must be an investigation. This is one of the reasons for the endless elaboration of "nonlethal" weapons—Tasers, plastic bullets, pepper spray, and the like—for purposes of crowd control: they are not freighted with the same restrictions. On the other hand, when police are engaged in actions *not* deemed to involve potentially lethal force, and that are not meant to lead to a suspect's eventual criminal conviction, there are almost no constraints on what they can do—certainly none that can be enforced in any way.[31]

So in the last of Van Creveld's categories, there are endless constraints. As for the other rules, anyone who has been involved in direct action can testify to the fact that the police systematically violate all of them. Police regularly engage in practices that, in war, would be considered outrageous, or at the very least, utterly dishonorable. Police regularly arrest mediators. If members of an affinity group occupy a building, and one does not but instead acts as police liaison, it might well end up that the liaison is the only one who is actually arrested. If one does negotiate an agreement with the police, they will almost invariably violate it. Police frequently attack or arrest those they have earlier offered safe passage. They regularly target medics. If those carrying out an action in one part of a city try to create "green zones" or safe spaces in another—in other words, if they try to set up an area in which everyone agrees not to break the law or provoke the authorities, as a way to distinguish combatants and noncombatants—the police will almost invariably attack the green zone.

Why? There are various reasons for this. Some are obviously pragmatic: you don't have to come to an understanding about how to treat prisoners if you can arrest protesters, but protesters can't arrest you. But in a broader sense such behavior is a means of refusing any suggestion of equivalency—the kind that would simply be assumed if fighting another army in a conventional war. Police represent the state; the state has a monopoly of the legitimate use of violence within its borders; therefore, within that territory, police are by definition incommensurable with anyone else. This is essential to understanding what police actually are. Many sociological studies have pointed out that maybe 6 percent of the average police officer's time is spent on anything that can even remotely be considered "fighting crime." Police are a group of armed, lower-echelon government administrators, trained in the scientific application of physical force to aid in the resolution of administrative problems.

They are bureaucrats with guns, and whether they are guarding lost children, talking rowdy drunks out of bars, or supervising free concerts in the park, the one common feature of the kind of situation to which they're assigned is the possibility of having to impose "non-negotiated solutions backed up by the potential use of force."[32] The key term here, I think, is *non-negotiated*. Police do not negotiate—at least when it comes to anything important—because that would imply equivalency. When they are forced to negotiate, they pretty much invariably break their word.[33]

In other words, police find themselves in a paradoxical position. Their job is to embody the state's monopoly of the use of coercive force; yet their freedom to employ that force is extremely limited. The refusal to treat the other side as honorable opponents, and therefore as equivalent in any way, seems to be the only way to maintain the principle of absolute incommensurability that representatives of the state must, by definition, maintain. This would appear to be the reason why, when restrictions on the use of force by police are removed, the results are catastrophic. Whenever you see wars that violate all the rules and involve horrific atrocities against civilians, they are invariably framed as "police actions."

Obviously, none of this actually answers the question of how rules of engagement are negotiated. But it does make it clear why it cannot be done directly. This seems particularly true in the United States; in many countries, from Italy to Madagascar, the rules of civil resistance can sometimes be worked quite explicitly, so that protest ends up becoming a kind of game in which the rules are clearly understood by each side. A good example is the famous *tute bianci* or "white overalls" tactics employed in Italy between 1999 and 2001, where protesters would fortify themselves with layers of padding and inflatable inner tubes and the like and rush the barricades, at the same time pledging to do no harm to another human being. Participants often admitted to me that the rules were, for the most part, directly negotiated: "You can hit us as hard as you like as long as you hit us on the padding; we won't hit you but we'll try to plow through the barricades; let's see who wins!" In fact, matters had come to such a pass that negotiation was expected: before the G8 meetings in Genoa, when the government opted for a policy of violent repression, they were forced to bring in the LAPD to train Italian police in how *not* to interact with protesters, or allow either side to be effectively humanized in the eyes of the other.[34] In the United States, however, police appear to object to such negotiations on principle—unless, that is, protesters are actually trying to get arrested, and are willing to negotiate the terms.

Still, it's obvious that on some level, negotiation must take place. What's more, whatever level that is, it is the real level of power: since, after all, as always in politics, real power is not the power to win a contest, but the power to define the rules and stakes; not the power to win an argument, but the power to define what the argument is about. Here it is clear that the power is not all on one side. Years of moral-political struggle, one might say, have created a situation in which the police, generally speaking, have to accept extreme restrictions on their use of force; this is much more true when dealing with people defined as "white," of course, but nonetheless it is a real limit on their ability to suppress dissent. The problem for those dedicated to the principle of direct action is that while these rules of engagement—particularly the levels of force police are allowed to get away with—are under constant renegotiation, this process is expected to take place through institutions to which anarchists, on principle, object. Normally, one is expected to employ the language of "rights" or "police brutality" to pursue one's case through the courts—with the help of liberal NGOs and sympathetic politicians—but most of all, one is expected to do battle in "the court of public opinion." This of course means through the corporate media, since "the public" in this context is little more than its audience. Of course for an anarchist, the very fact that human beings are organized into a "public," into a collection of atomized spectators, is precisely the problem. The solution for them is self-organization: they wish to see the public abandon their role as spectators and organize themselves into an endless and overlapping collection of directly democratic voluntary associations and communities. Yet according to the language normally employed by the media and political classes, the moment members of the public begin to do this, the moment they self-organize in any way—say, by forming labor unions or political associations—they are no longer the public but "special interest groups" presumed by definition to be opposed to the public interest. (This helps explain why even peaceful protesters at permitted events, expressing views shared by overwhelming majorities of Americans, are nonetheless never described as members of "the public.")

Negotiation, then, is supposed to take place indirectly. Each side is supposed to make its case via the media—mainly, through precisely the kind of calculated symbolic warfare that the police, in America, are willing to play quite aggressively, but activists, and particularly anarchists, are increasingly unwilling to play at all. Anarchists and their allies are above all trying to circumvent this game. To some degree they are trying to do so by creating their own media. To some degree, they are trying to do so by using the corporate media to convey images that they know are likely to alienate most suburban middle-class viewers, but that they hope will galvanize potentially revolutionary constituencies: oppressed minorities, alienated adolescents, the working poor. Many Black Bloc anarchists were quite delighted, after Seattle, to see the media "sensationalizing" property destruction for this very reason. To some degree, too, they are trying to circumvent the game by trying to seize the power to renegotiate the terms of engagement on the field of battle. It's the latter, I think, that the police see as fundamentally unfair.

SO WHY DO COPS HATE PUPPETS?

Let's return, then, to the notion of a "puppet intervention."

In Philly, on the evening of the first, we organized a press conference in which one of the few puppetistas who escaped arrest that morning was given center stage. During the press conference and subsequent talks with the media, we all emphasized that the puppet crews were, effectively, our peacekeepers. One of their main jobs was to intervene to defuse situations of potential violence. If the police were really primarily concerned with maintaining public order, as they maintained, peacekeepers seemed a strange choice for a preemptive strike.

By now, it should be easy enough to see why police might not see things this way. This is not to say we were not right to insist that the attack on the puppet warehouse was inspired by political motives, rather than a desire to protect the public.[35] It was. As we've seen, it appears, with its wild claims of acid and explosives, to have been part of a calculated campaign of symbolic warfare. At the same time, the *manner* in which puppets can be used to defuse situations of potential violence is completely different than, say, that which would be employed by protest marshals. Police tend to appreciate the presence of marshals, since marshals are organized into a chain of command that police tend immediately to treat as a mere extension of their own—and which, as a result, often effectively becomes so. Unlike marshals, puppets cannot be used to convey orders. Rather, like the clowns and Billionaires, they aim to transform and redefine situations of potential conflict.

It might be helpful here to reflect on the nature of the violence—"force," if you like—that police represent. A former LAPD officer writing about the Rodney King case pointed out that in most of the occasions in which a citizen is severely beaten by police, it turns out that the victim was actually innocent of any crime. "Cops don't beat up burglars," he observed. If you want to cause a policeman to be violent, the surest way is to *challenge their right to define the situation.* This is not something a burglar is likely to do.[36] This of course makes perfect sense if we remember that police are, essentially, bureaucrats with guns. Bureaucratic procedures are all about questions of definition. Or, to be more precise, they are about the imposition of a narrow range of preestablished schema to a social reality that is, usually, infinitely more complex: a crowd can be either orderly or disorderly; a citizen can be white, black, Hispanic, or Asian or Pacific Islander; a petitioner is or is not in possession of a valid photo ID. Such simplistic rubrics can be maintained only in the absence of dialogue; hence, the quintessential form of bureaucratic violence is the wielding of the truncheon when somebody "talks back."

I began by saying that this was to be an essay of interpretation. In fact, it has been just as much an essay about frustrated interpretation; about the limits of interpretation. Ultimately, I think this frustration can be traced back to the very nature of violence—bureaucratic or otherwise. Violence is in fact unique among forms of human action in that it holds out the possibility of affecting the actions of others about whom one understands nothing. If one wants to affect another's actions in any other way, one must at least have some idea of who they think they are, what they want, what they think is going on.

Interpretation is required, and that requires a certain degree of imaginative identification. Hit someone over the head hard enough, all this becomes irrelevant. Obviously, two parties locked in an equal contest of violence would usually do well to get inside each other's head, but when access to violence becomes extremely unequal, the need vanishes. This is typically the case in situations of structural violence: of systemic inequality that is ultimately backed up by the threat of force. Structural violence always seems to create extremely lopsided structures of imagination. Gender is actually a telling example here. Women almost everywhere know a great deal about men's work, men's lives, and male experience; men are almost always not only ignorant about women's lives, they often react with indignation at the idea they should even try to imagine what being a woman might be like. The same is typically the case in most relations of clear subordination: masters and servants, employers and employees, rich and poor. The victims of structural violence invariably end up spending a great deal of time imagining what it is like for those who benefit from it; the opposite rarely occurs. One concomitant is that the victims often end up identifying with, and caring about, the beneficiaries of structural violence—which, next to the violence itself, is probably one of the most powerful forces guaranteeing the perpetuation of systems of inequality. Another is that violence, as we've seen, allows the possibility of cutting through the subtleties of constant mutual interpretation on which ordinary human relations are based.

The details of this play of imagination against structural violence are endlessly complicated and this is hardly the place to work out the full theoretical ramifications. For now I only want to emphasize two crucial points.

The first is that the line of riot police is precisely the point where structural violence turns into the real thing. Therefore, it functions as a kind of wall against imaginative identification. Nonviolence training actually focuses on trying to break the barrier and teach activists how to constantly bear in mind what the cops are likely to be thinking, but even

here, we are usually dealing with thought on its most elemental, animal-
istic level ("a policeman will panic if he feels he is cornered," "never do
anything that he might interpret as reaching toward the gun" . . .). For
most anarchists, the existence of the imaginative wall is intensely frustrating, because anarchist morality is based on a moral imperative toward imaginative identification.[37] On many occasions, I have seen legal
trainers having to remind activists that, whatever their inclinations, one
should not engage in conversation with one's arresting officers, no matter how apparently open or interested they seem to be, because chances
are they are simply fishing for information that will help in a conviction.
And during the actions themselves, one tends to hear endless dismayed
speculation about what the cops must be thinking as they truncheon
or tear-gas nonviolent citizens; conversations that make clear, above all
else, that really, no one has the slightest idea. But this is precisely the police role. The point of military-style discipline is to make any individual
officer's actual feelings or opinions not just impenetrable, but entirely
irrelevant.

Obviously no wall is completely impenetrable. Given sufficient pressure, any wall will eventually begin to crumble. Most of those who help
to organize mass actions are keenly aware that historically, when anarchists actually win, when civil resistance campaigns of any sort topple
governments, it is usually at the point when the police refuse to fire on
them. This is one reason the image of police officers crying behind their
gas masks in Seattle was so important to them. Security officials seem to
understand this principle as well. That's why they spent so much energy,
in the months after Seattle, in trying to rally their troops.

So this is the first point: the imaginative wall.

The second point is that this juxtaposition of imagination and violence reflects a much larger conflict between two principles of political
action. One might even say, between two conceptions of political reality.
The first—call it a "political ontology of violence"—assumes that the
ultimate reality is one of forces, with "force" here largely a euphemism
for various technologies of physical coercion.

To be a "realist" in international relations, for example, has nothing to do with recognizing material realities—in fact, it is all about attributing "interests" to imaginary entities known as "nations"—but about willingness to accept the realities of violence. Nation-states are real because they can kill you.

Violence here really is what defines situations. The other could be described as a political ontology of the imagination. It's not so much a matter of giving "power to the imagination" as in recognizing that the imagination is the source of power in the first place (and here we might take note of the fact that next to the Situationists, the French theorist one will encounter the most often in anarchist bookstores is Cornelius Castoriadis).[38] This is why imaginative powers are seen as suffused with the sacred. What anarchists regularly try to do is to level a systematic and continual challenge to the right of the police, and the authorities in general, to define the situation. They do it by proposing endless alternative frameworks—or, more precisely, by insisting on the power to switch frameworks whenever they like.

Puppets are the very embodiment of this power.

What this means in the streets is that activists are trying to effectively collapse the political, negotiating process into the structure of the action itself. To win the contest, as it were, by continually changing the definition of what is the field, what are the rules, what are the stakes—and to do so on the field itself.[39] A situation that is sort of like nonviolent warfare becomes a situation that is sort of like a circus, or a theatrical performance, or a religious ritual, and might equally well slip back at any time.

Of course, from the point of view of the police, this is simply cheating. Protesters who alternate between throwing paint balls over their heads and breaking into song-and-dance numbers are not fighting fair. But of course, as we've seen, the police aren't fighting fair either. They systematically violate all the laws of combat. They systematically violate agreements. They have to, as a matter of principle, since to do otherwise would be to admit the existence of a situation of dual power; it would be to deny the absolute incommensurability of the state.

In a way, what we are confronting here is the familiar paradox of constituent power. As various German and Italian theorists are fond of reminding us, since no system can create itself (i.e., any God capable of instituting a moral order cannot be bound by that morality . . .), any legal/political order can be created only by some force to which that legality does not apply.[40] In modern Euro-American history, this has meant that the legitimacy of constitutions ultimately harkens back to some kind of popular revolution: at precisely the point, in my terms, where the politics of force does meet the politics of imagination. Now, of course, revolution is precisely what the people with the puppets feel they are ultimately about—even if they are trying to do so with an absolute minimum of actual violence. But it seems to me that what really provokes the most violent reactions on the part of the forces of order is precisely the attempt to make constituent power—the power of popular imagination to create new institutional forms—present not just in brief flashes, but continually. To permanently challenge the authorities' ability to define the situation. The insistence that the rules of engagement, as it were, can be constantly renegotiated on the field of battle, that you can constantly change the narrative in the middle of the story, is in this light just one aspect of a much larger phenomenon. It also explains why anarchists hate to think of themselves as having to rely in any way on the good offices of even well-meaning corporate media or liberal NGO groups, even the frequent hostility to would-be benefactors, who nonetheless demand, as a prerequisite to their help, the right to place anarchists within their own preset narrative frameworks. Direct action is, by definition, unmediated. It is about cutting through all such frameworks and bringing the power of definition into the streets. Obviously, under ordinary conditions—that is, outside of those magical moments when the police actually do refuse to fire—there is only a very limited degree to which one can actually do this. In the meantime, moral-political struggle in "the court of public opinion"—as well as the courts of law—would seem unavoidable. Some anarchists deny this. Others grudgingly accept it. All cling to direct action as the ultimate ideal.

This, I think, makes it easier to see why giant puppets, which are so extraordinarily creative but at the same time so intentionally ephemeral, which make a mockery of the very idea of the eternal verities that monuments are meant to represent, can so easily become the symbol of this attempt to seize the power of social creativity,[41] the power to re-create and redefine institutions. Why, as a result, they can end up standing in for everything—the new forms of organization, the emphasis on democratic process—that standard media portrayals of the movement make disappear. They embody the permanence of revolution. From the perspective of the "forces of order," this is precisely what makes them both ridiculous and somehow demonic. From the perspective of many anarchists, this is precisely what makes them both ridiculous and somehow divine.[42]

SOME VERY TENUOUS CONCLUSIONS

This essay thus ends where it should perhaps have begun, with the need to thoroughly rethink the idea of "revolution." While most of those engaged with the politics of direct action think of themselves as, in some sense, revolutionaries, few, at this point, are operating within the classic revolutionary framework where revolutionary organizing is designed to build toward a violent, apocalyptic confrontation with the state. Even fewer see revolution as a matter of seizing state power and transforming society through its mechanisms. On the other hand, neither are they simply interested in a strategy of "engaged withdrawal" (as in Virno's "revolutionary exodus") and the founding of new, autonomous communities.[43] In a way, one might say the politics of direct action, by trying to create alternative forms of organization in the very teeth of state power, means to explore a middle ground precisely between these two alternatives. Anyway, we are dealing with a new synthesis that, I think, is not yet entirely worked out.

If nothing else, some of the theoretical frameworks proposed in this essay provide an interesting vantage on the current historical moment. Consider here the notion of the "war on terror." Many have spoken with some dismay of the notion of permanent war that seems to be implied. In fact, while the twentieth century could be described as one of permanent war—almost the entire period between 1914 and 1991 was spent either fighting or preparing for world wars of one kind or another—it is

ON THE PHENOMENOLOGY OF GIANT PUPPETS   237

not at all clear whether the twenty-first could be described in the same terms. It might be better to say that what the United States is attempting to impose on the world is not really a war at all. It has, of course, become a truism that as nuclear weapons proliferate, declared wars between states no longer occur, and all conflicts come to be framed as "police actions." Still, it is also critical to bear in mind that police actions have their own, very distinctive, qualities. Police see themselves as engaged in a war largely without rules, against an opponent without honor, toward whom one is therefore not obliged to act honorably, but in which victory is ultimately impossible.

States have a strong tendency to define their relation to their people in terms of an unwinnable war of some sort or another. The American state has been one of the most flagrant in this regard: in recent decades we have seen a war on poverty degenerate into a war on crime, then a war on drugs (the first to be extended internationally), and finally, now, a war on terror. But as this sequence makes clear, the latter is not really a war at all but an attempt to extend this same, internal logic to the entire globe. It is an attempt to declare a kind of diffuse global police state. In the final analysis, I suspect the panic reaction on the part of the state was really more a reaction to the success of an ongoing, if subtle, global anticapitalist uprising than to the threat of Osama bin Laden—though the latter certainly provided the ultimate convenient excuse—it's just that on a global scale as well, moral-political struggle has created rules of engagement that make it very difficult for the United States to strike out directly at those against whom it would most like to strike out.[44]

To put it somewhat glibly: just as the structure of violence most appropriate for a political ontology based in the imagination is revolution, so is the structure of imagination most appropriate for a political ontology based in violence, precisely terror. One might add that the Bushes and Bin Ladens are working quite in tandem in this regard. (It is significant, I think, that if Al Qaeda does harbor some gigantic utopian vision—a reunification of the old Islamic Indian Ocean Diaspora? a restoration of the Caliphate?—they haven't told us much about it.)

Still, this is no doubt a bit simplistic. To understand the American

regime as a global structure, and at the same time to understand its contradictions, I think one must return to the cosmological role of the police
in American culture. It is a peculiar characteristic of life in the United
States that most American citizens, who over the course of the day can
normally be expected to try to avoid any circumstance that might lead
them to have to deal with police or police affairs, can also normally be
expected to go home and spend hours watching dramas that invite them
to see the world from a policeman's point of view. This was not always
so. It's actually quite difficult to identify an American movie from before
the 1960s where a policeman was a sympathetic hero. Over the course
of the '60s, however, police abruptly took the place previously held by
cowboys in American entertainment.[45] The timing seems hardly insignificant. Neither does the fact that by now, cinematic and TV images
of American police are being relentlessly exported to every corner of
the world, at the same time as their flesh-and-blood equivalents. What
I would emphasize here, though, is that both are characterized by an
extralegal impunity that, paradoxically, makes them able to embody a
kind of constituent power turned against itself. The Hollywood cop, like
the cowboy, is a lone maverick who breaks all the rules (this is permissible, even necessary, since he is always dealing with dishonorable opponents). In fact, it is usually precisely the maverick cop who engages in
the endless property destruction that provides so much of the pleasure
of Hollywood action films. In other words, police can be heroes in such
movies largely because they are the only figures who can systematically
ignore the law. It is constituent power turned on itself, of course, because
cops, on screen or in reality, are not trying to create (or constitute) anything. They are simply maintaining the status quo.

The moment cop movies rose to prominence, cowboy movies
effectively disappeared.

In one sense, this is the most clever ideological displacement of all—
the perfect complement to the aforementioned privatization of (consumer) desire. Insofar as the popular festival endures, it has become
pure spectacle, with the role of Master of the Potlatch granted to the
very figure who, in real life, is in charge of ensuring that any actual out-
breaks of popular festive behavior are forcibly suppressed.

Like any ideological formula, however, this one is extraordinarily unstable, riddled with contradictions—as the initial difficulties of the U.S. police in suppressing the globalization movement so vividly attest. It seems to me it is best seen as a way of managing a situation of extreme alienation and insecurity that itself can only be maintained by systematic coercion. Faced with anything that remotely resembles creative, nonalienated experience, it tends to look as ridiculous as a deodorant commercial during a time of national disaster. But then, I am an anarchist. The anarchists' problem remains how to bring that sort of experience, and the imaginative power that lies behind it, into the daily lives of those outside the small autonomous bubbles they have already created. This is a continual problem; but there seems to me every reason to believe that, were it possible, the power of the police cosmology, and with it, the power of the police themselves, would simply melt away.

PART IV THE REVOLT OF
THE CARING
CLASSES

Are You an Anarchist?

The Answer May Surprise You!

Chances are you have already heard something about who anarchists are and what they are supposed to believe. Chances are almost everything you have heard is nonsense. Many people seem to think that anarchists are proponents of violence, chaos, and destruction, that they are against all forms of order and organization, or that they are crazed nihilists who just want to blow everything up. In reality, nothing could be further from the truth. Anarchists are simply people who believe human beings are capable of behaving in a reasonable fashion without having to be forced to. It is really a very simple notion. But it's one that the rich and powerful have always found extremely dangerous.

At their very simplest, anarchist beliefs turn on two elementary assumptions. The first is that human beings are, under ordinary circumstances, about as reasonable and decent as they are allowed to be, and can organize themselves and their communities without needing to be

Originally appeared on nymaa.org, 2000.

told how. The second is that power corrupts. Most of all, anarchism is just a matter of having the courage to take the simple principles of common decency that we all live by, and to follow them through to their logical conclusions. Odd though this may seem, in most important ways you are probably already an anarchist—you just don't realize it.

Let's start by taking a few examples from everyday life.

If there's a line to get on a crowded bus, do you wait your turn and refrain from elbowing your way past others even in the absence of police?

If you answered "yes," then you are used to acting like an anarchist! The most basic anarchist principle is self-organization: the assumption that human beings do not need to be threatened with prosecution in order to be able to come to reasonable understandings with one another, or to treat one another with dignity and respect.

Everyone believes they are capable of behaving reasonably themselves. If they think laws and police are necessary, it is only because they don't believe that other people are. But if you think about it, don't those people all feel exactly the same way about you? Anarchists argue that almost all the antisocial behavior which makes us think it's necessary to have armies, police, prisons, and governments to control our lives is actually caused by the systematic inequalities and injustice those armies, police, prisons, and governments make possible. It's all a vicious circle. If people are used to being treated like their opinions do not matter, they are likely to become angry and cynical, even violent—which of course makes it easy for those in power to say that their opinions do not matter. Once they understand that their opinions really do matter just as much as anyone else's, they tend to become remarkably understanding. To cut a long story short: anarchists believe that for the most part it is power itself, and the effects of power, that make people stupid and irresponsible.

Are you a member of a club or sports team or any other voluntary organization where decisions are not imposed by one leader but made on the basis of general consent?

If you answered "yes," then you belong to an organization that works on anarchist principles! Another basic anarchist principle is voluntary association. This is simply a matter of applying democratic principles to ordinary life. The only difference is that anarchists believe it should be possible to have a society in which everything could be organized along these lines, all groups based on the free consent of their members, and therefore, that all top-down, military styles of organization like armies or bureaucracies or large corporations, based on chains of command, would no longer be necessary. Perhaps you don't believe that would be possible. Perhaps you do. But every time you reach an agreement by consensus, rather than threats, every time you make a voluntary arrangement with another person, come to an understanding, or reach a compromise by taking due consideration of the other person's particular situation or needs, you are being an anarchist—even if you don't realize it.

Anarchism is just the way people act when they are free to do as they choose, and when they deal with others who are equally free—and therefore aware of the responsibility to others that entails. This leads to another crucial point: that while people can be reasonable and considerate when they are dealing with equals, human nature is such that they cannot be trusted to do so when given power over others. Give someone such power, they will almost invariably abuse it in some way or another.

Do you believe that most politicians are selfish, egotistical swine who don't really care about the public interest? Do you think we live in an economic system that is stupid and unfair?

If you answered "yes," then you subscribe to the anarchist critique of today's society—at least, in its broadest outlines. Anarchists believe that power corrupts and those who spend their entire lives seeking power are the very last people who should have it. Anarchists believe that our present economic system is more likely to reward people for selfish and unscrupulous behavior than for being decent, caring human beings. Most people feel that way. The only difference is that most people don't think there's anything that can be done about it, or anyway—and this is what the faithful servants of the powerful are always most likely to insist—anything that won't end up making things even worse.

But what if that weren't true?

And is there really any reason to believe this? When you can actually test them, most of the usual predictions about what would happen without states or capitalism turn out to be entirely untrue. For thousands of years people lived without governments. In many parts of the world people live outside of the control of governments today. They do not all kill one another. Mostly they just get on about their lives the same as anyone else would. Of course, in a complex, urban, technological society all this would be more complicated: but technology can also make all these problems a lot easier to solve. In fact, we have not even begun to think about what our lives could be like if technology were really marshaled to fit human needs. How many hours would we really need to work in order to maintain a functional society—that is, if we got rid of all the useless or destructive occupations like telemarketers, lawyers, prison guards, financial analysts, public relations experts, bureaucrats, and politicians, and turned our best scientific minds away from working on space weaponry or stock market systems to mechanizing away dangerous or annoying tasks like coal mining or cleaning the bathroom, and distributed the remaining work among everyone equally? Five hours a day? Four? Three? Two? Nobody knows because no one is even asking this kind of question. Anarchists think these are the very questions we should be asking.

Do you really believe those things you tell your children (or that your parents told you)?

"It doesn't matter who started it." "Two wrongs don't make a right." "Clean up your own mess." "Do unto others . . ." "Don't be mean to people just because they're different." Perhaps we should decide whether we're lying to our children when we tell them about right and wrong, or whether we're willing to take our own injunctions seriously. Because if you take these moral principles to their logical conclusions, you arrive at anarchism.

Take the principle that two wrongs don't make a right. If you really took it seriously, that alone would knock away almost the entire basis for war and the criminal justice system. The same goes for sharing: we're always telling children that they have to learn to share, to be considerate of one another's needs, to help one another; then we go off into the real world where we assume that everyone is naturally selfish and competitive. But an anarchist would point out that, in fact, what we say to our children is right. Pretty much every great worthwhile achievement in human history, every discovery or accomplishment that's improved our lives, has been based on cooperation and mutual aid; even now, most of us spend more of our money on our friends and families than on ourselves; while likely as not there will always be competitive people in the world, there's no reason society has to be based on encouraging such behavior, let alone making people compete over the basic necessities of life. That only serves the interests of people in power, who want us to live in fear of one another. That's why anarchists call for a society based not only on free association but mutual aid. The fact is that most children grow up believing in anarchist morality, and then gradually have to realize that the adult world doesn't really work that way. That's why so many become rebellious, or alienated, even suicidal as adolescents, and finally, resigned and bitter as adults; their only solace, often, being the ability to raise children of their own and pretend to them that the world is fair. But what if we really could start to build a world that really was at least founded on principles of justice? Wouldn't that be the greatest gift to one's children one could possibly give?

Do you believe that human beings are fundamentally corrupt and evil, or that certain sorts of people (women, people of color, ordinary folk who are not rich or highly educated) are inferior specimens, destined to be ruled by their betters?

If you answered "yes," then, well, it looks like you aren't an anarchist after all. But if you answered "no," then chances are you already subscribe to 90 percent of anarchist principles, and, likely as not, are living your life largely in accord with them. Every time you treat another human with consideration and respect, you are being an anarchist. Every time you work out your differences with others by coming to reasonable compromise, listening to what everyone has to say rather than letting one person decide for everyone else, you are being an anarchist. Every time you have the opportunity to force someone to do something, but decide to appeal to their sense of reason or justice instead, you are being an anarchist. The same goes for every time you share something with a friend, or decide who is going to do the dishes, or do anything at all with an eye to fairness.

Now, you might object that all this is well and good as a way for small groups of people to get on with one another, but managing a city, or a country, is an entirely different matter. And of course there is something to this. Even if you decentralize society and put as much power as possible in the hands of small communities, there will still be plenty of things that need to be coordinated, from running railroads to deciding on directions for medical research. But just because something is complicated does not mean there is no way to do it democratically. It would just be complicated. In fact, anarchists have all sorts of different ideas and visions about how a complex society might manage itself. To explain them, though, would go far beyond the scope of a little introductory text like this. Suffice it to say, first of all, that a lot of people have spent a lot of time coming up with models for how a really democratic, healthy society might work; but second, and just as important, no anarchist claims to have a perfect blueprint. The last thing we want is to impose prefab models on society anyway. The truth is we probably can't even imagine half the problems that will come up when we try to create a democratic society; still, we're confident that, human ingenuity being what it is, such problems can always be solved, so long as it is in the spirit of our basic principles—which are, in the final analysis, simply the principles of fundamental human decency.

Army of Altruists

On the Alienated Right to Do Good

> You know, education, if you make the most of it, you
> study hard, you do your homework and you make an
> effort to be smart, you can do well. If you don't, you get
> stuck in Iraq.
>
> —JOHN KERRY (D-MASS.)

> Kerry owes an apology to the many thousands of
> Americans serving in Iraq, who answered their country's
> call because they are patriots and not because of any
> deficiencies in their education.
>
> —JOHN McCAIN (R-ARIZ.)

The one fleeting moment of hope for Republicans during the
lead-up to the 2006 congressional elections was afforded by
a lame joke by Senator John Kerry—a joke pretty obviously aimed at
George Bush—which they took to suggest that Kerry thought that only
those who flunked out of school end up in the military. It was all very
disingenuous. Most knew perfectly well Kerry's real point was to suggest
the president wasn't very bright.

Originally published in *Harper's Magazine*, January 2007, harpers.org.

But the right smelled blood. The problem with "aristo-slackers" like Kerry, wrote one *National Review* blogger, is that they assume "the troops are in Iraq not because they are deeply committed to the mission (they need to deny that) but rather because of a system that takes advantage of their lack of social and economic opportunities . . . We should clobber them with that ruthlessly until the day of the election—just like we did in '04—because it is the most basic reason they deserve to lose."

As it turned out, it didn't make a lot of difference, because most Americans decided they were not deeply committed to the mission either—insofar as they were even sure what the mission was. But it seems to me the question we should really be asking is: Why did it take a military catastrophe (and a strategy of trying to avoid any association with the kind of northeastern elites Kerry for so many typified) to allow the congressional Democrats to finally come out of the political wilderness? Or even more: Why has this Republican line proved so effective?

It strikes me that to get at the answer, one has to probe far more deeply into the nature of American society than most commentators, nowadays, are willing to go. We're used to reducing all such issues to an either/or: patriotism versus opportunity, values versus bread-and-butter issues like jobs and education. It seems to me though that just framing things this way plays into the hands of the right. Certainly, most people do join the army because they are deprived of opportunities. But the real question to be asking is: Opportunities to do what?

I'm an anthropologist and what follows might be considered an anthropological perspective on the question. It first came home to me a year or two ago when I was attending a lecture by Catherine Lutz, a fellow anthropologist from Brown who has been studying U.S. military bases overseas. Many of these bases organize outreach programs, in which soldiers venture out to repair schoolrooms or to perform free dental checkups for the locals. These programs were created to improve local relations, but in this task they often proved remarkably ineffective. Why, then, did the army not abandon them? The answer was that the programs had such enormous psychological impact on the soldiers, many of whom would wax euphoric when describing them: e.g., "This is why I joined the army"; "This is what military service is really all about—not just defending your country, but helping people." Professor Lutz is convinced that the main reason these programs continue to be funded is that soldiers who take part in them are more likely to reenlist. The military's own statistics are no help here: the surveys do not list "helping people" among the motives for reenlistment. Interestingly, it is the most high-minded option available—"patriotism"—that is the overwhelming favorite.

Certainly, Americans do not see themselves as a nation of frustrated altruists. Quite the opposite: our normal habits of thought tend toward a rough-and-ready cynicism. The world is a giant marketplace; everyone is in it for a buck; if you want to understand why something happened, first ask who stands to gain by it. The same attitudes expressed in the back rooms of bars are echoed in the highest reaches of social science. America's great contribution to the world in the latter respect has been the development of "rational choice" theories, which proceed from the assumption that all human behavior can be understood as a matter of economic calculation, of rational actors trying to get as much as possible out of any given situation with the least cost to themselves. As a result, in most fields, the very existence of altruistic behavior is considered a kind of puzzle, and everyone from economists to evolutionary biologists have made themselves famous through attempts to "solve" it—that is, to explain the mystery of why bees sacrifice themselves for hives or human beings hold open doors and give correct street directions to total strangers. At the same time, the case of the military bases suggests the possibility that in fact Americans, particularly the less affluent ones, are haunted by frustrated desires to do good in the world.

It would not be difficult to assemble evidence that this is the case. Studies of charitable giving, for example, have always shown the poor to be the most generous: the lower one's income, the higher the proportion of it that one is likely to give away to strangers. The same pattern holds true, incidentally, when comparing the middle classes and the rich: one study of tax returns in 2003 concluded that if the most affluent families had given away as much of their assets even as the average middle-class family, overall charitable donations that year would have increased by $25 billion. (All this despite the fact the wealthy have far more time and opportunity.) Moreover, charity represents only a tiny part of the picture. If one were to break down what the typical American wage earner does with his money one would likely find he gives most of it away. Take a typical male head of household. About a third of his annual income is likely to end up being redistributed to strangers, through taxes and charity—another third he is likely to give in one way or another to his children; of the remainder, probably the largest part is given to or shared with others: presents, trips, parties, the six-pack of beer for the local softball game.

One might object that this latter is more a reflection of the real nature of pleasure than anything else (who would want to eat a delicious meal at an expensive restaurant all by themselves?), but this is actually half the point. Even our self-indulgences tend to be dominated by the logic of the gift. Similarly, some might object that shelling out a small fortune to send one's children to an exclusive kindergarten is more about status than altruism. Perhaps: but if you look at what happens over the course of people's actual lives, it soon becomes apparent this kind of behavior fulfills an identical psychological need. How many youthful idealists throughout history have managed to finally come to terms with a world based on selfishness and greed the moment they start a family? If one were to assume altruism were the primary human motivation, this would make perfect sense: The only way they can convince themselves to abandon their desire to do right by the world as a whole is to substitute an even more powerful desire to do right by their children.

What all this suggests to me is that American society might well work completely differently than we tend to assume. Imagine, for a moment, that the United States as it exists today were the creation of some ingenious social engineer. What assumptions about human nature could we say this engineer must have been working with? Certainly nothing like rational choice theory. For clearly our social engineer understands that the only way to convince human beings to enter into the world of work and the marketplace (that is: of mind-numbing labor and cutthroat competition) is to dangle the prospect of thereby being able to lavish money on one's children, buy drinks for one's friends, and, if one hits the jackpot, to be able to spend the rest of one's life endowing museums and providing AIDS medications to impoverished countries in Africa. Where our theorists are constantly trying to strip away the veil of appearances and show how all such apparently selfless gestures really mask some kind of self-interested strategy, in reality, American society is better conceived as a battle over access to the right to behave altruistically. Selflessness—or at least, the right to engage in high-minded activity—is not the strategy. It is the prize. If nothing else, I think this helps us understand why the right has been so much better, in recent years, at playing to populist sentiments than the left. Essentially, they do it by accusing liberals of cutting ordinary Americans off from the right to do good in the world. Let me explain what I mean here by throwing out a series of propositions.

PROPOSITION I: Neither egoism nor altruism are natural urges; they in fact arise in relation to each other and neither would be conceivable without the market.

First of all, I should make clear that I do not believe that either egoism or altruism are somehow inherent to human nature. Human motives are rarely that simple. Rather, egoism or altruism are ideas we have about human nature. Historically, one tends to arise in response to the other. In the ancient world, for example, it is precisely in the times and places one sees the emergence of money and markets that one also sees the rise of world religions—Buddhism, Christianity, and Islam. If one sets aside a space and says, "Here you shall think only about acquiring material things for yourself," then it is hardly surprising that before long someone else will set aside a countervailing space, declaring, in effect: "Yes, but here we must contemplate the fact that the self, and material things, are ultimately unimportant." It was these latter institutions, of course, that first developed our modern notions of charity.

Even today, when we operate outside the domain of the market or of religion, very few of our actions could be said to be motivated by anything so simple as untrammeled greed or utterly selfless generosity. When we are dealing not with strangers but with friends, relatives, or enemies, a much more complicated set of motivations will generally come into play: envy, solidarity, pride, self-destructive grief, loyalty, romantic obsession, resentment, spite, shame, conviviality, the anticipation of shared enjoyment, the desire to show up a rival, and so on. These are the motivations that impel the major dramas of our lives, that great novelists like Tolstoy and Dostoevsky immortalize, but that social theorists, for some reason, tend to ignore. If one travels to parts of the world where money and markets do not exist—say, to certain parts of New Guinea or Amazonia—such complicated webs of motivation are precisely what one still finds. In societies where most people live in small communities, where almost everyone they know is a friend, a relative, or an enemy, the languages spoken tend even to lack words that correspond to self-interest or altruism, while including very subtle vocabularies for describing envy, solidarity, pride, and the like. Their economic dealings with one another likewise tend to be based on much more subtle principles. Anthropologists have created a vast literature to try to fathom the dynamics of these apparently exotic "gift economies," but if it seems odd to us to see, say, important men conniving with their cousins to finagle vast wealth, which they then present as gifts to bitter enemies in order to publicly humiliate them, it is because we are so used to operating inside impersonal markets that it never occurs to us to think how we would act if we had an economic system where we treated people based on how we actually felt about them.

Nowadays, the work of destroying such ways of life is largely left to missionaries—representatives of those very world religions that originally sprang up in reaction to the market long ago. Missionaries, of course, are out to save souls; but they rarely interpret this to mean their role is simply to teach people to accept God and be more altruistic.

Almost invariably, they end up trying to convince people to be more selfish and more altruistic, at the same time. On the one hand, they set out to teach the "natives" proper work discipline, and try to get them involved with buying and selling products on the market, so as to better their material lot. At the same time, they explain to them that ultimately, material things are unimportant, and lecture on the value of the higher things, such as selfless devotion to others.

PROPOSITION II: The political right has always tried to enhance this division, and thus claim to be champions of egoism and altruism simultaneously. The left has tried to efface it.

Might this not help to explain why the United States, the most market-driven industrialized society on earth, is also the most religious? Or, even more strikingly, why the country that produced Tolstoy and Dostoevsky spent much of the twentieth century trying to eradicate both the market and religion entirely?

Whereas the political left has always tried to efface this distinction—whether by trying to create economic systems that are not driven by the profit motive, or by replacing private charity with one or another form of community support—the political right has always thrived on it. In the United States, for example, the Republican Party is dominated by two ideological wings: the libertarian, and the "Christian right." At one extreme, Republicans are free-market fundamentalists and advocates of individual liberties (even if they see those liberties largely as a matter of consumer choice); on the other, they are fundamentalists of a more literal variety, suspicious of most individual liberties but enthusiastic about biblical injunctions, "family values," and charitable good works. At first glance it might seem remarkable that such an alliance manages to hold together at all (and certainly they have ongoing tensions, most famously over abortion). But in fact right-wing coalitions almost always take some variation of this form. One might say that the conservative approach always has been to release the dogs of the market, throwing all traditional verities into disarray; and then, in this tumult of insecurity, offering themselves up as the last bastion of order and hierarchy, the stalwart defenders of the authority of churches and fathers against the barbarians they have themselves unleashed. A scam it may be, but a remarkably effective one; and one effect is that the right ends up seeming to have a monopoly on value. They manage, we might say, to occupy both positions, on either side of the divide: extreme egoism and extreme altruism.

Consider, for a moment, the word *value*. When economists talk about value they are really talking about money—or more precisely, about whatever it is that money is measuring; also, whatever it is that economic actors are assumed to be pursuing. When we are working for a living, or buying and selling things, we are rewarded with money. But whenever we are not working or buying or selling, when we are motivated by pretty much anything other than the desire to get money, we suddenly find ourselves in the domain of "values." The most commonly invoked of these are of course "family values" (which is unsurprising, since by far the most common form of unpaid labor in most industrial societies is child-rearing and housework), but we also talk about religious values, political values, the values that attach themselves to art or patriotism—one could even, perhaps, count loyalty to one's favorite basketball team. All are seen as commitments that are, or ought to be, uncorrupted by the market. At the same time, they are also seen as utterly unique; where money makes all things comparable, "values" such as beauty, devotion, or integrity cannot, by definition, be compared. There is no mathematical formula that could possibly allow one to calculate just how much personal integrity it is right to sacrifice in the pursuit of art, or how to balance responsibilities to your family with responsibilities to your god. (Obviously, people do make these kinds of compromises all the time. But they cannot be calculated). One might put it this way: if value is simply what one considers important, then money allows importance to take a liquid form, enables us to compare precise quantities of importance and trade one off for the other. After all, if someone does accumulate a very large amount of money, the first thing they are likely to do is try to convert it into something unique, whether this be Monet's water lilies, a prize-winning racehorse, or an endowed chair at a university.

What is really at stake here in any market economy is precisely the ability to make these trades, to convert "value" into "values." We all are striving to put ourselves in a position where we can dedicate ourselves to something larger than ourselves. When liberals do well in America, it's because they can embody that possibility: the Kennedys, for example, are the ultimate Democratic icons not just because they started as poor Irish immigrants who made enormous amounts of money, but because they are seen as having managed, ultimately, to turn all that money into nobility.

PROPOSITION III: The real problem of the American left is that while it does try in certain ways to efface the division between egoism and altruism, value and values, it largely does so for its own children. This has allowed the right to paradoxically represent itself as the champions of the working class.

All this might help explain why the left in America is in such a mess. Far from promoting new visions of effacing the difference between egoism and altruism, value and values, or providing a model for passing from one to the other, progressives cannot even seem to think their way past it. After the last presidential election, the big debate in progressive circles was the relative importance of economic issues versus what was called the "culture wars." Did the Democrats lose because they were not able to spell out any plausible economic alternatives, or did the Republicans win because they successfully mobilized conservative Christians around the issue of gay marriage? As I say, the very fact that progressives frame the question this way not only shows they are trapped in the right's terms of analysis. It demonstrates they do not understand how America really works.

Let me illustrate what I mean by considering the strange popular appeal, at least until recently, of George W. Bush. In 2004, most of the American liberal intelligentsia did not seem to be able to get their heads around it. After the election, what left so many of them reeling was their suspicion that the things they most hated about Bush were exactly what so many Bush voters liked about him. Consider the debates, for example. If statistics are to be believed, millions of Americans who watched George Bush and John Kerry lock horns concluded that Kerry won, and then went off and voted for Bush anyway. It was hard to escape the suspicion that in the end, Kerry's articulate presentation, his skill with words and arguments, had actually counted against him.

This sends liberals into spirals of despair. They cannot understand why decisive leadership is equated with acting like an idiot. Neither can they understand how a man who comes from one of the most elite families in the country, who attended Andover, Yale, and Harvard, and whose signature facial expression is a self-satisfied smirk, could ever convince anyone he was a "man of the people." I must admit I have struggled with this as well. As a child of working-class parents who won a scholarship to Andover in the 1970s and, eventually, a job at Yale, I have spent much of my life in the presence of men like Bush, everything about them oozing self-satisfied privilege. But in fact, stories like mine—stories of dramatic class mobility through academic accomplishment—are increasingly unusual in America.

America, of course, continues to see itself as a land of opportunity, and certainly from the perspective of an immigrant from Haiti or Bangladesh, it is. No doubt in terms of overall social mobility, we still compare favorably with countries like Bolivia or France. But the United States has always been a country built on the promise of unlimited upward mobility. The working-class condition has been traditionally seen as a way station, as something one's family passes through on the road to something better. Lincoln used to stress that what made American democracy possible was the absence of a class of permanent wage laborers. In Lincoln's day, the ideal was that it was mainly immigrants who worked as wage laborers, and that they did so in order to save up enough money to do something else: if nothing else, to buy some land and become a homesteader on the frontier.

The point is not how accurate this ideal was; the point was most

Americans have found the image plausible. Every time the road is perceived to be clogged, profound unrest ensues. The closing of the frontier led to bitter labor struggles, and over the course of the twentieth century, the steady and rapid expansion of the American university system could be seen as a kind of substitute. Particularly after World War II, huge resources were poured into expanding the higher education system, which grew extremely rapidly, and all this was promoted quite explicitly as a means of social mobility. This served during the Cold War as almost an implied social contract, not just offering a comfortable life to the working classes but holding out the chance that their children would not be working-class themselves.

The problem, of course, is that a higher education system cannot be expanded forever. At a certain point one ends up with a significant portion of the population unable to find work even remotely in line with their qualifications, who have every reason to be angry about their situation, and who also have access to the entire history of radical thought. During the twentieth century, this was precisely the situation most likely to spark revolts and insurrections—revolutionary heroes from Chairman Mao to Fidel Castro almost invariably turn out to be children of poor parents who scrimped to give their children a bourgeois education, only to discover that a bourgeois education does not, in itself, guarantee entry into the bourgeoisie. By the late '60s and early '70s, the very point where the expansion of the university system hit a dead end, campuses were, predictably, exploding.

What followed could be seen as a kind of settlement. Campus radicals were reabsorbed into the university, but set to work largely at training children of the elite. As the cost of education has skyrocketed, financial aid has been cut back, and the government has begun aggressively pursuing student loan debts that once existed largely on paper, the prospect of social mobility through education—above all, liberal arts education—has been rapidly diminished. The number of working-class students in major universities, which steadily grew until at least the late '60s, has now been declining for decades. If working-class Bush voters tend to resent intellectuals more than they do the rich, then, the most likely reason is because they can imagine scenarios in which they might become rich, but cannot imagine one in which they, or any of their children, could ever become members of the intelligentsia. If you think about it, this is not an unreasonable assessment. A mechanic from Nebraska knows it is highly unlikely that his son or daughter will ever become an Enron executive. But it is possible. There is virtually no chance, on the other hand, that his child, no matter how talented, will ever become an international human rights lawyer, or a drama critic for *The New York Times*. Here we need to remember not just the changes in higher education, but also the role of unpaid, or effectively unpaid, internships. It has become a fact of life in the United States that if one chooses a career for any reason other than the money, for the first year or two one will not be paid. This is certainly true if one wishes to be involved in altruistic pursuits: say, to join the world of charities, or NGOs, or to become a political activist. But it is equally true if one wants to pursue values like Beauty or Truth: to become part of the world of books, or the art world, or an investigative reporter. The custom effectively seals off any such career for any poor student who actually does attain a liberal arts education. Such structures of exclusion had always existed, of course, especially at the top, but in recent decades fences have become fortresses.

If that mechanic's son—or daughter—wishes to pursue something higher, more noble, for a career, what options does she really have? Likely just two. She can seek employment with her local church, which is hard to get. Or she can join the army.

This is, of course, the secret of nobility. To be noble is to be generous, high-minded, altruistic, to pursue higher forms of value. But it is also to be able to do so because one does not really have to think too much about money. This is precisely what our soldiers are doing when they give free dental examinations to villagers: they are being paid (modestly, but adequately) to do good in the world. Seen in this light, it is also easier to see what really happened at universities in the wake of the 1960s— the "settlement" I mentioned above. Campus radicals set out to create a new society that destroyed the distinction between egoism and altruism, value and values. It did not work out, but they were, effectively, offered a kind of compensation: the privilege to use the university system to create lives that did so; in their own little way, to be supported in one's material needs while pursuing virtue, truth, and beauty, and above all, to pass that privilege on to their own children. One cannot blame them for accepting the offer. But neither can one blame the rest of the country for resenting the hell out of them. Not because they reject the project: as I say, this is what America is all about.

As I always ask activists engaged in the peace movement and counterrecruitment campaigns: Why do working-class kids join the army anyway? Because, like any teenager, they want to escape the world of tedious work and meaningless consumerism, to live a life of adventure and camaraderie in which they believe they are doing something genuinely noble. They join the army because they want to be like you.

Caring Too Much

That's the Curse of the Working Classes

W hy has the basic logic of austerity been accepted by everyone? Because solidarity has come to be viewed as a scourge.

"What I can't understand is, why aren't people rioting in the streets?" I hear this, now and then, from people of wealthy and powerful backgrounds. There is a kind of incredulity. "After all," the subtext seems to read, "we scream bloody murder when anyone so much as threatens our tax shelters; if someone were to go after my access to food or shelter, I'd sure as hell be burning banks and storming parliament. What's wrong with these people?"

It's a good question. One would think a government that has inflicted such suffering on those with the least resources to resist, without even turning the economy around, would have been at risk of political suicide. Instead, the basic logic of austerity has been accepted by almost

Originally published in *The Guardian*, March 26, 2014, theguardian.com.

everyone. Why? Why do politicians promising continued suffering win any working-class acquiescence, let alone support, at all?

I think the very incredulity with which I began provides a partial answer. Working-class people may be, as we're ceaselessly reminded, less meticulous about matters of law and propriety than their "betters," but they're also much less self-obsessed. They care more about their friends, families, and communities. In aggregate, at least, they're just fundamentally nicer.

To some degree this seems to reflect a universal sociological law. Feminists have long since pointed out that those on the bottom of any unequal social arrangement tend to think about, and therefore care about, those on top more than those on top think about, or care about, them. Women everywhere tend to think and know more about men's lives than men do about women, just as black people know more about white people's, employees about employers', and the poor about the rich.

And humans being the empathetic creatures that they are, knowledge leads to compassion. The rich and powerful, meanwhile, can remain oblivious and uncaring, because they can afford to. Numerous psychological studies have recently confirmed this. Those born to working-class families invariably score far better at tests of gauging others' feelings than scions of the rich, or professional classes. In a way it's hardly surprising. After all, this is what being "powerful" is largely about: not having to pay a lot of attention to what those around one are thinking and feeling. The powerful employ others to do that for them.

And who do they employ? Mainly children of the working classes. Here I believe we tend to be so blinded by an obsession with (dare I say, romanticization of?) factory labor as our paradigm for "real work" that we have forgotten what most human labor actually consists of.

Even in the days of Karl Marx or Charles Dickens, working-class neighborhoods housed far more maids, bootblacks, dustmen, cooks, nurses, cabbies, schoolteachers, prostitutes, and costermongers than employees in coal mines, textile mills, or iron foundries. All the more so today. What we think of as archetypally women's work—looking after people, seeing to their wants and needs, explaining, reassuring, anticipating what the boss wants or is thinking, not to mention caring for, monitoring, and maintaining plants, animals, machines, and other objects—accounts for a far greater proportion of what working-class people do when they're working than hammering, carving, hoisting, or harvesting things.

This is true not only because most working-class people are women (since most people in general are women), but because we have a skewed view even of what men do. As striking Tube workers recently had to explain to indignant commuters, "ticket takers" don't in fact spend most of their time taking tickets: they spend most of their time explaining things, fixing things, finding lost children, and taking care of the old, sick, and confused.

If you think about it, is this not what life is basically about? Human beings are projects of mutual creation. Most of the work we do is on one another. The working classes just do a disproportionate share. They are the caring classes, and always have been. It is just the incessant demonization directed at the poor by those who benefit from their caring labor that makes it difficult, in a public forum such as this, to acknowledge it.

As the child of a working-class family, I can attest this is what we were actually proud of. We were constantly being told that work is a virtue in itself—it shapes character or somesuch—but nobody believed that. Most of us felt work was best avoided, that is, unless it benefited others. But of work that did, whether it meant building bridges or emptying bedpans, you could be rightly proud. And there was something else we were definitely proud of: that we were the kind of people who took care of one another. That's what set us apart from the rich, who, as far as most of us could make out, could half the time barely bring themselves to care about their own children.

There is a reason the ultimate bourgeois virtue is thrift, and the ultimate working-class virtue is solidarity. Yet this is precisely the rope from which that class is currently suspended. There was a time when caring for one's community could mean fighting for the working class itself. Back in those days we used to talk about "social progress." Today we are seeing the effects of a relentless war against the very idea of working-class politics or working-class community. That has left most working people with little way to express that care except to direct it toward some manufactured abstraction: "our grandchildren"; "the nation"; whether through jingoist patriotism or appeals to collective sacrifice.

As a result everything is thrown into reverse. Generations of political manipulation have finally turned that sense of solidarity into a scourge. Our caring has been weaponized against us. And so it is likely to remain until the left, which claims to speak for laborers, begins to think seriously and strategically about what most labor actually consists of, and what those who engage in it actually think is virtuous about it.

The Revolt of the Caring Classes

This lecture marks the fiftieth anniversary of the beginning of the events that came to be known as May '68, the most dramatic moment of what Immanuel Wallerstein has referred to as "the world revolution of 1968," and I am here, I imagine, in part because of my own modest role in what he has also termed "the world revolution of 2011." So I thought it would be appropriate to consider some things that have changed between the two.

Nineteen sixty-eight is often presented as the last magnificent gasp of the insurrectionary dream of workers and intellectuals combining forces to rise up against bureaucracies of both state and capital. Its aftermath saw the lighting of a kind of vast intellectual bonfire, onto which all the tenets of previous radical orthodoxy, and particularly Marxist orthodoxy, were thrown one by one: dialectics, alienation, emancipation, critique, and above all, the notion that the proletariat, or probably anyone (the people, humanity itself), could be the proper revolutionary subject—or even be said to really exist. This put those inclined to rise

Lecture presented at the Collège de France, 2018.

up against the system in the obviously uncomfortable position of not knowing precisely in whose name they are rising up.

Of course, there have been a variety of efforts to solve this problem, from the post-workerist "multitude" to the more recent 99 percent. But rather than offer a critical appraisal, I thought it would be more interesting to start by looking at the sort of movements that have emerged leading up to 2011—starting those I've been involved with myself, from the Alterglobalization "movement of movements" to Occupy Wall Street— and in their immediate wake, to consider their common features, and to understand why they've taken the form they have. Generally these are not proletarian movements in the classic sense, though generally they contain strong working-class support, but neither have they been identity-based. Most are organized around an activist core that is fairly typical of the composition of nineteenth- or twentieth-century revolutionary vanguards—that is, a confluence of rebel children of the professional classes, and frustrated upwardly mobile children of the popular classes who have discovered that acquiring a bourgeois education does not actually win one entry into the bourgeoisie. (I would be a textbook example of the latter category.) What's really crucial, however, is the shifting nature of the primary constituency or support base for the movements, which was still somewhat opaque during the Alterglobalization movement, but had really become apparent a decade later, as the class of caregivers—that is, in the broadest possible definition, as anyone who saw their work primarily as helping, caring for, or furthering the development or flourishing of other human beings (or, arguably, living beings)—what I called the caring classes, or the class empathiques (Nafe Krandi-Mayor) or courgeoisie (Holly Wood).

I was particularly struck by surveying the "We are the 99%" tumblr page created in the early days of Occupy, where supporters too busy working to take part in the occupations could express support by holding up handwritten placards describing their situation, which always ended with "I am the 99%"—there were several thousand of these and I once spent an afternoon systematically reading through each and every one of them, and discovering that not only were they something like

75–80 percent from women, the overwhelming majority of them were involved in teaching, health, social service provision, or some field that directly involved helping or caring for others. And the complaints expressed were surprisingly uniform: essentially, that if one insisted on pursuing a career that allowed one to care for others, one considered socially useful, or even not socially destructive, one is inevitably paid so little, and left so deeply in debt, that one could not even take care of one's own family. This is how I first came to think of Occupy as "the revolt of the caring classes"—but it opens up a series of important questions about the changing organization of capitalism, the changing nature of work and assumptions about what is valuable about it, and of the composition of the workforce.

THE NATURE OF CONTEMPORARY CAPITALISM, IF IT CAN EVEN BE REFERRED TO AS SUCH

Here I am afraid I am obliged to move very quickly over a series of interlinked arguments that I have made elsewhere and which, though they depart somewhat from conventional understandings, I will have to simply summarize rather than demonstrate in any way. I will simply beg my audience's indulgence and list them.

1. ruling class—since the '70s and '80s, there has been a fusion of the upper echelons of corporate bureaucracies with finance, to which it had been previously opposed.
2. role of the state—since this new ruling class based its income increasingly on rent-taking, debt creation, and debt-trading ("financialization"), it changed the relation of state and capital; no longer primarily a guarantor of the property rights that allowed surplus extraction through the wage, the state increasingly played a direct role in that extraction ("by jural-political means") and this in turn meant state and corporate bureaucracies not only expanded, but fused, until the point where in many cases it's impossible to say where one starts and another

ends. This was most dramatically illustrated in the "too big to fail" bailouts in 2008, but it has become a basic feature of the new economic order.

3. organization of the workforce—the popular discourse was one of the rise of the "service economy," but in fact, the numbers of actual service providers, in the sense of waiters or hairdressers, have remained effectively unchanged for the last century at roughly 20 percent; what has changed dramatically is the number of clerical, administrative, information, and supervisory workers, which has expanded to well over half the workforce in wealthy countries over the last several decades. The remarkable thing about many of these jobs—and this includes whole industries that have ballooned, such as corporate law, telemarketing, lobbying, and university administration—is that the vast majority of those who work in such fields, at least in the lower echelons, are convinced their jobs are totally pointless.

This latter is the most surprising discovery of my own research on work, which was carried out at first in a relatively haphazard fashion, less as part of my academic work than it was political in motivation. It had long struck me that many of the standard justifications for capitalist inequalities having largely evaporated (I'm referring here to arguments based on capitalism producing rising living standards for the poor, a growing and politically stable middle class, or rapid technological advance), it is largely held in place to moral imperatives, the most powerful and universally accepted of these being the moral power of work and the moral power of debt. My research on the morality of debt, like that on contemporary forms of work, was essentially meant as political interventions: to try to understand the opponent's strengths as well as weaknesses. What I discovered was that over the course of the twentieth century, most people in developed economies really have internalized the morality of work—that is, that anyone not laboring harder than they would like to at something they do not much enjoy, preferably under the supervision of a hard taskmaster of some kind, is not really a full moral person, and probably does not deserve the support of his or her community—this very moral impulse had produced a perverse and paradoxical situation where enormous percentages of the workforce were convinced they were employed at absolutely nothing, and that were their jobs to disappear, it would make absolutely no difference whatsoever. The original piece I wrote in this regard, "On the Phenomenon of Bullshit Jobs" in 2013, was more in the way of a thought experiment than anything else: I speculated that this was the reason Keynes's predictions of a fifteen-hour work week never ended up coming about; perhaps, what Keynes called "technological unemployment"—which we're all supposed to believe was a false alarm warning of something that never really happened—actually did happen, but that, instead of reducing hours and redistributing the necessary work, we had, collectively, instead decided to make up meaningless jobs to keep unemployment rates steady at 5–8 percent. At the time I didn't much speculate on who the "we" in question really were, other than to observe that those running things were aware, and undoubtedly pleased, that, as George Orwell put it, "a population busy working, even at completely useless occupations, doesn't have time to do much else." The response was overwhelming and more than confirmed the premise: not only did the piece, published in a very obscure venue, go instantly viral, being translated within weeks into more than a dozen languages, but actual surveys followed that confirmed that, at least in the Netherlands and the UK, between 37 and 40 percent of employees in all occupations were convinced their jobs were completely unnecessary and pointless, and perhaps only half were entirely convinced their jobs served some viable social purpose.

This was much higher than I myself had anticipated.

*   *   *

The reasons for the rise of bullshit jobs are complex, but appear to be directly related to financialization: I have myself coined the term "managerial feudalism" for the endless multiplication of intermediate levels of administration, whether it's the dramatic increase of administrative staff in universities, since reorganizing education on corporate grounds has largely meant shifting power to a new faux-executive class of administrators who immediately insist on each commanding a small army of subordinates as a basic mark of status, to the creation of new layers of functionaries in corporate middle management, the creative industries (producers, curators, etc.) whose main jobs often seem to be forcing actual producers to devote increasing proportions of their time to internal marketing rituals. The surprising thing revealed by my own research is the intensity of the misery and social suffering these jobs create—a suffering all the more acute because there's almost no acceptable way to talk about it.

It also raises very interesting questions about popular theories of social value, because, of course, for a worker to believe her well-compensated administrative position to be socially "worthless" means she believes there is some standard for measuring worth other than market diktat. In fact, not only does the market assessment of the value of different forms of work not correspond to popular conceptions of what they actually contribute to society, but there actually seems to be an inverse relation: with few exceptions, the principle seems to be, the more one's work is seen as socially useful, the more it is recognized as helping others, the less one is likely to be paid for it. I should emphasize that this is not simply an effect of supply and demand—even though the initial instinct of economists, or those who believe our society really is governed by a market logic, would be to say that it must be. For instance, at the moment the United States has for some years been experiencing an acute shortage of trained nurses, and a glut of law school graduates. Yet the relative salaries of nurses and corporate lawyers remains unchanged. Clearly the real reasons for the price of labor, as with the price of most things actually, have little to do with market forces, and much to do with various forms of institutional power. But what I really want to draw attention to here—the really remarkable thing—is the degree to which people seem to feel that this is precisely as things *should* be. Perhaps the most well-articulated example of this are attitudes toward primary- or secondary-school teachers, who, it is often said, shouldn't be paid too generously, because, after all, "we wouldn't want people motivated primarily by money to be teaching our children." But this is seen to extend more generally: it's not just that employers feel that, if there's a task that anyone would conceivably do for any reason other than the money (for instance, translation work or graphic design) they really ought to contrive a way to get someone to do it for free; but that those who enjoy their work, or even are able to take pleasure in the fact that their work does indeed help others, shouldn't be paid, or at least, not nearly so much—it's only people who are working only for the money who deserve any appreciable amount of the stuff.

It's almost as if the old Stoic dictum *virtus ipsa pretium sui*, that virtue is (or ought to be) its own reward, has become a guiding principle for our economic life.

*   *   *

These sentiments have dramatic political repercussions. I genuinely believe it is impossible to understand the politics of austerity without them. In the UK, for instance, eight years of "austerity" have seen effective pay cuts to almost all of those who provide immediate and obvious benefits to the public—nurses, bus drivers, firefighters, railroad information booth workers, emergency medical personnel . . . It has come to the point where there are full-time nurses dependent on charity food banks. Yet creating this situation became such a point of pride for the party in power that parliamentarians were known to give out collective cheers on voting down bills proposing to give nurses or police a raise. The same party took a notoriously indulgent view of the sharply rising compensation of those City bankers who had almost crashed the world economy a few years before. Yet that government remained highly popular. There is a sense, it would seem, that an ethos of collective sacrifice for the common good *should* fall disproportionately on those who are already, by their choice of line of work, engaged in sacrifice for the common good.

*   *   *

One result is that national politics, in most countries, have come to be organized around—indeed, national life in a certain sense, to be held together by—a complex play of (often unstated) resentments. Those stuck in bullshit jobs resent those sectors of the working class who have traditionally productive labor, or whose work clearly helps others: hence, for instance, the strange ire directed, in the United States, against unionized auto workers or teachers when they have the temerity to demand decent wages and benefit packages, a rancor that never seems to be directed toward auto executives or school administrators. But at the same time, members of the working class have come to resent members of the intellectual and cultural elites far more than they do members of the economic elite. I'd long been puzzled by this fact—so regularly and skillfully exploited by right-wing populists. I think I cracked the riddle, at least to my own satisfaction, only by juxtaposing the hatred of the liberal elite with that other most effective right-wing populist refrain "support the troops," the unconditional adulation of—especially low-ranking—members of the military. There seemed a sense that these were connected but on the surface, at least, there seems no obvious reason. Then it occurred to me: this was really a conflict over different conceptions of nobility. What we are seeing is a resentment of a class of people who are seen as having monopolized all those jobs where one could be handsomely paid to pursue some form of value other than purely material.

A repairman in Nebraska or parking attendant in Detroit, after all, could imagine a scenario in which their child might become rich—unlikely though that might be. They found it impossible to imagine a scenario where their child might become drama critic of *The New York Times*, or an international human rights lawyer. And in this they were perfectly correct: the barriers are indeed higher. Those fields which are seen as cut off from the ordinary citizen are, in turn, precisely those where it is possible to pursue "values" rather than mere economic "value": truth (journalism, higher education), beauty (literature, the arts), justice (activism, human rights), charity, and so forth. Curiously, what are called "value voters" hate that class which purports to have monopolized the pursuit of value, just as they celebrate the armed forces. But this, too, makes sense: since, after all, if that repairman or parking attendant's son was determined to pursue a career where he was, indeed, paid a living wage and benefits to pursue something noble, something other than money, what options are really open to him? Perhaps to work in the church. More likely, to join the army. This is, for instance, why the particular animus directed toward Hollywood as the very epitome of this "liberal elite" also makes perfect sense: where once Hollywood was imagined as a magical place of potential social elevation, where poor farm girls go off to be discovered (it doesn't matter how often this really happened, though it did occasionally, so much so that people imagined it *could* happen), nowadays it appears to be dominated by an endogamous caste most of whose members can trace back generations of previous actors, writers, directors, and producers—which makes their pretenses toward a politics in favor of the little man seem all the more hypocritical to those who know they are permanently locked out of the worlds such figures inhabit.

I should add here that this also helps explain how and why racial politics takes the particular form that it does in the United States—and here the U.S. is, as it was in the earlier part of the twentieth century, the experimental ground, as it were, for certain forms of fascism that were later adopted in Europe and elsewhere around the world. Generally speaking, working-class immigrants and African Americans are the exception, and are not anti-intellectual in the same sense; most still see education as an honorable and legitimate means of advance rather than a mechanism of violent exclusion. This profound difference in orientation is one reason "working class" and "white working class" can become near-synonyms not only in the United States but so many other rich countries as well.

*   *   *

This state of affairs is clearly disastrous. But for the most part intellectuals have done an extremely poor job in analyzing these dynamics, let alone engaging in work that might contribute to supporting an effective opposition. Some key elements in the picture, such as the growth of useless employment, have barely been identified as a social problem or been the object of any sustained analysis in their own right. Let me devote the rest of this exposition to thinking about how we might do a better job.

Everything, in all these cases, revolves around different conceptions of value, and I don't think we can fully understand how we have come to accept the idea of there being a moral value in useless employment, and the various hatreds and resentments that ensue. Crucially, we need to consider the history of conceptions of work in what we somewhat dubiously call "the Western tradition." In both the story of the Garden of Eden, and the Hesiodic myth of Prometheus, work is seen as their punishment for defiance of a divine Creator, but at the same time as a more modest instantiation of the divine power of Creation itself. We are punished for defying God but forced to imitate God, forced to wield the divine power of creation against our will, but in a way guaranteed to produce misery.

Now, one could argue that this is simply in each case a poetic extrapolation of the two key aspects of what has become our common definition of work: first, that it is something no one would ordinarily wish to be doing for its own sake (hence, punishment); second, that we do it anyway to accomplish something beyond the work itself (hence, creation). But the fact that this "something beyond" should be conceived as "creation" is not self-evident. In fact, it's somewhat odd. After all, most work can't be said to "create" anything; most of it is a matter of maintaining and rearranging things.

Consider a coffee cup. We "produce" it once. We wash it a thousand times. Even work we do think of as "productive"—growing potatoes, forging a shovel, assembling a computer—could just as easily be seen as

tending, transforming, reshaping, and rearranging materials and elements that already exist.

This is why I would agree with Professor Descola that our concept
of "production," and our assumption that work is defined by its "productivity," is essentially theological. The Judeo-Christian God created
the universe out of nothing. (This in itself is slightly unusual; most Gods
work with existing materials.) His latter-day worshippers, and their descendants, have come to think of themselves as cursed to imitate God
in this regard. The sleight-of-hand involved, the way that most human
labor, which cannot in any sense be considered "production," is thus
made to disappear, is largely effected through gender. In the familiar
lines from the story of the Fall, God condemns men to till the soil—"by
the sweat of your brow you will eat your food"—and women to bear
children in similar unhappy circumstances: "I will make your pains in
childbearing very severe; with painful labor you will give birth to children" (Genesis 3:16). Male "productive" labor is thus being framed here
as the equivalent of childbirth, which from a male point of view (not so
much from a female one, but it is very much a male point of view being
presented here) can seem about as close to pure creation ex nihilo, the
infant appearing fully formed apparently out of nowhere, that human
beings are capable of.

Yet it is also painful "labor."

This conception is still with us, for instance, in the way social scientists speak of "production" and "reproduction." Etymologically, the
word *produce* derives from the Latin *producere*, "to bring forth" or "put
out," as in English one might still say, "she produced a wallet from her
handbag." Both the terms *production* and *reproduction* are based on
the same core metaphor: in the one case, objects seem to jump, fully
formed, out of factories; in the other, babies seem to jump, fully formed,
out of women's bodies. In neither case, of course, is this actually true.
But as in so many patriarchal social orders, men like to conceive themselves as doing socially, or culturally, what they like to think of women
as doing naturally. "Production" is thus simultaneously a variation on
a male fantasy of childbirth, and of the action of a male creator god

who similarly created the entire universe through the sheer power of his mind and words, just as men see themselves as creating the world from their minds and brawn, and see that as the essence of "work," leaving to women most of the actual labor of tidying and maintaining things to make this illusion possible.

These two elements—work as suffering, work as creation—have interacted in various ways over the last two thousand years or so but in northern Europe especially there is a third element, typically—but I think incorrectly—identified with Puritanism, or at least Protestantism, which is the sense of work as educational self-discipline and self-mortification. This is subtly different than the theological identification of work with punishment. In fact, its origins are not theological at all. Here it is crucial to understand that from at least the High Middle Ages onward, northern Europe was characterized by a phenomenon often called "life cycle service," where almost everyone, whatever their social class, was expected to spend their youth—and "youth" was generally seen as running from perhaps fourteen to twenty-eight or thirty—working as a paid servant in the household of someone, generally unrelated and of a slightly higher social class. This was true across the social spectrum: not only of craftspeople, with their apprentices and journeymen, but of peasants, with their milkmaids and "servants in husbandry," and even the nobility, with their knights' pages and "ladies in waiting." (Royal courts also hosted "gentlemen waiters," who were both "waiting on" the king and waiting for their inheritance.) Wage labor was thus seen as a stage of life, in which one devoted oneself to service, but simultaneously learned the self-discipline and acquired the skills and capital required to eventually marry and set up an autonomous household of one's own, and eventually, employ servants in one's own turn. It is no coincidence, I think, that the parts of Europe where life-cycle service were the norm were precisely those that embrace Protestantism, or that the emergence of capitalist social relations in those regions was also marked by self-conscious movements of social reform—the famous Puritan "reformation of manners," for instance—aimed at the working classes, since the creation of a permanent class of wage laborers meant that millions of people were suddenly trapped in permanent social adolescence, and the emerging bourgeoisie saw it as their duty to save them from their chaotic state by instilling a sense of industrious self-discipline. It was simply the logic of the Medieval household transposed onto the national level, with the difference that wage laborers could never really achieve full moral personhood, except perhaps in their leisure hours.

Now, if we examine how these three elements—work as punishment, work as imitation of divine creation, work as educational mortification and self-discipline—have played off against one another over the course of the last two hundred years, it becomes easier to see why it has become impossible for us to see the current situation, however absurd, as a problem. Time does not allow me to present more than a bullet-point style summary but we can sum up the developments roughly like this:

- the labor theory of value that was embraced first by the emerging industrial bourgeoisie starting in the mid to late eighteenth century, to deploy against the aristocracy and rentier classes, then even more avidly by the working classes against them.
- over the course of the nineteenth century the LToV came to be almost universally accepted, but took a particularly masculine, productivist—one might here say, creationist—form. This is perhaps not surprising considering the generalization of industrial capitalism at the time and the fact that the first workers' struggles took the form of demands that male heads of household, rather than women and children, be employed in the factories. In America, for instance, where industrial capitalism arrived fairly late, it often took an explicitly theological tone, as a "Gospel of Work."
- however, this productivism was its Achilles heel, since it allowed a skewed vision of what the working class actually was and what its work largely consisted of. Even today invoking the term "working class" instantly draws up images of men in overalls toiling on production lines, and it's common to hear otherwise

intelligent middle-class intellectuals suggest that, with the decline of factory work, the working class in say Britain or America
no longer exists—as if it were actually ingeniously constructed
androids that were driving their buses, trimming their hedges,
installing their cables, or changing their grandparents' bedpans.

- In fact, there was never a time most workers worked in factories.
Even in the days of Karl Marx, or Charles Dickens, working-class
neighborhoods housed far more maids, bootblacks, dustmen,
cooks, nurses, cabbies, schoolteachers, prostitutes, caretakers, and
costermongers than employees in coal mines, textile mills, or
iron foundries. Are these former jobs "productive"? In what
sense and for whom? It's because of such ambiguities that these
issues are regularly brushed aside when people are arguing about
value; but doing so blinds us to the reality that most working-
class labor, whether carried out by men or women, actually more
resembles what we archetypally think of as women's work, looking after people, seeing to their wants and needs, explaining,
reassuring, anticipating what the boss wants or is thinking, not
to mention caring for, monitoring, and maintaining plants, animals, machines, and other objects, than it involves hammering,
carving, hoisting, or harvesting things.

- the main ideological counterattack was coincident with the rise
of corporate bureaucratic capitalism in America and Germany.
The U.S. Gilded Age saw the self-conscious promotion of what
Andrew Carnegie called the "Gospel of Wealth," against the
Gospel of Work, an insistence that value springs from the minds
of entrepreneurs, workers are little different than the machines
they operate, that self-realization lies not in production but consumption; and which has over the last century become so successful that when one says "wealth creators" in popular discourse
it is automatically assumed one is speaking of rich people, rather
than workers.

- this, of course, left the question of how to validate work; and
the result was, increasingly, to fall back on a synthesis of work

as punishment and work as self-discipline. This explains the apparently contradictory situation revealed by almost all mid- to late-twentieth-century sociology-of-work studies, what I've called "the paradox of modern work," which in almost every case reveal

1. that most people's sense of dignity and self-worth is caught up in working for a living
2. that most people hate their jobs.

- Few seem willing to draw the obvious conclusion: that increasingly, people find a sense of dignity and self-worth in their jobs *because* they hate them. As one of my own informants told me, after describing how his coworkers would endlessly complain to one another about overwork in office jobs in which they were in fact doing next to nothing, there was an intense "pressure to value ourselves and others on the basis of how hard we work at something we'd rather not be doing . . . If you're not destroying your mind and body via paid work, you're not living right." It is, to be sure, more common among middle-class office workers than among migrant farm workers or short order chefs. But even in working-class environments, the attitude can be observed through its negation, since even those who do not feel they have to validate their existence, on a day-to-day basis, by boasting how overworked they are will nonetheless agree that those who avoid work entirely should probably drop dead.

We are constantly bombarded by propaganda insisting society is besieged by those who want something for nothing, that the poor (typically conceived in racist terms) are largely poor because they lack the will and discipline to work, that only those who do or have worked harder than they'd like to at something they would rather not be doing, preferably under a harsh taskmaster, deserve respect and consideration from their fellow citizens. As a result, the sadomasochistic element in work, which many remark becomes ever more pronounced the more the work itself is bereft of purpose and meaning, rather than being an ugly, if predictable side effect to top-down chains of command in the workplace, has actually become central to what validates work itself. Suffering has become a badge of economic citizenship, in much the same way as having a home address. Without it, you have no right to make any other claim.

To sum up: Bullshit jobs proliferate today in large part because of the peculiar nature of managerial feudalism that has come to dominate wealthy economies—and to an increasing degree, all economies. They cause misery because human happiness is always caught up in a sense of having effects on the world; a feeling that most people, when they speak of their work, express through a language of social value. Yet at the same time they are aware that the greater the social value produced by a job, the less one is likely to be paid to do it. Millions are faced with the choice between doing useful and important work like taking care of children but being effectively told that the gratification of helping others should be its own reward, and it's up to them to figure out how to pay their bills, or accepting pointless and degrading work that destroys their mind and body for no particular reason, other than a widespread feeling that if one does not engage in labor that destroys the mind and body, whether or not there is a reason to be doing it, one does not deserve to live.

In nineteenth-century Britain, the great pioneer of the contemporary conception of work, as a value in itself, was Thomas Carlyle, who believed God had intentionally left the world unfinished so as to allow humans to partake of the divine. In one essay he engages in a peculiar diatribe against happiness; responding to the utilitarian doctrines of men like Jeremy Bentham, who had proposed that human pleasure could be precisely quantified, and therefore all morality reduced to calculating what would provide "the greatest happiness for the greatest number." Happiness, he wrote, is an ignoble concept.

The only happiness a brave man ever troubled himself with asking much about was, happiness enough to get his work done.

All work, even cotton-spinning, is noble; work is alone noble, be that here said and asserted once more. And in like manner too, all dignity is painful. A life of ease is not for any man . . . Our highest religion is named the Worship of Sorrow. For the son of man there is no noble crown, well worn or even ill worn, but there is a crown of thorns!

Bentham and the Utilitarians, who saw no purpose of human life other than the pursuit of pleasure, can be seen as the philosophical ancestors of modern consumerism, which is still justified by an economic theory of "utility." But Carlyle's perspective isn't really the negation of Bentham's; or if it is, then only in the dialectical sense, where two apparent opposites remain permanently at war, their advocates unaware that in their struggle, they constitute a higher unity which would be impossible without both. The belief that what ultimately motivates human beings has always been, and must always be, the pursuit of wealth, power, comforts, and pleasure has always and must always be complemented by a doctrine of work as self-sacrifice, as valuable precisely *because* it is the place of misery, sadism, emptiness, and despair.

CARING AS WORK DIRECTED TOWARD FACILITATING OTHERS' FREEDOM

This may seem bleak but I think that the very fact that so many recognize their work to be pointless, and are so concerned about the matter, and the indignation over the fact that people are effectively punished for seeking employment that actually helps others, can be seen as marking the beginning of a reformulation of the very idea of what a working class actually is and always has been.

As Marx himself pointed out, until the emergence of capitalism, it never occurred to anyone to write a book on the conditions that would create the most wealth; they argued about the conditions that would create the best people, and even if one sees the world in productivist terms, the production of commodities is ultimately a subordinate moment in the production of human beings; the ultimate pathology of capitalism is that it sees "social reproduction" as an adjunct to material production rather than the other way around. But increasingly, social struggles in wealthy countries focus specifically on the terms of human production. In the United States, for instance, in quite a number of large cities, the two largest employers are universities and hospitals; that is, factories of human production divided in good Cartesian fashion between mind and body—and right-wing populism, again, in its creationist and anti-abortion campaigns, takes direct aim at the moral authority of those running each. This latter, however, is something of a rearguard action, since in America—and this seems true in most places—the mainstream left is just as firmly in control of the apparatus of human production as the mainstream right is in control of the means of production of things; realistically, the prospect of right populists in America wresting control of it is about as likely as the prospect of a socialist party taking power in America and collectivizing heavy industry.

In this way the situation appears to be a classic standoff. And this is as true in America as in most of the contemporary world. The strategic question, then, from the perspective of a revolutionary such as myself, at any rate, is how exactly could what I've called the "caring classes"—the travailleurs empathiques or courgeoisie—break through this impasse, and effectively become the vehicle for what—to borrow a term from the Italian autonomist tradition—we might call the recomposition of the working class as a whole. It is certainly true that labor mobilizations in Europe and North America have increasingly centered on those whose work involves the benevolent shaping of others and the maintenance of benevolent environments—hospital workers, teachers, cleaners, etc. One might call these the proletariat of these factories for the production of people. If it is really true that digitization and robotization threaten to eliminate an increasing number of jobs, this will only become more true—since caring professions are precisely those which least lend themselves to digitization, or at least, that most of us would least like to see being performed by anything other than a human being. (It's also true that if Marx was right and surplus value can be extracted only through human labor, then capitalist exploitation in its classic form—as opposed to rent-seeking bureaucratic or managerial feudalism—will end up concentrating almost exclusively on care workers.)

But there are some serious impediments to their effective organization as a political force.

I'll start with what I think to be the central contradiction of robotization: that while the application of such technology does indeed vastly increase productivity in the production of material commodities, thus creating what's been called de facto "technological deflation," if applied to caring labor, it has exactly the opposite effect: since more and more of the care worker's time has to be devoted to rendering qualitative activities and effects into formats that can even be recognized by a computer, the result is reduced productivity and inflation—hence the dramatic increases in the cost of education and health services in particular, despite the lack of any notable improvement in quality. One effect is that the immediate class enemies, one might say, of the caring classes are the professional managerial classes, who insist on this endless bullshitization, and ultimately finance, which presides over an economic order where absolutely everything has to be translated into quantifiable terms. The problem is that it is precisely the professional managerial classes that have become the core constituency of what used to be working-class-based left political parties, such as the Democrats in America, Labour in the UK, various Socialists and Social Democrats in France, Germany, and elsewhere in Europe—and finance, in many cases, their ultimate backers. Hence nurses' unions in America ended up supporting Hillary Clinton's Democrats despite the fact that hospital administrators were core supporters of that very party; teachers in the United States have an even worse dilemma, since school administrators are actually represented by the same union. Clearly any real mobilization of the caring classes would have to involve a profound break with existing "left" institutions.

*   *   *

New institutional forms would have to also involve new conceptions of the value of labor, and here, I think we're likely going to have to transcend the very notion of production of human beings (though I think it's still useful for certain forms of analysis) to move beyond the theology of creation, as suffering or otherwise. Here, of course, the work of feminist theorists on caring and caring labor are crucial, ranging from the Marxist feminist Leopoldina Fortunati, Mariarosa Dalla Costa, Silvia Federici, to newer but no less important thinkers like Bev Skeggs, economists like Nancy Folbre, and theorists of it as an ethos or practice more generally, such as Carol Gilligan, Nel Noddings, Ruddick, Held, Tronto, and Kittay. (The somewhat ludic version of caring theory presented here was developed in part in tandem with Erica Lagalisse.) As Folbre notes, all labor can be conceived as caring labor in the sense that it "helps meet the needs of others"—that is, even if one is building a bridge, it can be seen as caring labor insofar as one does it because one cares that others can get across the river—and this seems to be very much part of the tacit criteria applied by workers in declaring their work to be without social value. A key aspect of caring is that it is about the creation and maintenance of relationships, a rejection of the patriarchal ideal of autonomy for an acceptance of interdependency, but, at the same time, a rejection too of the mere "empathic" projection of self onto another; rather, it is a self-effacing openness to the reality of others, their needs and desires. All this implies the caring is not actually a value but the prime means for the creation of value, and it is easy to see that almost all working-class labor already involves such a caring element—at least as much and generally much more so than a productive one. But then the question has to become, what precisely is it, what form of value, that is being produced here. Here there is no real consensus in the literature, which is full of terms like *growth*, *needs*, *flourishing*, *interest*, drawn from a variety of other psychological, philosophical, or economic disciplinary traditions. I'd like to end by making my own rather idiosyncratic suggestion here.

It seems to me that caring labor is best conceived as labor that is directed, ultimately, at maintaining and enhancing its object's freedom.

The existing literature has tended to avoid this formulation, I think, because it sees "freedom" in patriarchal liberal terms essentially as autonomy, as lack of dependency on others, and therefore as the opposite of caring relations, but this is by no means the only possible definition of freedom. Take, for instance, Marx's remarks about the nature of communism in Volume 3 of *Capital*, where he talks about leaving the domain of necessity for the domain of freedom, which is action, creative or otherwise, that is performed not as a means to an end, but as an end in itself. Action for its own sake could be considered one definition of freedom but it is also a common definition of play. An argument could be made that the principle of freedom, as the expression of powers for their own sake, exists on every level of physical reality, and certainly every aspect of what we call the natural world. Facilitating such play, ensuring and maintaining the possibility of such play, is the ultimate aim of caring labor. If this seems odd, consider the fact that the almost invariable paradigm for caring labor is maternal nurture: tending to the needs and desires of infants and small children. Now, one can conceive this as directed toward biological needs or a process of growth, but if one sees the matter in terms of action, and asks what sort of action on the part of children is primarily being facilitated by maternal care, the obvious answer is: play. Mothers take care of children, feed, clean, and protect them, in order to provide an environment that facilitates play—and, of course, they play with children themselves, as an integral part of the caring relation. And yes, play itself is a key element in a child's discovery of the world, education, growth, but it is also an end in itself.

*   *   *

So rather than production carried out for the sake of private consumption in the domestic sphere, we can reconceive value-creating labor as care carried out for the sake of enhancing freedom in all aspects of human existence. Such a view is already tacit in people's sense of the social value—or lack of it—in their own labor, and if teased and developed, in the same way that theorists like Marx teased out and developed the full implications of the productivist version of the labor theory of value embraced by the working class of his own day, it could have profound implications for how we view every aspect of the economy (one need only pause to consider what it might mean for the role of money). Even more, perhaps, if translated into theoretical common sense in the same way the productivist version of the labor theory of value was in the nineteenth century, it has potentially revolutionary implications in every sense of the term.

PART V

WHAT'S THE POINT IF WE CAN'T HAVE FUN?

Another Art World, Part I

Art Communism and Artificial Scarcity

We would like to offer some initial thoughts on exactly how the art world can operate simultaneously as a dream of liberation and a structure of exclusion; how its guiding principle is both that everyone should really be an artist, and that this is absolutely and irrevocably not the case. The art world is still founded on Romantic principles; these have never gone away; but the Romantic legacy contains two notions: one, a kind of democratic notion of genius as an essential aspect of any human being, even if it can only be realized in some collective way, and another, that those things that really matter are always the product of some individual heroic genius. The art world, essentially, dangles the ghost of one so as to ultimately, aggressively, insist on the other.

In May 2019, just married a week before, we arrived at the Venice Biennale. It wasn't exactly a honeymoon; or if it was, it was more a work-

Coauthored with Nika Dubrovsky; originally published in *e-flux*, no. 102, September 2019, e-flux.com.

ing honeymoon: we had the idea to make the Biennale the basis of our first joint writing project, though we weren't sure precisely what that project was going to be.

We spent much of our first day in the Arsenale—a nearly thousand-year-old structure reputed to have once held one of the world's first arms factories—trying to get past the guards.

Apparently there were levels and degrees of press access, and it was necessary to negotiate our way through a complex system of authorization numbers, bar codes, and color-coded passes, encountering a variety of security personnel with different badges and uniforms and means of communication manning physical and conceptual barriers. Scores of well-dressed participants stood dutifully in line, argued in a dozen languages, shuffled from room to room, recuperated in specially provided café bookshops while strategizing over dinner invitations or borrowed ID cards, or assessing the relative importance of the parties they'd be attending later in the day. There was an extraordinary lack of humor about the whole business. People were flustered, stoic, self-righteous, intent; almost no one, in this cathedral of irony, seemed bemused.

The seriousness! It seemed important to establish that something of great consequence was happening here. It was not clear why. Just as there was no obvious reason to proliferate multiple degrees of advanced access in the first place, there was no reason for everyone else to feel so invested in the consequences. It only really made sense if exclusion was itself one of the main objects being produced: it was not just that everyone was playing a game whose rules were shifting and opaque, it seemed important that all players, even the haughtiest oligarch or most consummate broker, stood at least occasionally in danger of being foiled and humiliated. Or at the very least flustered and annoyed.

The art world, for all the importance of its museums, institutes, foundations, university departments, and the like, is still organized primarily around the art market. The art market in turn is driven by finance capital. Being the world's least regulated market among shady businesses, tax shelters, scams, money laundering, etc., the art world might be said to represent a kind of experimental ground for the hammering-out of a certain ideal of freedom appropriate to the current rule of finance capital.

A case can certainly be made that contemporary art is in effect an extension of global finance (which is itself, of course, closely tied to empire). Artsy neighborhoods tend to cluster around the financial districts of major cities. Artistic investment follows the same logic as financial speculation. Still—if contemporary art were simply an extension of finance capital, works designed to look good in banks, or in bankers' homes, why should we even care? It's not as if cultural critics spend a lot of time debating the latest design trends in luxury yachts. Why should changing trends in decorative objects that the owners of such yachts like to place in their sitting rooms be considered relevant, in any way, to the lives or aspirations of bus drivers, maids, bauxite miners, telemarketers, or pretty much anyone outside the charmed circle of the "art world" itself?

There are two traditional ways to answer this question and they pull in opposite directions.

1. Contemporary art defines the very pinnacle of a much larger structure of aesthetic value, which ultimately encompasses all forms of meaning-making and cultural expression, and therefore plays a key role in reproducing the larger structure of social relations which ensure drivers, maids, miners, and telemarketers will continue to be told their lives and concerns are uninteresting and unimportant, and relegate the aesthetic forms and cultural expressions that speak to their hearts to second- or third-tier status.

2. While co-opted by the rich, as well as public and private managers and bureaucrats, contemporary art still embodies, or is even the primary embodiment, of alternative conceptions of value that have the potential to explode that larger structure of social relations, and that are either unavailable, or not nearly so readily available, anywhere else.

Obviously both of these things probably can be and are true at the same time. It might even be said that the revolutionary potential of art is a large part of what makes it so effective as a principle of control. Even children of ragpickers, sweatshop laborers, and refugees, after all, are mostly sent to school, where they are exposed to the works of Leonardo and Picasso, play with paints, learn that art and culture are the highest achievements of humanity and perhaps the most obvious justification for humanity's continued existence on the planet (despite all the damage we inflict); they are taught to aspire to lead lives where their children can live in comfort so that their children's children can pursue forms of creative expression. And for the most part, since that is the game everyone is playing, they do aspire to such things. The world's cities are full of young people who do see a life of expression as the ultimate form of freedom, and even those who dream of becoming soap opera stars or hip-hop video producers recognize that as things are currently organized, the "art world" is the crowning height of that larger domain of "arts," and as such, its regulatory principle, that which holds the elaborate ranks and hierarchies of genres and forms of art—so strangely reminiscent of earlier ranks and hierarchies of angels—in their proper place. This remains true even for those who have nothing but bemused contempt for the very idea of contemporary art, or are entirely unaware of it, insofar as they exist within a world where those who produce the forms of artistic expression they do appreciate, or their children, insofar as they aspire to move up in the world, will necessarily have to exist in a world where contemporary art is seen as the purest expression of human creativity—and creativity as the ultimate value.

The easiest way to measure the stubborn centrality of such structures, perhaps, is to consider how difficult it is to get rid of them. Attempts are always being made. There always seems to be someone in the art world trying to create participatory programs, explode the boundaries between high and low genres, include members of marginalized groups as producers or audiences or even patrons.

Sometimes they draw a lot of attention. Always in the end they fade away and die, leaving things more or less exactly as they were before.

In the 1970s and '80s, for example, there was a concerted effort in America to challenge the border between high art and popular music, even to the point where a few of the artists (Brian Eno, Talking Heads, Laurie Anderson, Jeffrey Lohn) actually did create work that hit the charts, and played to sold-out theaters full of young people who had never heard of Hugo Ball or Robert Rauschenberg. Critics declared that the very idea of high and low genres was quickly dissolving away. But it wasn't true. In a few years, it was all just another forgotten musical trend, an odd sidebar in the history of rock 'n' roll.

Hardly surprising perhaps, since the art market, and the music industry, always operated on entirely different economic principles: the one mainly financed by rich collectors and governments, the other by mass marketing to the general public. Still, if there was a real challenge to the logic of exclusion anywhere in the arts, during the twentieth century, it was precisely in the domain of music, where a defiant tradition from folk to rock and punk and hip-hop actually came closest to realizing the old avant-garde dream that everyone could be an artist—though one can, of course, debate precisely how close this really came. At the very least, it established the idea that creativity is a product of small collectives as easily as individual auteurs. All this happened, significantly, at a certain distance from actual self-proclaimed artistic avant-gardes; and it is telling that the brief mutual flirtation with the art world in the '80s was a prelude to a backlash that left music far more corporatized, individualized, and with far fewer spaces for experimentation than it had since at least the 1950s.

Any market, of course, must necessarily operate on a principle of scarcity. In a way, the art market and the music industry face similar problems: materials are mostly cheap and talent is widespread; therefore, for profits to be made, scarcity has to be produced. Of course, in the art world, this is what the critical apparatus is largely about: the production of scarcity; which is, in turn, why even the most sincerely radical anticapitalist critics, curators, and gallerists will tend to draw the line at the possibility that everyone really could be an artist, even in the most diffuse possible sense. The art world remains overwhelmingly a world of heroic individuals, even when it claims to echo the logic of movements and collectives—even when the ostensible aim of those collectives is to annihilate the distinction between art and life.

Even the Dadaists and Surrealists are remembered today as a handful of romantic geniuses, whatever they might have claimed to be about.

It is also noteworthy that the only time a significant number of people believed that structures of exclusion really were dissolving, that a society in which everyone could become an artist was actually conceivable, occurred in the midst of social revolutions when it was genuinely believed that capitalism was in its death spirals, and markets themselves were about to become a thing of the past. Many of these trends, unsurprisingly, emerge directly from Russia, where the period from the revolution of 1905 to the avant-garde heyday of the 1920s saw an almost brutal efflorescence of new ideas of what artistic communism might be like.

ART COMMUNISM

> In a Commune everyone is a creator. Every Man should
> be an artist, everything can become fine art.
>
> —OSIP BRIK

Consider the case of Kazimir Malevich, who arrived in Moscow in 1904 from the hinterland of Ukraine to become one of the most influential theorists of twentieth-century art. In his 1920 essay "The Question of Imitative Art," he asserts: "We are moving towards a world where everyone will create . . . We must set creativity's path in such a way that all the masses will take part in the development of every creative thought that appears, without turning it into mechanized production or cliché."

The new, revolutionary art, he insists, was to be based on creativity as "the human essence . . ." "as the aim of life, and as the perfection of oneself."

For Malevich—and he was hardly alone—artists were not only the prophets of this new world, but they were to become the foundation of it, its model. As we all know, such ideas were largely stifled with the suppression of the avant-garde under Stalin. Though as Tzvetan Todorov and Boris Groys have both recently pointed out, what happened is a little more complicated. The main reason avant-garde painters, designers, and sculptors had to be killed or brought under heel was because the political avant-garde ultimately adopted a version of the most radically exclusionary form of that exact same tradition, where Stalin himself—much like Mussolini and Hitler—became the individual heroic genius reshaping life itself according to a single aesthetic vision.

Todorov argues that in the twentieth century at least, this is what always happens in revolutionary moments. Artists start to demand not just new rights to create and distribute their artworks; above all they demand to preside over a transformation of social reality and the ways culture reproduces itself. But in the end they invariably fail. To achieve their dreams they are obliged to rely on politicians, who have no intention of sharing power with them; therefore, after a short creative surge, almost always coinciding with an opening of political horizons (Malevich himself published his first essays in a journal called, simply, *Anarchy*), a deep and harsh reaction ensues, and the politicians, inspired to carve out their own aesthetic visions on the flesh and sinews of humanity, end up doing absolutely terrible things.

Conservatives have always insisted that this will inevitably happen—in fact, this is the essential definition of what conservativism is, the assertion that applying anyone's aesthetic vision to the public sphere must always end in disaster—and in this sense, at least, conservative impulses reign. We are taught to consider figures like Malevich terrifying in their naivete. But what did his vision of true communism actually consist of? It's not just one of a future society in which everyone would be free from the struggle for survival (this, just about everyone was anticipating at the time). It was also a vision in which the "pursuit of happiness" would mean that everyone was able to pursue some sort of artistic or scientific project. This of course was founded on the assumption that people had both the capacity and the inclination, even if it just meant puttering about trying to create a perpetual motion device or perfecting a stand-up comedy routine. Malevich's vision implied that curiosity and a desire for self-expression are essential components of whatever it is we are defining as "humanity"—or perhaps all life (some Russian avant-gardists were also interested in the liberation of cows)—and that therefore freedom is more a matter of removing impediments than fundamentally reshaping human nature. This is why Malevich could argue that the basis of a new artistic world would have to be economic—though like so many other revolutionaries, he was also interested in the creation of a new universal aesthetic language. Malevich himself came from the national outskirts; he was a Pole who grew up in a Ukrainian village, and who never mastered literary Russian or received a "proper" art education. His squares and triangles were a way of transcending all that. In a similar way, the Russian avant-garde project was also educational, designed not to create the "new man" (as the Stalinists later put it) but to include those previously most excluded—the poor and provincials, the inhabitants of the national suburbs—to give them the minimal tools they would need to join in the collective.

Did Malevich's vision definitively fail? It might seem that things could not have possibly gone more wrong. Millions died in the civil war and under Stalin, and even afterward, the dream of communism was indefinitely postponed. Still, there was a side of Soviet society—and state socialist society more generally—that we rarely acknowledge. It was almost impossible to get fired from one's job. As a result it was quite possible to work three or four hours a day, or even two or three days a week, and thus to concentrate one's energies on other projects, or, for that matter, on not much of anything at all. There was plenty of time to "think and walk," and since capitalist-style consumer pleasures were not widely available, and cultural resources like libraries, free lectures and lessons, and so forth, were, the Brezhnev years in particular saw whole generations of "watchmen and street-sweepers," as they were called—people who intentionally found undemanding jobs, managed to live whole lives on the small bits of money guaranteed by the state, and used their free time to write poetry, make pictures, and argue about the meaning of life.

All this obviously was under the watchful eye of the totalitarian state, but one could well argue that this is precisely why those running the state felt it had to remain totalitarian. The revolution had produced a society where almost everyone was in a position to become a thinker or artist, to plot and scheme, to question everything. So they had to be directly suppressed. In the capitalist West, most people simply didn't have the time to do any of these things.

We are taught to dismiss the revolutionary avant-gardists as romantics. It's not clear if all of them would have refused the designation. The revolutionary tradition—Marx included—in many ways traces back directly to Romanticism, and while nowadays this is generally seen to be precisely what was wrong with it, it seems to us that the real history is decidedly more complicated.

Let us then proceed step by step to explain why we believe this to be the case.

THE CONFUSING LEGACY OF ROMANTICISM

Romanticism in general has come into very bad color nowadays; it is seen as silly and possibly dangerous. *Romanticizing* has become a term for sentimental idealization, whether of nature, peasants, noble savages, the poor, or imagined creative geniuses. The political embrace of Romanticism is seen as leading most naturally to some kind of authoritarian nationalism, or at worst, the Third Reich. But the avant-garde tradition is similarly almost entirely rooted in Romanticism.

Part of the problem is that nowadays, few are aware of what early Romantic thinkers actually said—though to be fair, they often didn't help things much by writing contradictory things in a deliberately obscure and difficult style. Still, certain consistent strains can be unraveled, and they are not what we commonly imagine them to be.

As an example, consider the endless modernist fascination with comparing art produced by what Hal Foster famously labeled "the privileged triad of the primitive, the child, and the insane." What did these three really seem to have in common? In the twentieth century, the usual assumption was that the collapse of the cultural authority of the Church had left Europeans without a common visual language, and that by studying the similarities between savages, lunatics, and children, it might be possible to recover some kind of pure, presocial, and therefore universal visual language on which a new one could be built. As we've seen, revolutionary avant-gardes could sometimes take up a version of these ideas as well. But the original Romantic conception was far more radical. It was in fact closely tied to the concept of culture—itself originally an invention of German Romanticism. The idea that the language, folklore, manners, myths, sensibilities, and even forms of happiness typical of a nation or social group all form a kind of expressive unity, products of some kind of "popular genius," was rooted in the assumption that everyone was, in a sense, already engaged in artistic expression. In this view of culture, our very perceptions of the world around us are given meaning and emotional color by generations of ancestral creativity. "We see through hearing," Herder wrote, because the myths and poetry of our childhood define what we actually see when we look at a mountain, forest, or another human being. But the creation of culture is ongoing. As the German poet and philosopher Novalis famously wrote, "Every person is meant to be an artist." Artistic genius is simply "an exemplification and intensification of what human beings always do."

The problem, Romantics insisted, was that bourgeois society had created social pressures and expectations so stifling and atrocious that very few make it to adulthood with their humanity and freedom intact. Bourgeois education had the effect of murdering the imagination. What children and unschooled "primitives" were really thought to have in common, then, was simply that they had not (or not yet) been crushed. In a pathological society such as our own, in contrast, those individuals who do somehow manage to preserve that inborn artistic "genius" with which all children begin their lives, do so at tremendous personal cost; they are typically driven half mad by the experience. German Romantic novels, like those of E.T.A. Hoffmann, typically counterpose some half-mad artistic or spiritual loner and a monotonously monstrous set of provincial types—the doctor, mayor, mayor's wife, and mistress—united against him, since they perceive his very existence as an attack on their petty and hypocritical reality.

True, the early, democratic phase of German Romanticism gradually descended into conservative nationalism. But those core ideas fundamentally reshaped all subsequent thinking about both politics and art.

This is in particular evident in the legacy of the French Revolution. On the face of it, most of the French revolutionaries, with their cult of Reason, might seem about as far as one could get from the tradition of German Romanticism. True, Rousseau embraced some Romantic ideas, but for the most part, the language and sensibilities could hardly be more different. Still, one of the most radical Romantic ideas was simply that, if everyone is born a free and ingenious child, then the lack of freedom and genius, or the spread of stupidity, malice, and hypocrisy in that society can only be the product of social conditions. This was considered shocking at the time. French revolutionaries were often so determined to prove it that they sometimes placed aristocratic children with the families of drunks—just to prove that they would turn out to be drunks themselves.

The notion of the avant-garde, however, emerges from the immediate wake of arguments about how that revolution lost its way. (Incidentally, so did modern conservativism, and social science.) Reactionaries argued that the cult of Reason would lead inevitably to the Terror. But so would the cult of Imagination. Attempting to wipe the slate clean and start over would inevitably mean destroying everything that held society together and made life meaningful: community, solidarity, status, authority . . . basically all those things which have become the themes of social theory ever since. Those who believed social change was good and inevitable nonetheless took such objections very seriously. The notions of the artistic avant-garde and the political vanguard emerged directly from the resultant debates. Originally, in fact, they were assumed to be exactly the same thing.

Here we are obliged to provide a somewhat brutal summary of a very complicated history, but suffice it to say that the debate in France, typified by arguments between the followers of Count Henri de Saint-Simon and those of his onetime secretary Auguste Comte, largely came down to an argument about how to manage the transition from an agrarian feudal social order to a commercial and industrial civilization.

Medieval lords—so the argument went—might have been harsh and often arbitrarily violent; they might in many ways have been little more than so many bands of thieves. But they had the Church, and the Church was capable of mobilizing structures of beauty and meaning to give everyone a sense of precisely where they stood in the larger social order. This was precisely what they saw as lacking in industrial society. The Church was now useless. But the captains of industry seemed to feel that the material bounty they provided should simply speak for itself. Clearly, it didn't. Political chaos and social anomie was thus the direct result of the lack of any new class to fulfill the priestly function. Comteans imagined these to be scientists: hence Comte's eventual creation of the religion of Positivism, in which sociologists would play the role of clerics. Saint-Simon cast about a bit (for a while he focused on engineers) but ultimately settled on artists as the vanguard who would lead the way toward a culture of freedom and equality, one in which the coercive mechanisms, he believed, would ultimately wither away.

For over a century, would-be revolutionary vanguards continued to debate whether they would be more like scientists or more like artists, while painters and sculptors formed themselves into sects. Revolutionary parties endlessly tried to patch together alliances between the least alienated and most oppressed. The dream of the collapse of the barriers between art and life, which would eventually return us to a society in which Novalis's vision would be realized, was always an inherent part of the revolutionary project. By the twentieth century, many of the best-known avant-garde artists were no longer even producing much in the way of immortal works of art, but instead largely plans on how to share their power and freedom with others. As a result, the supreme twentieth-century avant-garde genre, or at least the most accomplished and original, was not even the collage but the manifesto.

At this point we can return to Russia.

The Russian revolutionary avant-garde was rooted squarely in the tradition we have just described. Its imagined "people of the future" (*Budetlyans*) would not only be liberated from those unfair and malicious social conditions that stifled their creativity; they would also have the freedom of children. Obviously, no one was so naïve as to believe they would live like children in any literal sense, that communism would create a world free from death, betrayal, existential fear, morbid obsession, or unrequited love. Only real children would experience such a paradise. Rather, it would create a world where future people would have the right, duty, and opportunity to reflect on those inevitable, adult, existential problems in startlingly beautiful ways. Communism would be a world no longer divided into mad geniuses and dull, obedient fool–spectators, either uncomprehending or adulatory. Everyone would become both at the same time.

The Museum of Care

Imagining the World After the Pandemic

Or more precisely, we are imagining a sane world after the virus, one where, instead of just trying to put things back the way they were, we act on what we've learned. For instance, a huge proportion of office work, especially administrative, managerial, marketing, legal, finance, consultancy, and the like, have shown themselves to be pure bullshit. If they disappeared, it would either make no difference or the world might even be a slightly better place. The proof is that during the crisis, most of them did disappear and the world kept spinning. So imagine for a moment we are sane and don't just go back to pretending there's some reason to have all these people bluffing to make us think they work all day but instead got rid of the bullshit jobs. Well, one question would be: What would we do with all the buildings where they used to work? Obviously, those actually useful workers who kept us

Coauthored with Nika Dubrovsky; originally published in *Arts of the Working Class*, May 30, 2022, artsoftheworkingclass.org.

alive and cared for us during the epidemic—doctors, nurses, cleaners, couriers, electricians, farmers—don't need giant glass buildings to make them feel important. Some can be blown up. This will be good because it means there will be less energy used to keep them heated, cooled, and so forth, which will reduce carbon emissions. But surely we wouldn't want to blow up all of them.

After the French and Russian revolutions, the royal palaces were turned into state museums. That might point to one sane way to use them. But there's also a crazy way: a return to "normalcy." The model for this might be what happened after the large-scale deindustrialization of Western metropolises, when former factories and warehouses were turned into private art centers, offices, and condominiums for the kind of people who worked in them. Many find it hard to imagine this won't happen again, if there is rapid de-bullshitization of work, but no real change to the financial system, or structures of wealth and power more generally. Empty offices would be bought up by investors, who would turn them into expensive condominiums or private art spaces whose presence will give the real estate additional market value. The only alternative usually put on the table is if the state takes over everything, either in the form of state socialism (which is basically just state-monopoly capitalism) or its right-wing "national socialist" variant (in whatever updated twenty-first-century form).

In that future, those empty offices not used to house bureaucrats or secret police will be turned into state museums: conservative, elitist institutions whose general ambience balances somewhere between that of a cemetery and that of a bank. We would like to insist on the possibility—perhaps not the likelihood, but at least the possibility—of sanity. Imagine that the experience of lockdown and economic collapse actually allows us to see the world as it really is and we acknowledge that what's referred to as "an economy" is simply the way we collectively keep one another alive, provision one another with the things we need, and generally take care of one another. Say we also reject the notion of social control.

Prisons, after all, provide food, shelter, and even basic medical care.

Still, they are not "caring" institutions. What they provide is not care because real care is directed not just at supplying material needs, not even just to allow others to grow and thrive, but also, to maintain or enhance their freedom. Imagine we jettison the idea of production and consumption being the sole purpose of economic life and substitute care and freedom. What would we do with the buildings then?

In a world built around care and solidarity, much of this vast and absurd office space would indeed be blown up, but some could be turned into free city universities, social centers, and hotels for those in need of shelter. We could call them "Museums of Care"—precisely because they are spaces that do not celebrate production of any sort but rather provide the space and means for the creation of social relationships and the imagining of entirely new forms of social relations.

What's the Point If We Can't Have Fun?

My friend June Thunderstorm and I once spent half an hour sitting in a meadow by a mountain lake, watching an inchworm dangle from the top of a stalk of grass, twist about in every possible direction, and then leap to the next stalk and do the same thing. And so it proceeded, in a vast circle, with what must have been a vast expenditure of energy, for what seemed like absolutely no reason at all.

"All animals play," June had once said to me. "Even ants." She'd spent many years working as a professional gardener and had plenty of incidents like this to observe and ponder. "Look," she said, with an air of modest triumph. "See what I mean?"

Most of us, hearing this story, would insist on proof. How do we know the worm was playing? Perhaps the invisible circles it traced in the air were really just a search for some unknown sort of prey. Or a mating ritual. Can we prove they weren't? Even if the worm was playing, how do we know this form of play did not serve some ultimately practical purpose: exercise, or self-training for some possible future inchworm emergency?

Originally published in *The Baffler*, no. 24, January 2014, thebaffler.com.

This would be the reaction of most professional ethologists as well. Generally speaking, an analysis of animal behavior is not considered scientific unless the animal is assumed, at least tacitly, to be operating according to the same means/end calculations that one would apply to economic transactions. Under this assumption, an expenditure of energy must be directed toward some goal, whether it be obtaining food, securing territory, achieving dominance, or maximizing reproductive success—unless one can absolutely prove that it isn't, and absolute proof in such matters is, as one might imagine, very hard to come by.

I must emphasize here that it doesn't really matter what sort of theory of animal motivation a scientist might entertain: what she believes an animal to be thinking, whether she thinks an animal can be said to be "thinking" anything at all. I'm not saying that ethologists actually believe that animals are simply rational calculating machines. I'm simply saying that ethologists have boxed themselves into a world where to be scientific means to offer an explanation of behavior in rational terms— which in turn means describing an animal *as if* it were a calculating economic actor trying to maximize some sort of self-interest—whatever their theory of animal psychology, or motivation, might be.

That's why the existence of animal play is considered something of an intellectual scandal. It's understudied, and those who do study it are seen as mildly eccentric. As with many vaguely threatening, speculative notions, difficult-to-satisfy criteria are introduced for proving animal play exists, and even when it is acknowledged, the research more often than not cannibalizes its own insights by trying to demonstrate that play must have some long-term survival or reproductive function.

Despite all this, those who do look into the matter are invariably forced to the conclusion that play does exist across the animal universe. And exists not just among such notoriously frivolous creatures as monkeys, dolphins, or puppies, but among such unlikely species as frogs, minnows, salamanders, fiddler crabs, and yes, even ants—which not only engage in frivolous activities as individuals, but also have been observed since the nineteenth century to arrange mock wars, apparently just for the fun of it.

Why do animals play? Well, why shouldn't they? The real question is: Why does the existence of action carried out for the sheer pleasure of acting, the exertion of powers for the sheer pleasure of exerting them, strike us as mysterious? What does it tell us about ourselves that we instinctively assume that it is?

SURVIVAL OF THE MISFITS

The tendency in popular thought to view the biological world in economic terms was present at the nineteenth-century beginnings of Darwinian science. Charles Darwin, after all, borrowed the phrase "survival of the fittest" from the sociologist Herbert Spencer, that darling of robber barons. Spencer, in turn, was struck by how much the forces driving natural selection in *On the Origin of Species* jibed with his own laissez-faire economic theories. Competition over resources, rational calculation of advantage, and the gradual extinction of the weak were taken to be the prime directives of the universe.

The stakes of this new view of nature as the theater for a brutal struggle for existence were high, and objections were registered very early on. An alternative school of Darwinism emerged in Russia emphasizing cooperation, not competition, as the driver of evolutionary change. In 1902 this approach found a voice in a popular book, *Mutual Aid: A Factor of Evolution*, by the naturalist and revolutionary anarchist pamphleteer Peter Kropotkin. In an explicit riposte to social Darwinists, Kropotkin argued that the entire theoretical basis for social Darwinism was wrong: those species that cooperate most effectively tend to be the most competitive in the long run. Kropotkin, born a prince (he renounced his title as a young man), spent many years in Siberia as a naturalist and explorer before being imprisoned for revolutionary agitation, escaping, and fleeing to London. *Mutual Aid* grew from a series of essays written in response to Thomas Henry Huxley, a well-known social Darwinist, and summarized the Russian understanding of the day, which was that while competition was undoubtedly one factor driving both natural and social evolution, the role of cooperation was ultimately decisive.

The Russian challenge was taken quite seriously in twentieth-century biology—particularly among the emerging subdiscipline of evolutionary psychology—even if it was rarely mentioned by name. It came, instead, to be subsumed under the broader "problem of altruism"—another phrase borrowed from the economists, and one that spills over into arguments among "rational choice" theorists in the social sciences. This was the question that already troubled Darwin: Why should animals ever sacrifice their individual advantage for others? Because no one can deny that they sometimes do. Why should a herd animal draw potentially lethal attention to himself by alerting his fellows that a predator is coming? Why should worker bees kill themselves to protect their hive? If to advance a scientific explanation of any behavior means to attribute rational, maximizing motives, then what, precisely, was a kamikaze bee trying to maximize?

We all know the eventual answer, which the discovery of genes made possible. Animals were simply trying to maximize the propagation of their own genetic codes. Curiously, this view—which eventually came to be referred to as neo-Darwinian—was developed largely by figures who considered themselves radicals of one sort or another. Jack Haldane, a Marxist biologist, was already trying to annoy moralists in the 1930s by quipping that, like any biological entity, he'd be happy to sacrifice his life for "two brothers or eight cousins." The epitome of this line of thought came with the militant atheist Richard Dawkins's book *The Selfish Gene*—a work that insisted all biological entities were best conceived of as "lumbering robots," programmed by genetic codes that, for some reason no one could quite explain, acted like "successful Chicago gangsters," ruthlessly expanding their territory in an endless desire to propagate themselves. Such descriptions were typically qualified by remarks like, "Of course, this is just a metaphor, genes don't *really* want or do anything." But in reality, the neo-Darwinists were practically driven to their conclusions by their initial assumption: that science demands a rational explanation, that this means attributing rational motives to all behavior, and that a truly rational motivation can only be one that, if observed in humans, would normally be described as selfishness or greed.

As a result, the neo-Darwinists went even further than the Victorian variety. If old-school social Darwinists like Herbert Spencer viewed nature as a marketplace, albeit an unusually cutthroat one, the new version was outright capitalist. The neo-Darwinists assumed not just a struggle for survival, but a universe of rational calculation driven by an apparently irrational imperative to unlimited growth.

This, anyway, is how the Russian challenge was understood. Kropotkin's actual argument is far more interesting. Much of it, for instance, is concerned with how animal cooperation often has nothing to do with survival or reproduction, but is a form of pleasure in itself. "To take flight in flocks merely for pleasure is quite common among all sorts of birds," he writes. Kropotkin multiplies examples of social play: pairs of vultures wheeling about for their own entertainment, hares so keen to box with other species that they occasionally (and unwisely) approach foxes, flocks of birds performing military-style maneuvers, bands of squirrels coming together for wrestling and similar games:

> We know at the present time that all animals, beginning with the ants, going on to the birds, and ending with the highest mammals, are fond of plays, wrestling, running after each other, trying to capture each other, teasing each other, and so on. And while many plays are, so to speak, a school for the proper behavior of the young in mature life, there are others which, apart from their utilitarian purposes, are, together with dancing and singing, mere manifestations of an excess of forces—"the joy of life," and a desire to communicate in some way or another with other individuals of the same or of other species—in short, a manifestation of sociability proper, which is a distinctive feature of all the animal world.

To exercise one's capacities to their fullest extent is to take pleasure in one's own existence, and with sociable creatures, such pleasures are proportionally magnified when performed in company. From the Russian perspective, this does not need to be explained. It is simply what life is. We don't have to explain why creatures desire to be alive. Life is an end in itself. And if what being alive actually consists of is having powers—to run, jump, fight, fly through the air—then surely the exercise of such powers as an end in itself does not have to be explained either. It's just an extension of the same principle.

Friedrich Schiller had already argued in 1795 that it was precisely in play that we find the origins of self-consciousness, and hence freedom, and hence morality. "Man plays only when he is in the full sense of the word a man," Schiller wrote in his *On the Aesthetic Education of Man*, "and he is wholly a Man only when he is playing." If so, and if Kropotkin was right, then glimmers of freedom, or even of moral life, begin to appear everywhere around us.

It's hardly surprising, then, that this aspect of Kropotkin's argument was ignored by the neo-Darwinists. Unlike "the problem of altruism," cooperation for pleasure, as an end in itself, simply could not be recuperated for ideological purposes. In fact, the version of the struggle for existence that emerged over the twentieth century had even less room for play than the older Victorian one. Herbert Spencer himself had no problem with the idea of animal play as purposeless, a mere enjoyment of surplus energy. Just as a successful industrialist or salesman could go home and play a nice game of cribbage or polo, why should those animals that succeeded in the struggle for existence not also have a bit of fun? But in the new full-blown capitalist version of evolution, where the drive for accumulation had no limits, life was no longer an end in itself, but a mere instrument for the propagation of DNA sequences—and so the very existence of play was something of a scandal.

WHY ME?

It's not just that scientists are reluctant to set out on a path that might lead them to see play—and therefore the seeds of self-consciousness, freedom, and moral life—among animals. Many are finding it increasingly difficult to come up with justifications for ascribing any of these things even to human beings. Once you reduce all living beings to the equivalent of market actors, rational calculating machines trying to propagate their genetic code, you accept that not only the cells that make up our bodies, but whatever beings are our immediate ancestors, lacked anything even remotely like self-consciousness, freedom, or moral life—which makes it hard to understand how or why consciousness (a mind, a soul) could ever have evolved in the first place.

The American philosopher Daniel Dennett frames the problem quite lucidly. Take lobsters, he argues—they're just robots. Lobsters can get by with no sense of self at all. You can't ask what it's like to be a lobster. It's not like anything. They have nothing that even resembles consciousness; they're machines. But if this is so, Dennett argues, then the same must be assumed all the way up the evolutionary scale of complexity, from the living cells that make up our bodies to such elaborate creatures as monkeys and elephants, who, for all their apparently human-like qualities, cannot be proved to think about what they do. That is, until suddenly, Dennett gets to humans, which—while they are certainly gliding around on autopilot at least 95 percent of the time—nonetheless do appear to have this "me," this conscious self grafted on top of them, that occasionally shows up to take supervisory notice, intervening to tell the system to look for a new job, quit smoking, or write an academic paper about the origins of consciousness. In Dennett's formulation,

> Yes, we have a soul. But it's made of lots of tiny robots. Somehow, the trillions of robotic (and unconscious) cells that compose our bodies organize themselves into interacting systems that sustain the activities traditionally allocated to the soul, the ego or self. But since we have already granted that simple robots are unconscious (if toasters and thermostats and telephones are unconscious), why couldn't teams of such robots do their fancier projects without having to compose me? If the immune system has a mind of its own, and the hand–eye coordination circuit that picks berries has a mind of its own, why bother making a super-mind to supervise all this?

Dennett's own answer is not particularly convincing: he suggests we develop consciousness so we can lie, which gives us an evolutionary advantage. (If so, wouldn't foxes also be conscious?) But the question grows more difficult by an order of magnitude when you ask *how* it happens—the "hard problem of consciousness," as David Chalmers calls it. How do apparently robotic cells and systems combine in such a way as to have qualitative experiences: to feel dampness, savor wine, adore cumbia but be indifferent to salsa? Some scientists are honest enough to admit they don't have the slightest idea how to account for experiences like these, and suspect they never will.

DO THE ELECTRON(S) DANCE?

There is a way out of the dilemma, and the first step is to consider that our starting point could be wrong. Reconsider the lobster. Lobsters have a very bad reputation among philosophers, who frequently hold them out as examples of purely unthinking, unfeeling creatures. Presumably, this is because lobsters are the only animal most philosophers have killed with their own two hands before eating. It's unpleasant to throw a struggling creature in a pot of boiling water; one needs to be able to tell oneself that the lobster isn't really feeling it. (The only exception to this pattern appears to be, for some reason, France, where Gérard de Nerval used to walk a pet lobster on a leash and where Jean-Paul Sartre at one point became erotically obsessed with lobsters after taking too much mescaline.) But in fact, scientific observation has revealed that even lobsters engage in some forms of play—manipulating objects, for instance, possibly just for the pleasure of doing so. If that is the case, to call such creatures "robots" would be to shear the word *robot* of its meaning. Machines don't just fool around. But if living creatures are not robots after all, many of these apparently thorny questions instantly dissolve away.

What would happen if we proceeded from the reverse perspective and agreed to treat play not as some peculiar anomaly, but as our starting point, a principle already present not just in lobsters and indeed all living creatures, but also on every level where we find what physicists, chemists, and biologists refer to as "self-organizing systems"?

This is not nearly as crazy as it might sound.

Philosophers of science, faced with the puzzle of how life might emerge from dead matter or how conscious beings might evolve from microbes, have developed two types of explanations.

If living creatures are not robots after all, many of these apparently thorny questions instantly dissolve away.

The first consists of what's called emergentism. The argument here is that once a certain level of complexity is reached, there is a kind of qualitative leap where completely new sorts of physical laws can "emerge"— ones that are premised on, but cannot be reduced to, what came before. In this way, the laws of chemistry can be said to be emergent from physics: the laws of chemistry presuppose the laws of physics, but can't simply be reduced to them. In the same way, the laws of biology emerge from chemistry: one obviously needs to understand the chemical components of a fish to understand how it swims, but chemical components will never provide a full explanation. In the same way, the human mind can be said to be emergent from the cells that make it up.

Those who hold the second position, usually called panpsychism or panexperientialism, agree that all this may be true but argue that emergence is not enough. As the British philosopher Galen Strawson recently put it, to imagine that one can travel from insensate matter to a being capable of discussing the existence of insensate matter in a mere two jumps is simply to make emergence do too much work. Something has to be there already, on every level of material existence, even that of subatomic particles—something, however minimal and embryonic, that does some of the things we are used to thinking of life (and even mind) as doing—in order for that something to be organized on more and more complex levels to eventually produce self-conscious beings. That "something" might be very minimal indeed: some very rudimentary sense of responsiveness to one's environment, something like anticipation, something like memory. However rudimentary, it would have to exist for self-organizing systems like atoms or molecules to self-organize in the first place.

All sorts of questions are at stake in the debate, including the hoary problem of free will. As innumerable adolescents have pondered—often while stoned and first contemplating the mysteries of the universe—if the movements of the particles that make up our brains are already determined by natural laws, then how can we be said to have free will? The standard answer is that we have known since Heisenberg that the movements of atomic particles are not predetermined; quantum physics can predict to which positions electrons, for instance, will *tend* to jump, in aggregate, in a given situation, but it is impossible to predict which way any particular electron will jump in any particular instance. Problem solved.

Except not really—something's still missing. If all this means is that the particles that make up our brains jump around randomly, one would still have to imagine some immaterial, metaphysical entity ("mind") that intervenes to guide the neurons in nonrandom directions. But that would be circular: you'd need to already have a mind to make your brain act like a mind.

If those motions are not random, in contrast, you can at least begin to think about a material explanation. And the presence of endless forms of self-organization in nature—structures maintaining themselves in equilibrium within their environments, from electromagnetic fields to processes of crystallization—does give panpsychists a great deal of material to work with. True, they argue, you can insist that all these entities must either simply be "obeying" natural laws (laws whose existence does not itself need to be explained) or just moving completely randomly . . . but if you do, it's really only because you've decided that's the only way you are willing to look at it. And it leaves the fact that you have a mind capable of making such decisions an utter mystery.

Granted, this approach has always been the minority position. During much of the twentieth century, it was put aside completely. It's easy enough to make fun of. ("Wait, you aren't seriously suggesting that tables can think?" No, actually, no one's suggesting that; the argument is that those self-organizing elements that make up tables, such as atoms, evince extremely simple forms of the qualities that, on an exponentially more complex level, we consider thought.) But in recent years, especially with the newfound popularity, in some scientific circles, of the ideas of philosophers such as Charles Sanders Peirce (1839–1914) and Alfred North Whitehead (1861–1947), we have begun to see something of a revival.

Curiously, it's largely physicists who have proved receptive to such ideas. (Also mathematicians—perhaps unsurprisingly, since Peirce and Whitehead themselves both began their careers as mathematicians.) Physicists are more playful and less hidebound creatures than, say, biologists—partly, no doubt, because they rarely have to contend with religious fundamentalists challenging the laws of physics. They are the poets of the scientific world. If one is already willing to embrace thirteen-dimensional objects or an endless number of alternative universes, or to casually suggest that 95 percent of the universe is made up of dark matter and energy about whose properties we know nothing, it's perhaps not too much of a leap to also contemplate the possibility that subatomic particles have "free will" or even experiences. And indeed, the existence of freedom on the subatomic level is currently a heated question of debate.

What evolutionary psychologists can't explain is why fun is fun.

Is it meaningful to say an electron "chooses" to jump the way it does? Obviously, there's no way to prove it. The only evidence we *could* have (that we can't predict what it's going to do), we do have. But it's hardly decisive. Still, if one wants a consistently materialist explanation of the world—that is, if one does not wish to treat the mind as some supernatural entity imposed on the material world, but rather as simply a more complex organization of processes that are already going on, at every level of material reality—then it makes sense that something at least a little like intentionality, something at least a little like experience, something at least a little like freedom, would have to exist on every level of physical reality as well.

Why do most of us, then, immediately recoil at such conclusions?

Why do they seem crazy and unscientific? Or more to the point, why are we perfectly willing to ascribe agency to a strand of DNA (however "metaphorically"), but consider it absurd to do the same with an electron, a snowflake, or a coherent electromagnetic field? The answer, it seems, is because it's pretty much impossible to ascribe self-interest to a snowflake. If we have convinced ourselves that rational explanation of action can consist only of treating action as if there were some sort of self-serving calculation behind it, then by that definition, on all these levels, rational explanations can't be found. Unlike a DNA molecule, which we can at least pretend is pursuing some gangster-like project of ruthless self-aggrandizement, an electron simply does not have a material interest to pursue, not even survival. It is in no sense competing with other electrons. If an electron is acting freely—if it, as Richard Feynman is supposed to have said, "does anything it likes"—it can only be acting freely as an end in itself. Which would mean that at the very foundations of physical reality, we encounter freedom for its own sake—which also means we encounter the most rudimentary form of play.

SWIM WITH THE FISHES

Let us imagine a principle. Call it a principle of freedom—or, since Latinate constructions tend to carry more weight in such matters, call it a principle of ludic freedom. Let us imagine it to hold that the free exercise of an entity's most complex powers or capacities will, under certain circumstances at least, tend to become an end in itself. It would obviously not be the only principle active in nature. Others pull other ways. But if nothing else, it would help explain what we actually observe, such as why, despite the second law of thermodynamics, the universe seems to be getting more, rather than less, complex. Evolutionary psychologists claim they can explain—as the title of one recent book has it—"why sex is fun." What they can't explain is why fun is fun.

I don't deny that what I've presented so far is a savage simplification of very complicated issues. I'm not even saying that the position I'm suggesting here—that there is a play principle at the basis of all physical reality—is necessarily true. I would just insist that such a perspective is at least as plausible as the weirdly inconsistent speculations that currently pass for orthodoxy, in which a mindless, robotic universe suddenly produces poets and philosophers out of nowhere. Nor, I think, does seeing play as a principle of nature necessarily mean adopting any sort of milky utopian view. The play principle can help explain why sex is fun, but it can also explain why cruelty is fun. (As anyone who has watched a cat play with a mouse can attest, a lot of animal play is not particularly nice.) But it gives us ground to unthink the world around us.

Years ago, when I taught at Yale, I would sometimes assign a reading containing a famous Taoist story. I offered an automatic A to any student who could tell me why the last line made sense. (None ever succeeded.)

> Zhuangzi and Huizi were strolling on a bridge over the Hao River, when the former observed, "See how the minnows dart between the rocks! Such is the happiness of fishes."
>
> "You not being a fish," said Huizi, "how can you possibly know what makes fish happy?"
>
> "And you not being I," said Zhuangzi, "how can you know that I don't know what makes fish happy?"
>
> "If I, not being you, cannot know what you know," replied Huizi, "does it not follow from that very fact that you, not being a fish, cannot know what makes fish happy?"
>
> "Let us go back," said Zhuangzi, "to your original question. You asked me how I knew what makes fish happy. The very fact you asked shows that you knew I knew—as I did know, from my own feelings on this bridge."

The anecdote is usually taken as a confrontation between two irreconcilable approaches to the world: the logician versus the mystic. But if that's true, then why did Zhuangzi, who wrote it down, show himself to be defeated by his logician friend?

After thinking about the story for years, it struck me that this was the entire point. By all accounts, Zhuangzi and Huizi were the best of friends. They liked to spend hours arguing like this. Surely, that was what Zhuangzi was really getting at. We can each understand what the other is feeling because, arguing about the fish, we are doing exactly what the fish are doing: having fun, doing something we do well for the sheer pleasure of doing it. Engaging in a form of play. The very fact that you felt compelled to try to beat me in an argument, and were so happy to be able to do so, shows that the premise you were arguing must be false. Since if even philosophers are motivated primarily by such pleasures, by the exercise of their highest powers simply for the sake of doing so, then surely this is a principle that exists on every level of nature—which is why I could spontaneously identify it, too, in fish.

Zhuangzi was right. So was June Thunderstorm. Our minds are just a part of nature. We can understand the happiness of fishes—or ants, or inchworms—because what drives us to think and argue about such matters is, ultimately, exactly the same thing.

Now wasn't that fun?

Notes

There Never Was a West

1. Samuel P. Huntington, "The Clash of Civilizations?" *Foreign Affairs* 72 (3), Summer 1993: 22–49.
2. Samuel P. Huntington, "The West: Unique, Not Universal," *Foreign Affairs* 75 (6), November–December 1996: 28–46.
3. Huntington, "The West."
4. Karl Deutsch, "On Nationalism, World Regions, and the Nature of the West," in Per Torvik, ed., *Mobilization, Center-Periphery Structures and Nation-Building* (Bergen: Universitetsforlaget, 1981), p. 77.
5. Lucien Lévy-Bruhl, *How Natives Think*, trans. Lilian Clare (Salem, MA: Ayer, 1986 [1926]).
6. Bernard Manin, "On Legitimacy and Political Deliberation," in Mark Lilla, ed., *New French Thought: Political Philosophy* (Princeton, NJ: Princeton University Press, 1994).
7. David Graeber, *Fragments of an Anarchist Anthropology* (Chicago: University of Chicago Press, 2004).
8. Michel-Rolph Trouillot, *Global Transformations: Anthropology and the Modern World* (New York: Palgrave, 2003).
9. Paul Gilroy, *The Black Atlantic: Modernity and Double Consciousness* (Cambridge, MA: Harvard University Press, 1993); Ron Sakolsky and James Koehnline, eds., *Gone to Croatan: The Origins of North American Dropout Culture* (Brooklyn: Autonomedia, 1993); Marcus Rediker, "'Under the Banner of King Death': The Social World of Anglo-American Pirates, 1716–1726," *William*

and Mary Quarterly 38 (2): 203–27; Marcus Rediker, Between the Devil and the Deep Blue Sea: Merchant Seamen, Pirates, and the Anglo-American Maritime World, 1700–1750 (Cambridge: Cambridge University Press, 1987); Peter Linebaugh and Marcus Rediker, The Many-Headed Hydra: Sailors, Slaves, Commoners, and the Hidden History of the Revolutionary Atlantic (Boston: Beacon Press, 2000).

10. Paul Veyne, Le Pain et le Cirque: Sociologie Historique d'un Pluralisme Politique (Paris: Editions du Seuil, 1976); Donald G. Kyle, Spectacles of Death in Ancient Rome (New York: Routledge, 1988); Kathryn Lomar and Tim Cornell, eds., Bread and Circuses: Euergetism and Municipal Patronage in Roman Italy (London: Routledge, 2003).

11. Cornelius Castoriadis, Philosophy, Politics, Autonomy: Essays in Political Philosophy (New York: Oxford University Press, 1991); Jacques Godbout, "Pas de représentation sans représentativité?" Revue du MAUSS Semestrielle, no. 26: 90–104.

12. Francis Dupuis-Déri, "The Political Power of Words: The Birth of Pro-Democratic Discourse in the Nineteenth Century in the United States and Canada," Political Studies 52 (2004): 118–34. See also Francis Dupuis-Déri, "L'Esprit Anti-Démocratique des Fondateurs des 'Démocraties' modernes," Agone 22 (1999): 95–113.

13. John Adams, Defense of the Constitutions of Government of the United States of America, Against the Attack of M. Turgot in His Letter to Dr. Price (Philadelphia: W. Cobbet, 1797).

14. John Markoff, "Where and When Was Democracy Invented?" Comparative Studies in Society and History 41 (4) (1999): 660–90.

15. Dupuis-Déri, "L'Esprit Anti-Démocratique"; Dupuis-Déri, "The Political Power of Words."

16. Arlene W. Saxonhouse, "Athenian Democracy: Modern Mythmakers and Ancient Theorists," PS: Political Science and Politics 26 (3): 486–90.

17. Chris GoGwilt, "True West: The Changing Idea of the West from the 1880s to the 1920s," in Enduring Western Civilization: The Construction of the Concept of Western Civilization and Its "Others," ed. Silvia Federici (London: Praeger, 1995); Martin W. Lewis and Kären E. Wigen, The Myth of Continents: A Critique of Metageography (Berkeley: University of California Press, 1997).

18. Silvia Federici, ed., Enduring Western Civilization.

19. Giovanni Arrighi, Iftikhar Ahmad, and Min-weh Shih, "Beyond Western Hegemonies," paper presented at the XXI Meeting of the Social Science History Association, New Orleans, Louisiana, October 10–13, 1996.

20. Arrighi et al., "Beyond Western Hegemonies," p. 34.

21. Arrighi et al., "Beyond Western Hegemonies," p. 25.

22. Engseng Ho, "Empire Through Diasporic Eyes: A View From the Other Boat," Comparative Studies in Society and History 46 (2) (2004): 210–46.

23. Bruce Johansen, Forgotten Founders: How the American Indian Helped Shape

Democracy (Boston: Harvard Common Press, 1982); Donald A. Grinde and Bruce E. Johansen, *Exemplar of Liberty: Native America and the Evolution of Democracy* (Los Angeles: University of California Los Angeles, 1990).

24. Samuel B. Payne, "The Iroquois League, the Articles of the Confederation, and the Constitution," *William and Mary Quarterly* 53 (3) (1997): 605–20.

25. Elizabeth Tooker, "The United States Constitution and the Iroquois League," *Ethnohistory* 35 (1998): 305–36; Dean R. Snow, *The Iroquois* (London: Blackwell, 1994); Bruce Johansen, *Debating Democracy: Native American Legacy of Freedom* (Santa Fe: Clear Light, 1998).

26. Michael Newman, "Founding Feathers: The Iroquois and the Constitution," *The New Republic* 199 (19) (1998): 17–21.

27. Adams, *Defense of the Constitutions*, p. 296; Philip A. Levy, "Exemplars of Taking Liberties: The Iroquois Influence Thesis and the Problem of Evidence," *William and Mary Quarterly* 53 (3) (1996): 587–604; Payne, p. 618.

28. Markoff, p. 673 n. 62.

29. Marcus Rediker, *Villains of All Nations: Atlantic Pirates in the Golden Age* (Boston: Beacon Press, 2004).

30. Rediker, *Villains of All Nations*, p. 53.

31. Colin Calloway, *New Worlds for All: Indians, Europeans, and the Remaking of Early America* (Baltimore: Johns Hopkins, 1997). See James Axtell, *The Invasion Within: The Contest of Cultures in Colonial North America* (Oxford: Oxford University Press, 1985).

32. Calloway, p. 192.

33. Sakolsky and Koehnline; Linebaugh and Rediker.

34. B. H. Quain, "The Iroquois," in Margaret Mead, ed., *Cooperation and Competition Among Primitive Peoples* (New York: McGraw-Hill, 1937), pp. 240–81.

35. William Pietz, "The Problem of the Fetish I," *RES: Journal of Anthropology and Aesthetics* 9 (1985): 5–17; William Pietz, "The Problem of the Fetish II: The Origin of the Fetish," *RES: Journal of Anthropology and Aesthetics* 13 (1987): 23–45; and William Pietz, "The Problem of the Fetish IIIa: Bosman's Guinea and the Enlightenment Theory of Fetishism," *RES: Journal of Anthropology and Aesthetics* 16 (1988): 105–23.

36. Wyatt MacGaffey, "African Objects and the Idea of the Fetish," *RES: Journal of Anthropology and Aesthetics* 25 (1994): 123–31; David Graeber, "Fetishism and Social Creativity, or Fetishes Are Gods in Process of Construction," *Anthropological Theory* 5 (4) (2005): 407–38.

37. Arthur Lovejoy, "The Chinese Origin of a Romanticism," in *Essays in the History of Ideas* (New York: George, 1955).

38. Steven Muhlberger and Phil Paine, "Democracy's Place in World History," *Journal of World History* 4 (1) (1993): 23–45; Jean Baechler, *Démocraties* (Paris: Calmann–Lévy, 1985).

39. Martha Lamberg-Karlovsky, ed., *The Breakout: The Origins of Civilization* (Cambridge: Harvard University Press, 2000).

324 NOTES TO PAGES 42–118

40. K. C. Chang, *Art, Myth, and Ritual: The Path to Political Authority in Ancient China* (Cambridge, MA: Harvard University Press, 1983).
41. C. C. Lamberg-Karlovsky, "The Eastern 'Breakout' and the Mesopotamian Social Contract," in *The Breakout*, p. 122.
42. Mason Hammond, "The Indo-European Origins of the Concept of a Democratic Society," in *The Breakout*, p. 59.
43. Gordon R. Willey, "Ancient Chinese, New World, and Near Eastern Ideological Traditions: Some Observations," in Martha Lamberg-Karlovsky, ed., *The Breakout: The Origins of Civilization* (Cambridge, MA: Harvard University Press, 2000).
44. Linda Schele, "Sacred Landscape and Maya Kingship," in Martha Lamberg-Karlovsky, ed., *The Breakout: The Origins of Civilization* (Cambridge, MA: Harvard University Press, 2000).
45. George A. Collier with Elizabeth Lowery Quaratiello, *Basta!: Land & The Zapatista Rebellion in Chiapas* (Oakland: Food First Books, 1999); John Ross, *The War Against Oblivion: The Zapatista Chronicles* (Monroe, ME: Common Courage Press, 2000); Jan Rus, Aída Hernandez, and Shannan L. Mattiace, *Mayan Lives, Mayan Utopias: The Indigenous Peoples of Chiapas and the Zapatista Rebellion* (Lanham, MD: Rowman and Littlefield, 2003).
46. Walter D. Mignolo, "The Many Faces of Cosmo-polis: Border Thinking and Critical Cosmopolitanism," in *Cosmopolitanism* (Durham, NC: Duke University Press, 2002).
47. Mignolo, p. 180.
48. Giovanni Sartori, *The Theory of Democracy Revisited* (Chatham, NJ: Chatham House, 1987), p. 279.
49. Francis Dupuis-Déri, "The Struggle Between Political Agoraphobia and Agoraphilia" (2002). Paper presented at the Massachusetts Institute of Technology, political science workshop.
50. Walter Benjamin, "Critique of Violence," in *Reflections: Essays, Aphorisms, and Autobiographical Writings* (New York: Harcourt Brace, 1978).
51. Michael Mann, "The Dark Side of Democracy: The Modern Tradition of Ethnic and Political Cleansing," *New Left Review* 235 (1999): 18–45.
52. Mann, p. 19.

Culture as Creative Refusal

1. Marilyn Strathern, *Negative Strategies in Melanesia*. In *Localizing Strategies: Regional Traditions of Ethnographic Writing*, ed. Richard Fardon (Edinburgh: Scottish Academic Press, 1990), pp. 204–16.
2. Marcel Mauss, *Techniques, Technologies, and Civilizations*, ed. Nathan Schlanger (London: Berghan, 2006).
3. Peter Lamborn Wilson, "The Shamanic Trace," in *Escape from the Nineteenth Century and Other Essays* (Brooklyn: Autonomedia, 1998), pp. 72–142.
4. Wilson, p. 91.

5. See Thomas Gibson and Kenneth Silander, eds., *Anarchic Solidarity: Autonomy, Equality, and Fellowship in Southeast Asia* (New Haven: Yale University Press, 2011), and James C. Scott, *The Art of Not Being Governed: An Anarchist History of Upland Southeast Asia* (New Haven: Yale University Press, 2011).

6. David Graeber, *Debt: The First 5,000 Years* (Brooklyn: Melville House, 2011), building my argument on that of the feminist historian Gerda Lerner.

7. Hector Munro Chadwick, *The Heroic Age* (Cambridge: Cambridge University Press, 1926).

8. David Wengrow, *What Makes Civilization? The Ancient Near East and the Future of the West* (New York: Oxford University Press), and Wengrow, "'Archival' and 'Sacrificial' Economies in Bronze Age Eurasia: An Interactionist Approach to the Hoarding of Metals," in *Interweaving Worlds: Systemic Interactions in Eurasia, 7th to the 1st Millennia BC*, eds. T. C. Wilkinson, S. Sherratt, and J. Bennet (Oxbow: Oxford, 2011).

9. Georges Dumézil, *Mythe et Épopée* (Paris: Galimard, 1968–73).

10. Paul Treherne, "The Warrior's Beauty: The Masculine Body and Self-Identity in Bronze Age Europe," *Journal of European Archaeology* 3 (1): 105–44.

11. Marshall Sahlins, *Islands of History* (Chicago: University of Chicago Press, 1985).

12. Alvin W. Gouldner, *Enter Plato* (New York: Basic Books, 1965).

13. See Bernard Manin, *The Principles of Representative Government* (Cambridge: Cambridge University Press, 1997), and Oliver Dowlen, *The Political Potential of Sortition: A Study of the Random Selection of Citizens for Public Office* (London: Imprint Academic, 2009).

14. O. C. Dahl, *Malgache et Maanyan: Une comparaison linguistique*, Avhandlinger utgitt av Instituttet 3 (Oslo: Egede Instituttet, 1951), and O. C. Dahl, "La Subdivision de la famille Barito et la place du Malgache," *Acta Orientalia* (Copenhagen) 38 (1977): 77–134.

15. Conrad P. Kottak, "A Cultural Adaptive Approach to Malagasy Social Organization," in *Social Exchange and Interaction*, ed. E. Wilmsen. Anthropological Paper No. 46, Museum of Anthropology (Ann Arbor, MI: 1972); Conrad P. Kottak, "The Origin of Prostitution in Ancient Mesopotamia," *Signs* 11 (2) (1980): 236–54; Kent V. Flannery, "Divergent Evolution," in *The Cloud People: Divergent Evolution of the Zapotec and Mixtec Civilizations* (New York: Academic Press, 1983).

16. Matthew E. Hurles et al., "The Dual Origin of the Malagasy in Island Southeast Asia and East Africa: Evidence from Maternal and Paternal Lineages," *The American Society of Human Genetics* 16 (2005): 894–901; M. P. Cox et al., "A Small Cohort of Island Southeast Asian Women Founded Madagascar," *Proceedings of the Royal Society of Biological Sciences* 279 (1739) (2012): 2761–68. I find this biological evidence gratifying, as I have long pointed out that discussions of the origins of human habitation in Madagascar are a classic example of the pitfalls of sexist language. Archaeologists still regularly ask 'when

did Man come to Madagascar?' often noting that there is, in fact, evidence for human activity—particularly, the mass killing of dwarf hippopotamuses—from as early as the first century CE. Yet there is no sign of ongoing settlement. Obviously, the real question to be asked is 'when did women come to Madagascar?' since a band of men hunting to provision ships, for example, or even settling in after shipwrecks, would have no enduring significance; without women, one cannot have a population.

17. K. A. Adelaar, "Malay Influence on Malagasy: Linguistic and Culture-Historical Inferences," *Oceanic Linguistics* 28 (1) (1989): 1-46; K. A. Adelaar, "New Ideas on the Early History of Malagasy," in *Papers in Austronesian Linguistics* no. 1 (1991), ed. H. Steinhauer, 1-22. Pacific Linguistics Series A, No. 81 (Canberra: Department of Linguistics, Research School of Pacific Studies, Australian National University); K. A. Adelaar, "Malay and Javanese Loanwords in Malagasy, Tagalog and Siraya (Formosa)," *Bijdragen tot de Taal-, Land- en Volkenkunde* 150 (1995): 50-65; K. A. Adelaar, "The Asian Roots of Malagasy: A Linguistic Perspective," *Bijdragen tot de Taal-, Land- en Volkenkunde* 151 (1995): 325-56; K. A. Adelaar, "Borneo as a Cross-Roads for Comparative Austronesian Linguistics," in *The Austronesians: Historical and Comparative Perspectives* (2nd ed.), ed. P. Bellwood, J. J. Fox, and D. Tryon (Canberra: Australian National University Press, 2005); K. A. Adelaar, "Towards an Integrated Theory about the Indonesian Migrations to Madagascar," in *Ancient Human Migrations*, ed. P. Pergine, I. Peiros, and M. Feldman (Salt Lake City: University of Utah Press, 2009); R. M. Blench, "The Ethnographic Evidence for Long-Distance Contacts Between Oceania and East Africa," in *The Indian Ocean in Antiquity*, ed. J. Reade (New York: Kegan Paul/British Museum, 1994); R. M. Blench, "New Palaeozoogeographical Evidence for the Settlement of Madagascar," *Azania* 42 (2007): 69-82; Philippe Beaujard, "Les Arrivées austronésiennes à Madagascar: vagues ou continuum? (Partie I)," *Etudes Océan Indien* 35-36 (2003): 59-128; Philippe Beaujard, "East Africa, the Comoros Islands and Madagascar before the Sixteenth Century," *Azania* 42 (2007): 15-35; Philippe Beaujard, "The First Migrants to Madagascar and Their Introduction of Plants: Linguistic and Etymological Evidence," *Azania* 46 (2011): 169-89.

18. Adelaar, "The Asian Roots of Malagasy," p. 328.

19. See Anthony Reid, ed., *Slavery, Bondage, Dependency in Southeast Asia* (New York: St. Martin's Press, 1983), and Gwyn Campbell, *The Structure of Slavery in Indian Ocean Africa and Asia* (London: Frank Cass, 2004).

20. R. M. Blench, "The Austronesians in Madagascar and Their Interaction with the Bantu of East African Coast: Surveying the Linguistic Evidence for Domestic and Translocated Animals," *Philippines Journal of Linguistics* 18 (2) (2008): 18-43; R. M. Blench, "Bananas and Plantains in Africa: Re-Interpreting the Linguistic Evidence," *Ethnobotany Research and Applications* 7 (2009): 363-80; Beaujard, "The First Migrants to Madagascar."

21. For a good summary from a Malagasy perspective, see Beaujard, "East Africa," and Randall L. Pouwels, "Eastern Africa and the Indian Ocean to 1800: Reviewing Relations in Historical Perspective," *International Journal of African Historical Studies* 35 (2/3) (2002): 385–425; Thomas Vernet, "Les Réseaux de traite de l'Afrique orientale: côte swahili, Comores et nordouest de Madagascar (vers 1500–1750)," *Cahiers des Anneaux de la Mémoire* 9 (2006): 67–107; Thomas Vernet, "Slave Trade and Slavery on the Swahili Coast (1500–1750)," in *Slavery, Islam and Diaspora*, ed. B. A. Mirzai, I. M. Montana, and P. Lovejoy (Trenton, NJ: Africa World Press, 2009).

22. Marie de Chantal Radimilahy, *Mahilaka: An Archaeological Investigation of an Early Town in Northwestern Madagascar* (Uppsala, Sweden: Dept. of Archaeology and Ancient History, 1998).

23. Robert E. Dewar, "Of Nets and Trees: Untangling the Reticulate and Dendritic in Madagascar's Prehistory," *World Archaeology* 26 (3) (1995): 301–18.

24. Radimilahy, pp. 24–25.

25. Maurice Bloch, *Placing the Dead: Tombs, Ancestral Villages, and Kinship Organization in Madagascar* (London: Seminar Press, 1971).

26. Frantz Fanon, *Black Skin, White Masks* (London: MacGibbon and Kee, 1968).

27. Pouwels, "Eastern Africa and the Indian Ocean."

28. Pouwels, "Eastern Africa and the Indian Ocean."

29. Jacques Lombard, "Zatovo qui n'a pas été créé par Dieu: un conte sakalava traduit et commenté," *Asie du Sud Est et Monde Insulindien* 7 (1976): 165–223.

30. Charles Renel, *Contes de Madagascar* (Paris: E. Leroux, 1910), pp. 268–70.

31. Renel, *Contes de Madagascar*, pp. 270–74.

32. Beaujard, *Mythe et société*.

33. David Graeber, *Lost People: Magic and the Legacy of Slavery in Madagascar* (Bloomington: Indiana University Press, 2007).

34. Pierre Vérin, *The History of Civilisation in North Madagascar* (Rotterdam: A. A. Balkema, 1986). See, e.g., R. J. Barendse, *The Arabian Seas: The Indian Ocean World of the Seventeenth Century* (Armonk, NY: M. E. Sharpe, 2002).

Dead Zones of the Imagination

1. This essay is based on the 2006 Malinowski Memorial Lecture entitled "Beyond Power/Knowledge: An Exploration of the Relation of Power, Ignorance and Stupidity." It is a substantially revised version of the one that, for some years, was available online at the London School of Economics website. This version is now meant to be considered the official one for reference purposes.

2. Michael Herzfeld, *The Social Production of Indifference: Exploring the Symbolic Roots of Western Bureaucracy* (New York: Berg, 1992), p. 3.

3. Herzfeld, *The Social Production of Indifference*, p. 8. For a good recent summary of the anthropological literature on bureaucracy, see Colin Hoag, "Assembling Partial Perspectives: Thoughts on the Anthropology of Bureaucracy," *PoLAR* 34 (1) (2011): 81–94.

4. See Yael Navaro-Yashin, *Faces of the State: Secularism and Public Life in Turkey* (Princeton, NJ: Princeton University Press, 2002).

5. Max Weber, *The Protestant Ethic and the Spirit of Capitalism* (London: Scribner's, 1958), p. 181.

6. Eric B. Ross, "Cold Warriors Without Weapons," *Identities* 4 (3–4) (1998): 475–506. Just to give a sense of the connections here, Geertz was a student of Clyde Kluckhohn at Harvard, who was not only "an important conduit for CIA area studies funds," but had contributed the section on anthropology to Parsons and Shils's famous Weberian manifesto for the social sciences, *Toward a General Theory of Action* (1951). Kluckhohn connected Geertz to MIT's Center for International Studies, then directed by the former CIA director of economic research, which in turn convinced him to work on development in Indonesia. The Center had as its declared aim the development of "an alternative to Marxism" largely through what came to be known as modernization theory—again, on Weberian grounds. See Ben White, "Clifford Geertz: Singular Genius of Interpretive Anthropology," *Development and Change* 38 (6) (2007): 1187–208.

7. Talcott Parsons and Edward A. Shils, eds., *Toward a General Theory of Action* (Cambridge: Harvard University Press, 1951).

8. Johann Galtung, "Violence, Peace, and Peace Research," *Journal of Peace Research* 6 (1969): 167–91; Galtung, *Peace: Research, Education, Action: Essays in Peace Research*, vol. 1 (Copenhagen: Christian Ejlers, 1975).

9. Philippe Bourgois, "The Power of Violence in War and Peace: Post-Cold War Lessons from El Salvador," *Ethnography* 2 (1) (2001): 5–34; Paul Farmer, "An Anthropology of Structural Violence," *Current Anthropology* 45 (3) (2004): 305–25; Paul Farmer, *Pathologies of Power: Health, Human Rights, and the New War on the Poor* (Berkeley: University of California Press, 2005); Akhil Gupta, *Red Tape: Bureaucracy, Structural Violence, and Poverty in India* (Durham, NC: Duke University Press, 2012).

10. Farmer, *Pathologies*, p. 40.

11. Nancy Scheper-Hughes, *Death Without Weeping: The Violence of Everyday Life in Brazil* (Berkeley: University of California Press, 1992); Carolyn Nordstrom and Joann Martin, eds., *The Paths to Domination, Resistance, and Terror* (Berkeley: University of California Press, 1992).

12. Hence feminists often note that "violence against women is structural" (e.g., Rosa-Linda Fregoso, *Terrorizing Women: Feminicide in the Americas* [Durham, NC: Duke University Press, 2010], p. 141) in the sense that actual physical attacks and threats underpin the very institutions and arrangements that can then be described as "structural violence" because of their effects. Similarly, Catia Confortini observes that once one understands "structures" as material processes, one can see not only that "direct violence is a tool used to build, perpetuate, and reproduce structural violence," but it makes possible our very categories of masculinity and femininity to begin with. Hartsock makes

analogous points in her critique of Foucault (Nancy Hartsock, "Foucault on Power: A Theory for Women?" in *Feminism/Postmodernism*, ed. Linda Nicholson [New York: Routledge, 1989]).

13. Catia Confortini, "Galtung, Violence, and Gender: The Case for a Peace Studies/Feminism Alliance," *Peace and Change* 31 (3) (2006): 333–67.

14. To be fair, one reason that so many who use the term "structural violence" imagine that it is possible to have such structures unbacked by physical violence is that they are employing a typically liberal definition of "violence" as physical attacks on others, or even a typically conservative definition of violence as unauthorized damage to persons or property, rather than the more typically radical definition of violence as including threats of physical attack (C. A. J. Coady, "The Idea of Violence," *Journal of Applied Philosophy* 3 (1) (1986): 3–19; cf. David Graeber, *Direct Action: An Ethnography* [Oakland: AK Press, 2009), pp. {2009), pp. 48–49] } 448–49].

15. Keith Breckenridge, "Power Without Knowledge: Three Nineteenth Century Colonialisms in South Africa," *Journal of Natal and Zulu History* 26 (2008): 3–31. Available online: researchspace.ukzn.ac.za/server/api/core/bitstreams /aa887df2-6c36-4561-9326-4c6cc3c1d223/content.

16. Keith Breckenridge, "Verwoerd's Bureau of Proof: Total Information in the Making of Apartheid," *History Workshop Journal* 59 (2005): 84.

17. Andrew S. Mathews, "Power/Knowledge, Power/Ignorance: Forest Fires and the State in Mexico," *Human Ecology* 33 (6) (2005): 795–820; Andrew S. Mathews, *Instituting Nature: Authority, Expertise, and Power in Mexican Forests, 1926–2011* (Cambridge, MA: MIT Press, 2011).

18. David Apter, *The Politics of Modernization* (Chicago: University of Chicago Press, 1965); David Apter, *Choice and the Politics of Allocation: A Developmental Theory* (New Haven: Yale University Press, 1971).

19. Neil Whitehead, ed., *Violence* (Santa Fe: School of American Research Press, 2004).

20. Whitehead, *Violence*, pp. 9–10.

21. Obviously, the immediate reason teenage boys object to imagining themselves as girls is homophobia; but one then has to ask why that homophobia is so powerful in the first place, and why it takes the form that it does. After all, many teenage girls are equally homophobic, but it does not seem to stop them from taking pleasure in imagining themselves as boys.

22. bell hooks, "Representations of Whiteness in the Black Imagination," in *Black Looks: Race and Representation* (Boston: South End Books, 1992), p. 165.

23. The key texts on Standpoint Theory, by Patricia Hill Collins, Donna Haraway, Sandra Harding, Nancy Hartsock, and others, are collected in Sandra Harding, ed., *The Feminist Standpoint Theory Reader: Intellectual and Political Controversies* (London: Routledge, 2004). I might add that the history of this very essay provides a telling example of the sort of gendered obliviousness I'm describing. When I first framed the problem, I wasn't even aware of this body

of literature, though my argument had clearly been indirectly influenced by it—it was only the intervention of a feminist friend, Erica Lagalisse, who put me on to where many of these ideas were actually coming from.

24. Egon Bittner, *Aspects of Police Work* (Boston: Northeastern University Press, 1970); Egon Bittner, "The Capacity to Use Force as the Core of the Police Role," in *Moral Issues in Police Work*, eds. Frederick Elliston and Michael Feldberg (Savage, MD: Rowman and Littlefield, 1985); P. A. J. Waddington, *Policing Citizens: Authority and Rights* (London: University College London Press, 1999); Mark Neocleous, *The Fabrication of Social Order: A Critical Theory of Police Power* (London: Pluto Press, 2000).

25. Edmund Leach, *Rethinking Anthropology* (Cambridge: Cambridge University Press, 1959).

26. Marc Cooper, "Dum Da Dum-Dum," *The Village Voice*, April 16, 1991: 28–33.

27. Jean Piaget, *The Origins of Intelligence in Children* (New York: W. W. Norton & Company, 1936 [1963]).

28. I have explored some of these implications—concerning both alienation and liberatory politics—further in an essay called "Revolution in Reverse."

29. Renato Rosaldo, "From the Door of His Tent: The Fieldworker and the Inquisitor," in *Writing Culture: The Poetics and Politics of Fieldwork*, eds. George Marcus and James Clifford (Berkeley: University of California Press, 1986).

30. In fact, the way the image of the panopticon has been adopted in the academy, as an argument *against* the primacy of violence in contemporary forms of power, might be considered a perfect example of how academics can become complicit in the process by which structures founded on violence can represent themselves as something else.

31. It would be interesting to document the ebb and flow of ethnographic interest within different historical empires to see if there are any consistent patterns. As far as I'm aware, the first large empire that gathered systematic ethnographic, culinary, medical, and similar information from within the empire were the Mongols.

32. Douglas H. Johnson, "Colonial Policy and Prophecy: the 'Nuer Settlement,' 1929–1930," *Journal of the Anthropological Society of Oxford* X/1 (1979): 1–20; Douglas H. Johnson, "Evans-Pritchard, the Nuer, and the Sudan Political Service," *African Affairs* 81 (323) (1982): 231–46; Douglas H. Johnson, *Nuer Prophets* (Oxford: Clarendon Press, 1994).

33. Johnson, "Evans-Pritchard," p. 245.

34. There has been of late a minor boomlet in anthropological studies of ignorance, and some of the more recent examples even take some of the arguments of my original Malinowski lecture into consideration. But even here, one can observe at least a slight tug pulling in the opposite direction, as when High, Kelly, and Mair suggest, in their introduction, that while a political critique approach to the subject is not invalid, a distinctively "ethnographic approach" must mean seeing ignorance not in purely negative terms, as the absence of

knowledge, but "as a substantive phenomenon with its own history" and therefore to understand its "productivity" (Casey High, Ann H. Kelly, and Jonathan Mair, eds., *The Anthropology of Ignorance: An Ethnographic Approach* [London: Palgrave, 2012], pp. 15–16). This of course sounds very much like Foucault on power. Ethnography abhors a vacuum. But vacuums do exist.

35. Elaine Scarry, *The Body in Pain: The Making and Unmaking of the World* (Oxford: Oxford University Press, 1985), p. 28.

The Bully's Pulpit

1. Still, before we let adult males entirely off the hook, I should observe that the argument for military efficiency cuts two ways: even those societies whose men refuse to organize themselves effectively for war also do, in the overwhelming majority of cases, insist that women should not fight at all. This is hardly very efficient. Even if one were to concede that men are, generally speaking, better at fighting (and this is by no means clear; it depends on the type of fighting), and one were to simply choose the most able-bodied half of any given population, then some of them would be female. Anyway, in a truly desperate situation it can be suicidal not to employ every hand you've got. Nonetheless, again and again we find men—even those relatively nonbelligerent ones—deciding they would rather die than break the code saying women should never be allowed to handle weapons. No wonder we find it so difficult to sympathize with male atrocity victims: they are, to the degree that they segregate women from combat, complicit in the logic of male violence that destroyed them. But if we are trying to identify that key flaw or set of flaws in human nature that allows for that logic of male violence to exist to begin with, it leaves us with a confusing picture. We do not, perhaps, have some sort of inbuilt proclivity for violent domination. But we do have a tendency to treat those forms of violent domination that do exist—starting with that of men over women—as moral imperatives unto themselves.

On the Phenomenology of Giant Puppets

1. I'm adopting here the name most commonly employed by participants in North America. Most firmly reject the term "anti-globalization." I have in the past proposed simply "globalization movement," but some find this confusing. In Europe, the terms "alternative" or "alter-globalization" are often used, but these have yet to be widely adopted in the United States.

2. Obviously, this assumes that the groups in question are broadly on the same page; if a group were overtly racist or sexist no one would ask about their internal decision-making process. The point is that questions of process are far more important than the kind of sectarian affiliations that had so dominated radical politics in the past: i.e., Anarcho-Syndicalists versus Social Ecologists, or Platformists, etc. Sometimes these factors do enter in. But even then, the objections are likely to be raised in process terms.

3. That policy can be summed up by *The New York Times*'s senior news editor Bill Borders, who, when challenged by FAIR, a media watchdog group, to explain why the *Times* provided almost no coverage of two thousand inauguration protests (the second-largest inauguration protests in American history), replied that they did not consider the protests themselves to be a news story, but "a staged event," "designed to be covered," and therefore not genuine news ("ACTIVISM UPDATE: *New York Times* Responds on Inauguration Criticism": news release [February 22, 2001], Fairness and Accuracy in Reporting). FAIR replied by asking in what sense the inauguration parade itself was any different.)

4. One effect of the peculiar definition of violence adopted by the American media is that Gandhian tactics do not, generally speaking, work in the United States. One of the aims of nonviolent civil disobedience is to reveal the inherent violence of the state, to demonstrate that it is prepared to brutalize even dissidents who could not possibly be the source of physical harm. Since the 1960s, however, the U.S. media has simply refused to represent authorized police activity of any sort as violent. In the several years immediately preceding Seattle, for instance, forest activists on the West Coast had developed lockdown techniques by which they immobilized their arms in concrete-reinforced PVC tubing, making themselves at once obviously harmless and very difficult to remove. It was a classic Gandhian strategy. The police response was to develop what can only be described as torture techniques: rubbing pepper spray in the eyes of incapacitated activists. When even that didn't cause a media furor (in fact, courts upheld the practice), many concluded Gandhian tactics simply didn't work in America. It is significant that a large number of the Black Bloc anarchists in Seattle, who rejected the lockdown strategy and opted for more mobile and aggressive tactics, were precisely forest activists who had been involved in tree-sits and lockdowns in the past.

5. Those with puppets have been attacked and arrested frequently as well, but to my knowledge the corporate media has never reported this.

6. In *The Black Bloc Papers*, compiled by David and X of the Green Mountain Anarchist Collective (Baltimore: Black Clover Press, 2002), p. 53. The references to diverting forms of exchange value into use values is clearly directly inspired by Situationist manifestos.

7. I owe the phrase to Ilana Gershon.

8. Ristin Cooks, "Puppet Masters: Paper Hand Puppet Intervention Brings Its Brand of Political Theater Back to Chapel Hill," *Independent Online*, August 8, 2001, indyweek.com/culture/art/puppet-masters.

9. Similar themes recur in many interviews with radical puppeteers. This is from Mattyboy of the Spiral Q Puppet Theater in Philadelphia: "OK, I'm 23. I've lost 13 friends to AIDS. This is wartime, it's a plague. This is the only way for me to deal with it. With puppets I create my own mythology. I bring them back as gods and goddesses" ("The Puppets Are Coming," Daisy Freid, *Philadelphia City Paper*, January 16–23, 1997). One illustrated volume on Bread and Puppet

is actually called *Rehearsing with Gods: Photographs and Essays on the Bread & Puppet Theater*, by Ronald T. Simon and Marc Estrin (White River Junction, VT: Chelsea Green, 2004).

10. Barbara Epstein, *Political Protest and Cultural Revolution: Nonviolent Direct Action in the 1970s and 1980s* (Berkeley: University of California Press, 1993).

11. The Pagan Bloc has been a regular fixture in large-scale actions since Seattle, and, unlike the Quakers and other Christian proponents of civil disobedience, was willing, ultimately, to recognize Black Bloc practice as a form of nonviolence and even to form a tacit alliance with them.

12. Videographers documented police commanders on the first day reassuring activists that the Seattle police "had never attacked nonviolent protesters and never would." Within hours the same commanders had completely reversed course.

13. The best source I've found on these events is in Joseph Boski's "The Costs of Global Governance: Security and International Meetings since WTO Seattle," paper presented at the CYBER Conference, Globalization: Governance and Inequality, May 31–June 1, 2002, Ventura, California.

14. Blocking a street is in fact technically not even a crime, but an "infraction" or "violation": that is, the legal equivalent of jaywalking, or a parking ticket. If one violates such ordinances for nonpolitical purposes one can normally expect to receive some kind of ticket, but certainly not to be taken to a station or spend the night in jail.

15. Jose Martinez, "Police Prep for Protests over Biotech Conference at Hynes," *Boston Herald*, March 4, 2000.

16. *The New York Times*, June 6, Corrections, p. A2. The original story was significantly entitled "Detroit Defends Get-Tough Stance," June 4, 2000, p. A6. The correction reads: "An article on Sunday about plans for protests in Detroit and in Windsor, Ontario, against an inter-American meeting being held in Windsor through today referred incorrectly to the protests last November at the World Trade Organization meeting in Seattle. The Seattle protests were primarily peaceful. The authorities there said that any objects thrown were aimed at property, not people. No protesters were accused of throwing objects, including rocks and Molotov cocktails, at delegates or police."

17. This document was transcribed and widely circulated on activist LISTSERVs at the time. According to one story in the *Miami Herald* ("Trade Protesters Mean Business, Analyst Warns," Joan Fleischman, October 1, 2003), it derived from "retired DEA agent Tom Cash, 63, now senior managing director for Kroll Inc., an international security and business consulting firm." Cash in turn claimed to derive his information from "police intelligence" sources.

18. A number of Molotovs were thrown in Quebec City, apparently by local people. But francophone Canada has a very different tradition of militancy.

19. See, for example, Brendan I. Koerner, "Can Miami Really Ban Giant Puppets?," *Slate*, November 12, 2003, www.slate.com/id/2091139.

20. One has to wonder where they actually get these things. A typical example from my own experience comes from the World Economic Forum protests in New York in early 2002. Police at one point attacked a group of protesters who were part of a crowd waiting to begin a permitted march when they observed them distributing large plexiglass posters that were designed to double as shields. Several were dragged off and arrested. Police later circulated several different stories for the reasons for the attack but the one they eventually fixed on was a claim that the arrestees were preparing to attack the nearby Plaza Hotel; they claimed to have discovered "lead pipes and jars full of urine" on their persons—though in this case they did not actually produce the evidence. This is a case on which I have some firsthand knowledge, since I knew the arrestees and had been standing a few feet away from them when it happened. They were, in fact, undergraduate students from a small New England liberal arts college who had agreed to have their preparations and training before the march videotaped by a team of reporters from ABC's *Nightline* (the reporters, though, unfortunately, were not actually there at the time). A less likely group of thugs would have been hard to imagine. Needless to say, they were startled and confused to discover police were claiming that they had come to the march equipped with jars of urine. In such cases, claims that urine or excrement were involved is considered, by activists, instant and absolute proof that the police had planted the evidence.

21. There is also no clear evidence that '60s protesters spat on soldiers any more than early feminists actually burned bras. At least, no one has managed to come up with a contemporary reference to such an act. The story seems to have emerged in the late '70s or early '80s, and, as the recent documentary *Sir! No Sir!* nicely demonstrates, the only veteran who has publicly claimed this happened to him is likely to be lying.

22. I have been unable to trace who first publicly announced such claims, though my memory from the time was that they were voiced almost simultaneously from Mayor Riordan of Los Angeles and a Philadelphia Democratic Party official, during the preparations for those cities' respective primaries. The claim was obviously also meant to appeal to conservative stereotypes of liberals as members of a "cultural elite"—but it had surprisingly wide influence. As Stevphen Shukaitis has pointed out, it has been reproduced even by sympathetic voices in the NGO community ("Space, Imagination // Rupture: The Cognitive Architecture of Utopian Political Thought in the Global Justice Movement," *University of Sussex Journal of Contemporary History* 8, 2005). While I have not conducted systematic surveys of the socioeconomic background of anarchists in the course of my own research, I can rely on six years of personal experience to say that, in fact, "trust fund babies" in the movement are extremely rare. Any major city is likely to have one or two, often prominent simply because of their access to resources, but I myself know at least two or three anarchists from military families for every one equipped with a trust fund.

23. One common fear is that wooden dowels used in their construction could be detached and used as cudgels, or to break windows.

24. Monday, August 21, "Convention Protests Bring Mixed Reactions" (Reuters/Zogby). "In a Zogby America survey of 1,004 adults, 32.9% said they were proud of the protesters, while another 31.2% said they were wary. Another 13.2% said they were sympathetic and 15.7% irritated and 6.9% said they were unsure." Considering the almost uniform hostility of the coverage, the fact that a third of the audience were nonetheless "proud," and that fewer than one in six were sure their reaction was negative, is quite remarkable.

25. Probably the destruction of productive capacity as well, which must be endlessly renewed.

26. It might be significant here that the United States' main exports to the rest of the world consist of (a) Hollywood action movies and (b) personal computers. If you think about it, they form a kind of complementary pair to the brick-through-window/giant puppet set I've been describing—or rather, the brick/puppet set might be considered a kind of subversive, desublimated reflection of them—the first involving paeans to property destruction, the second, the endless ability to create new, but ephemeral, insubstantial imagery in the place of older, more permanent forms.

27. Some of this history is retold, and the story brought forward to Reclaim the Streets and the current carnivals against capitalism, in an essay by Gavin Grindon called "The Breath of the Possible," in *Constituent Imagination: Militant Investigation, Collective Research*, eds. David Graeber and Stevphen Shukaitis (Oakland: AK Press, 2006).

28. For one good example of such reflections, see "History of Radical Puppetry" by the Wise Fool Puppet Collective (www.zeitgeist.net/wfca/radpup.htm). Wise Fool traces its art more back to Medieval mystery plays than festivals but it provides a nice historical perspective.

29. Where they will normally turn on shows that take the perspective of the same police in charge of getting them off the streets to begin with; more on this later.

30. Martin Van Creveld, *The Transformation of War* (New York: Free Press, 1991).

31. See Egon Bittner, *Aspects of Police Work* (Boston: Northeastern University Press, 1990), for a good summary of police sociology's understanding of these constraints and the general issue of "discretion." Since most Americans assume that police are normally engaged in preventing or investigating crimes, they assume that police conduct is freighted with endless bureaucratic restraints. In fact, one of the great discoveries of police sociology is that police spend a surprisingly small percentage of their time on criminal matters.

32. Bittner's phrase. See also Mark Neocleous, *The Fabrication of Social Order: A Critical Theory of Police Power* (London: Pluto Press, 2000).

33. Consider here the fact that "police negotiators" are generally employed in hostage situations; in other words, in order to actually get the police to negotiate, one has to literally be holding a gun to someone's head. And in such situations

police can hardly be expected to honor their promises; in fact, they could well argue they are morally obliged not to.

34. Organizers at Genoa uniformly spoke of their shock during the actions when, suddenly, all the police commanders whose cell phone numbers they had assembled suddenly refused to answer calls from activists.

35. I have yet to hear of a passing pedestrian or other member of "the public" who was injured by even the rowdiest anarchist tactics; in any large-scale action, large numbers of passing pedestrians are likely to end up gassed, injured, or arrested by police.

36. Marc Cooper, "Dum Da Dum-Dum," *The Village Voice*, April 16, 1991, pp. 28–33. I have developed these themes in much greater detail elsewhere: see my Malinowski lecture of 2006, "Beyond Power/Knowledge: An Exploration of the Relation of Power, Ignorance and Stupidity."

37. Peter Kropotkin, still probably the most famous anarchist thinker to have developed an explicit ethical theory, argued that all morality is founded on the imagination. Most contemporary anarchists would appear to follow him on this, at least implicitly.

38. Particularly Castoriadis's "Imaginary Institution of Society." Again, this is a theme that I can only fully develop elsewhere, but one could describe the history of left-wing thought since the end of the eighteenth century as revolving around the assumption that creativity and imagination were the fundamental ontological principles. This is obvious in the case of Romanticism, but equally true of Marx—who insisted in his famous comparison of architects and bees that it was precisely the role of imagination in production that made humans different from animals. Marx, in turn, was elaborating on perspectives already current in the workers' movement of his day. This helps explain, I think, the notorious affinity that avant-garde artists have always felt with revolutionary politics. Right-wing thought has always tended to accuse the left of naivete in refusing to take account of the importance of the "means of destruction," arguing that ignoring the fundamental role of violence in defining human relations can only end up producing pernicious effects.

39. One might draw an analogy here to the collapse of levels typical of consensus decision-making. One way to think of consensus process is an attempt to merge the process of deliberation with the process of enforcement. If one does not have a separate mechanism of coercion that can force a minority to comply with a majority decision, majority voting is clearly unadvisable—the process of finding consensus is meant to produce outcomes that do not need a separate mechanism of enforcement because compliance has already been guaranteed within the process of decision-making itself.

40. I am referring here of course to Karl Schmitt, Walter Benjamin, and more recently, to Toni Negri and Giorgio Agamben.

41. The T-shirt of the Arts in Action collective that actually makes many of these puppets features a quote from Brecht: "We see art not as a mirror to hold up to reality but as a hammer with which to shape it."

42. It is interesting to observe that there is a long-standing tradition in American thought that sees creativity as inherently antisocial, and therefore, demonic. It emerges particularly strongly in racial ideologies. This, however, is properly the subject for another essay.

43. See Paolo Virno and Michael Hardt, eds., *Radical Thought in Italy: A Potential Politics* (Minneapolis: University of Minnesota Press, 1996).

44. The fact that almost all the principal figures involved in the repression of protest in America ended up as "security consultants" in Baghdad after the American conquest of Iraq seems rather telling here. Of course, they rapidly discovered their usual tactics were not particularly effective against opponents who really *were* violent, capable, for example, of dealing with IMF and World Bank officials by actually blowing them up.

45. Clint Eastwood, of course, in his shift from spaghetti Western to *Dirty Harry*, was the very avatar of the transformation.

Index

religion: art and, 300, 302; culture and,
8–10; hatred and, 142–43; money
and, 253–55; patriarchy and, 120;
rejection of, 124, 130–35; work and,
275–76, 281–82
Republicans, 83, 249–50, 255–57;
protests at 2000 convention against,
203–204, 209–10, 215, 216–17,
222–25, 230–31; *see also* right wing/
conservatives
republic model, 7, 20–24, 38, 48, 50
revolts, 266–67; of Atlantic proletariat,
17, 18; civilizational collapse and,
44, 119; debt and, 65; education
and, 259; against imperialism, 27;
in Madagascar, 136; monuments
and, 203; police refusal and, 233; in
Roman empire, 142; by students, 157,
214–15
revolutions, xiv, 266–67, 305–306;
American, 30, 50, 107; art and,
296–99, 301–303; as festival, 219–21,
335n27; French, 22, 50, 143, 301–302,
305; prefigurative, 51, 236; Russian,
94, 296–303, 305; subjects of,
266–68, 286–87
right wing/conservatives: altruism and,
249–50, 253, 255–57; on hatred, 143;
human production and, 283; violence
and, 329n14, 336n38; work and, 83
Riordan, Richard, 334n22
rioting, 21
Romantics, xix, 291, 299–302
Rome, ancient: competition in, 21, 123;
conquering of, 32–33; debt crisis in,
106–107; freedom in, xiii–xiv; hatred
in, 141–42; republic model in, 7,
20–24, 38, 48, 50
Rosaldo, Renato, 172
Rousseau, Jean-Jacques, 16, 301
Ruddick, Sara, 285
Russia, 255; art in, xix, 296–99, 303;
jobs in, 80, 298; revolution in, 94,
296–303, 305; Stalin and, 143, 225,
297, 298; thinkers from, xvii, 220,
254, 309–12, 336n37

sacrifice, 118, 122, 123, 134–35
Sahlins, Marshall, xvi–xvii, 121,
130
Saint-Simon, Henri de, 302
Saramago, José, 154
Sartre, Jean-Paul, 314
Scarry, Elaine, 174
Schele, Linda, 43
Schiller, Friedrich, 312
schizmogenesis, 115–39
Schmookler, Andrew Bard, 180
Schumann, Peter, 206
Schwarzkopf, Norman, 177
science, 307–20
Scotland, protests in, 63
Seattle, WTO/N30 in (1999), ix, 46,
62, 195, 196, 204, 332n4; Black Bloc
at, 201–202; mythologization of,
211–12, 333n16; policing at,
207–208, 233, 333n12; puppets
at, 205–206
self-consciousness, origins of,
312–14
self-defense, 182–83, 186–87
self-esteem, 185, 191–92
self-organization, 244, 314–17; *see also*
anarchists; consensus
September 11, 2001, 179, 236–37;
repression after, 63, 195, 212
sexual assault, 189–92
shamanism, 42, 43, 118
Shih, Min-wen, 26–28
Shils, Edward, 157, 328n6
Shukaitis, Stevphen, 334n22
Sieyés, Emmanuel Joseph, 49
silver, 76, 90–92
Sir! No Sir!, 334n21
Situationists, 201, 218–20, 332n6
Skeggs, Bev, 285
Skidelsky, Robert, 89–98
slavery, 17, 161, 174; Classical, xiii–xiv,
3; debt and, 105; in Madagascar, 124,
125, 127, 129–30, 137, 161; money
and, 76, 90; in South Asia, 41; in
U.S., 24, 34, 35; wage, 76; witnesses
to, 181

Permissions Acknowledgments

Grateful acknowledgment is made for permission to reprint the following material:

"There Never Was a West": Originally published in *Possibilities: Essays on Hierarchy, Rebellion, and Desire* (Oakland, CA: AK Press, 2007).

"Finance Is Just Another Word for Other's People's Debts": David Graeber, "Finance Is Just Another Word for Other People's Debts: An Interview with David Graeber," by Hannah Chadeayne Appel, originally published in *Radical History Review*, no. 118, Fall 2014, pp. 159–73. Copyright 2014, MARHO: The Radical Historians' Organization, Inc. All rights reserved. Reprinted by permission of the publisher, Duke University Press. www.dukeupress .edu.

"On the Phenomenon of Bullshit Jobs: A Work Rant": Originally published in *STRIKE! Magazine*, no. 3, Summer 2013.

"Against Economics": Originally published as "Against Economics," *The New York Review of Books*, December 5, 2019. Copyright © 2019 David Graeber.

"Soak the Rich" (debate with Thomas Piketty): Originally published in *The Baffler*, no. 25, July 2014.

"Culture as Creative Refusal": Originally published in *Cambridge Anthropology*, volume 31, no. 2, Autumn 2013, pp. 1–19.

"Hatred Has Become a Political Taboo: Originally published in *Bad Feelings*, by Arts Against Cuts, published by Book Works, 2015.

"Dead Zones of the Imagination": This essay is based on the 2006 Malinowski Memorial Lecture entitled "Beyond Power/Knowledge: An Exploration of the Relation of Power, Ignorance and Stupidity." It is a substantially revised version that was published in *HAU: Journal of Ethnographic Theory*, vol. 2, no. 2, Fall 2012, pp. 105–28.

"The Bully's Pulpit: On the Elementary Structure of Domination": Originally published in *The Baffler*, no. 28, July 2015.

"I Didn't Understand How Widespread Rape Was. Then the Penny Dropped": Originally published in *The Guardian*, November 5, 2017.

"On the Phenomenology of Giant Puppets": Originally published in *Possibilities: Essays on Hierarchy, Rebellion, and Desire* (Oakland, CA: AK Press, 2007).

"Are You an Anarchist?": Originally published by NYMAA on nymaa.org in 2000.

"Army of Altruists": Copyright © 2007 Harper's Magazine. All rights reserved. Reproduced from the January issue by special permission.

"Caring Too Much": Originally published in *The Guardian*, March 26, 2014.

"The Revolt of the Caring Classes": Lecture presented at the Collège de France, 2018.

"Another Art World, Part I": Originally published in *e-flux*, no. 102, September 2019.

"The Museum of Care: Imagining the World After the Pandemic": Originally published in *Arts of the Working Class*, May 30, 2022.

"What's the Point If We Can't Have Fun?": Originally published in *The Baffler*, no. 24, January 2014.

A Note About the Author

David Graeber was a professor of anthropology at the London School of Economics. He was the author of *Pirate Enlightenment, or the Real Libertalia*; *Debt: The First 5,000 Years*; and *Bullshit Jobs*, among many other books, and the coauthor, with David Wengrow, of *The Dawn of Everything*, a *New York Times* bestseller. An iconic thinker and a renowned activist, he died in 2020.